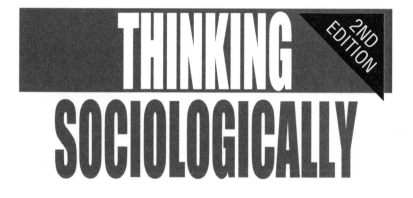

THINKING
SOCIOLOGICALLY

2ND EDITION

Zygmunt Bauman and Tim May

Blackwell
Publishing

350 Main Street, Malden, MA 02148-5020, USA
108 Cowley Road, Oxford OX4 1JF, UK
550 Swanston Street, Carlton, Victoria 3053, Australia

First published 1990 by Blackwell Publishing Ltd
Second edition published 2001
11 2010

Library of Congress Cataloging-in-Publication Data

Bauman, Zygmunt.
   Thinking sociologically / Zygmunt Bauman and Tim May. — 2nd ed.
      p.   cm.
   Includes bibliographical references and index.
   ISBN 978-0-631-21928-6 (alk. paper) — ISBN 978-0-631-21929-3 (pb.: alk. paper)
   I. Sociology.   I. May, Tim.   II. Title.

HM51.B364   2001
301-dc21

                                                    00-069768

A catalogue record for this title is available from the British Library.

Set in 10 on 12 pt Times
by Ace Filmsetting Ltd, Frome, Somerset
Printed and bound in Singapore
by Ho Printing Singapore Pte Ltd

For further information on
Blackwell Publishing, visit our websi
http://www.blackwellpublishing.com

contents

preface to the second edition

Writing the second edition of a book which was originally written by Zygmunt Bauman was a task that I approached with some trepidation. The original, after all, was written in a distinctive style that was attractive to numerous readers in several languages. At the same time, Zygmunt felt that a new, updated edition would benefit from my input. In the face of this, quite how I was to preserve this uniqueness, while adding my own materials, was bound to require some care.

The end result is a totally revised and expanded edition. Original chapters have been altered and we have introduced new ones, whilst materials have been added throughout the entire text: for example, on health and fitness, intimacy, time, space and disorder, risk, globalization, organizations and new technologies. In the end, both of us believe that we have produced a book that maintains the best parts of the first edition, but adds to it in ways that significantly improve its overall appeal.

We are both concerned that *Thinking Sociologically* is attractive to a wide audience. In terms of those who are studying sociology, we have sought to anticipate the different topics that are taught within the curriculum, while writing in a way that we hope is illuminating to practising social scientists in general. We are also keen that the book appeals to a wider audience who may wish to learn more of a discipline that is gaining greater attention for the insights it offers into society and social relations. For us, the reasons for this are clear: sociology provides a valuable and often neglected perspective on the issues that face us all in the twenty-first century.

As two sociologists, separated by two generations, we are both devoted to our subject in terms of the understanding it offers for making sense of our experiences within the social environments we inhabit. Thinking sociologically not only helps us in our understanding of each other and ourselves, but also offers important explanations for the dynamics of societies and social relations in general. We hope, therefore, that you will emerge from reading this book and agree with us that sociology is an illuminating, exciting, practical and challenging discipline.

acknowledgements

I would first like to thank Zygmunt for asking me to co-author this book. I would also like to thank the following for their support and encouragement: Richard Brown, Lyn Bryant, Alan Bryman, Graeme Gilloch, Alan Harding, Frank Lee, Linda McKie, Simon Marvin, Ken Parsons, Bev Skeggs, Paula Surridge, Carole Sutton, Paul Sweetman, Paul Taylor and Malcolm Williams. My love and gratitude to Dee, who has put up with moving from Plymouth to Durham and now to Manchester in the last five years. The reasons for this were because of circumstances over which we had little control, and our thanks are now due to those who have enabled us to feel 'at home' in our new area. My love also to our children, Calum and Cian, who keep me in check by exercising a healthy disdain for my publishing activities!

Zygmunt and I have enjoyed the production of this book and hope that you find the discipline of sociology exciting and insightful. Finally, we would both like to thank the editorial and production teams at Blackwell in both the USA and UK, including Valery Rose, Christine Firth, Susan Rabinowitz and Ken Provencher.

INTRODUCTION: THE DISCIPLINE OF SOCIOLOGY

In this chapter we wish to examine the idea of thinking sociologically and its importance for understanding ourselves, each other and the social environments in which we live. For this purpose we are going to consider the idea of sociology as a disciplined practice with its own set of questions for approaching the study of society and social relations.

$$\triangledown$$

In Search of Distinction

Sociology not only encompasses a disciplined set of practices, but also represents a considerable body of knowledge that has been accumulated over the course of its history. A glance at the section in libraries entitled 'Sociology' leads one to see a collection of books that represents sociology as a binding tradition. These books provide volumes of information for newcomers to the field, whether they want to become practising sociologists or merely to expand their understanding of the world in which they live. Here are places in which readers can avail themselves of whatever sociology may offer and so consume, digest, appropriate and expand upon this body of knowledge. In this way sociology becomes a site of constant flux with newcomers adding new ideas and studies of social life to those same shelves. Sociology, in this sense, is a site of continuing activity that tests received wisdom against new experiences and so adds to knowledge and changes the form and content of the discipline in the process.

The above seems to make sense. After all, when we ask ourselves 'What is sociology?' we may well refer to a collection of books in a library as indicative of the output of the discipline. Such ways of thinking about sociology seem obvious. After all, if asked 'What is a lion?' we might take a book on animals and indicate a particular picture. In this way we are pointing to links between certain words and objects. Thus, words refer to objects. Such objects become a word's referent and thus we make links between a word and an object under particular conditions. Without this process of common understanding, everyday communication, which we take for granted, would be inconceivable. This, however, does not suffice for a fuller, more sociological, understanding of this connection.

The above does not give us knowledge about the object itself. We now have to ask supplementary questions: for example, in what ways is this object peculiar? In what ways does it differ from other objects, so that referring to it by a separate name is justified? If calling this animal a lion is correct, but calling it a tiger is not, there must be something that lions have that tigers do not. There must be some distinguishing differences between them. Only by discovering this difference can we know what characterizes a lion – as distinct from knowing what the object the word 'lion' stands for. So it is with trying to characterize a way of thinking that we call sociological.

We are satisfied that the word 'sociology' stands for a certain body of knowledge and for certain practices which employ this accumulated knowledge. However, what is it that makes the knowledge and practices distinctly 'sociological'? What makes them different from other bodies of knowledge and other disciplines that have their own practices? Going back to our lion example to answer this question, we could seek to distinguish sociology from other disciplines. In most libraries we might discover that the closest shelves to sociology carry the labels 'History', 'Anthropology', 'Political science', 'Law', 'Social policy', 'Accounting', 'Psychology', 'Management studies', 'Economics', 'Criminology' 'Philosophy', 'Social policy', 'Linguistics', 'Literature' and 'Human geography'. The librarians who arranged such shelves might have assumed that the readers browsing through the sociology section would occasionally reach for a book on one of these subjects. In other words, the subject matter of sociology might have been assumed to be nearer to those bodies of knowledge than others. Perhaps the differences between sociology books and the books placed in their immediate vicinity are then less pronounced than those between, say, sociology and organic chemistry?

A librarian cataloguing in this way makes sense. The neighbouring bodies of knowledge have much in common. They are all concerned with the human-made world: that which would not exist but for the actions of human beings. These subjects are concerned, in their different ways, with human actions and their consequences. However, if they explore the same territory, what sets them apart? What makes them so different that they justify different names?

We are prompted to give a simple answer to these questions: divisions between bodies of knowledge must reflect the divisions in the world they investigate. It is the human actions (or the aspects of the human actions) which differ from each other, and the divisions between bodies of knowledge simply take account of this fact. Thus, history is about the actions that took place in the past, whereas sociology concentrates on current actions. Similarly, anthropology tells us of human societies that are assumed to be at different stages of development from our own (however that may be defined). In the case of some other close relatives of sociology, political science tends to discuss actions relating to power and the government; economics tends to deals with actions related to the use of resources in terms of the maximization of utility for individuals who are held to be 'rational' in a particular sense of the word, as well as the production and distribution of goods; law and criminology are interested in interpretation and application of the law and the norms that regulate human behaviour and in the way such norms are articulated, made obligatory, enforced and with what consequences? However, as soon as we begin to justify the boundaries between disciplines in this manner, the issue becomes problematic, for we assume that the human world reflects such neat divisions that then become specialist branches of investigation. We now reach an important issue: like most beliefs which appear to be self-evident, they remain obvious only as long as we refrain from examining the *assumptions* that underpin them.

So where do we get the idea that human actions may be divided into certain categories in the first place? From the fact that they have been classified in such a way and that each file in this classification has been given a separate name? From the fact that there are groups of credible experts, regarded as knowledgeable and trustworthy people, who claim exclusive rights to study aspects of society and then furnish us with informed opinions? Yet does it make sense, from the point of view of our experiences, that society can be split into economics, politics or social policy? We do not live now in the realm distinguished by political science, then in economics, nor do we move from sociology to anthropology when travelling from England to part of, say, South America, or from history to sociology when we grow a year older!

If we are able to separate these domains of activity in our experiences and so categorize our actions in terms of the political at one moment and the economic at another, is it because we have been taught to make such distinctions in the first place? Therefore, what we know is not the world itself, but what we are doing in the world in terms of how our practices are informed by an image of that world. It is a model that is put together from the building blocks derived from the relations between *language* and *experience*. Thus, there is no natural division of the human world that is reflected in different scholarly disciplines. It is, on the contrary, a division of labour between the scholars who examine human actions and this is reinforced by the mutual separation of respective experts, along with the exclusive rights that each group enjoys to decide what does and what does not belong to their areas of expertise.

In our quest to find the 'difference that makes the difference', how do the practices of these branches of study differ from each other? There is a similarity between their attitudes towards whatever they selected as their objects of study. After all, they all claim obedience to the same rules of conduct when dealing with their respective objects. All seek to collect relevant facts and ensure that they are valid and then check and recheck those facts in order that the information about them is reliable. In addition, they all try to put the propositions they make about the facts in a form in which they can be clearly, unambiguously understood and tested against evidence. In so doing they seek to pre-empt or eliminate contradictions between propositions in order that no two different propositions can be true at the same time. In short, they all try to live up to the idea of a systematic discipline and to present their findings in a responsible manner.

We can now say that there is no difference in how the task of the expert and their trademark – scholarly responsibility – is understood and practised. Those people claiming to be scholarly experts seem to deploy similar strategies to collect and to process their facts: they observe aspects of human actions, or employ historical evidence and seek to interpret them within modes of analysis that make sense of those actions. It seems, therefore, that our last hope of finding our difference is in the kinds of questions that motivate each discipline: that is, those that determine the points of view (cognitive perspectives) from which human actions are observed, explored, described and explained by scholars belonging to these different disciplines.

Consider the types of questions that motivate economists. Here, consideration would turn to the relationship between the costs and benefits of human action. They may consider human action from the point of view of the management of scarce resources and how these may be used to their best advantage. Also, the relationships between actors would be examined as aspects of the production and exchange of goods and services, all of which is assumed to be regulated by market relations of supply and demand and the desire of actors to pursue their preferences according to a model of rational action. The findings would then be arranged into a model of the process through which resources are created, obtained and allocated among various demands. Political science, on the other hand, is more likely to be interested in those aspects of human actions that change, or are changed by, the actual or anticipated conduct of other actors in terms of power and influence. In this sense actions can be viewed in terms of the asymmetry between power and influence and so some actors emerge from interaction with their behaviour modified more significantly than other partners to the interaction. It might also organize its findings around concepts like power, domination, the state, authority, and so on.

The concerns of economics and political science are by no means alien to sociology. This is readily apparent from works within sociology that are written by scholars who may self-identify as historians, political scientists, anthropologists or geographers. Yet sociology, like other branches of social study, has its own cognitive perspectives that inform sets of questions for interrogating human actions, as well as its own principles of interpretation. From this point of view we can say that sociology is distinguished through viewing human actions as elements of wider figurations: that is, of a non-random assembly of actors locked together in a web of mutual dependency (dependency being a state in which the probability that the action will be undertaken and the chance of its success change in relation to what other actors are, do or may do). Sociologists ask what consequences this has for human actors, the relations into which we enter and the societies of which we are a part. In turn, this shapes the object of sociological inquiry and so figurations, webs of mutual dependence, reciprocal conditioning of action and expansion or confinement of actors' freedom are among the most prominent preoccupations of sociology.

Individual actors come into the view of sociological study in terms of being members or partners in a network of interdependence. Given that, regardless of what we do, we are dependent upon others, the central questions of sociology, we could say, are: how do the types of social relations and societies that we inhabit relate to how we see each other, ourselves and our knowledge, actions and their consequences? It is these kinds of questions – part of the practical realities of everyday life – that constitute the particular area of sociological discussion and define sociology as a relatively autonomous branch of the human and social sciences. Therefore, we may conclude that thinking sociologically is a way of understanding the human world that also opens up the possibility for thinking about the same world in different ways.

Sociology and Common Sense

Thinking sociologically is also distinguished by its relationship with so-called 'common sense'. Perhaps more than other branches of scholarship, sociology finds its relation with common sense informed by issues that are important for its standing and practice. Physical and biological sciences do not appear to be concerned with spelling out their relationship to common sense. Most sciences settle for defining themselves in terms of the boundaries that separate them from other disciplines. They do not feel that they share sufficient ground to concern themselves with drawing boundaries or bridges with this rich yet disorganized, non-systematic, often inarticulate and ineffable knowledge that we call common sense.

Such indifference may have some justification. Common sense, after all, appears to have nothing to say of the matters that preoccupy physicists, chemists or astronomers. The subjects they deal with do not fall within the daily experiences and sights of ordinary women and men. Thus, non-experts do not normally consider themselves able to form opinions about such matters unless aided by the scientists. After all, the objects explored by the physical sciences appear only under very special circumstances, for example, through the lens of gigantic telescopes. Only the scientists can see them and experiment with them under these conditions and so can claim a monopolistic possession of the given branch of science. Being the sole owners of the experience that provides the raw material for their study, the process, analysis and interpretation of the materials are within their control. Products of such processing then have to withstand the critical scrutiny of other scientists. They will not have to compete with common sense for the simple reason that there is no commonsensical point of view with respect to the matters they pronounce upon.

We now have to ask some more sociological questions. After all, is the characterization as simple as the above implies? The production of scientific knowledge contains social factors that inform and shape its practice, while scientific findings may have social, political and economic implications that, in any democratic society, are not for scientists to have the last words upon. We cannot, in other words, so easily separate the means of scientific research from the ends to which it may be put, nor practical reason from science itself. After all, how research is funded and by whom may, in some instances, have a bearing upon the results of that research. Recent public concerns over the quality of the food we eat, the environment in which we live, the role of genetic engineering and the patenting of genetic information on populations by large corporations, are just a few of the matters that science alone cannot determine for they are about not only the justification of knowledge, but also its application and implications for the lives we lead. These matters are about our experiences and their relationship to our everyday practices, the control we have over our lives and the direction in which our societies are unfolding.

These issues provide the raw material for sociological investigations. All of us live in the company of other people and interact with each other. In the process we display an extraordinary amount of *tacit knowledge* that enables us to get on with the business of everyday life. Each of us is a skilled actor. Yet what we get and what we are depend on what other people do. After all, most of us have lived through the agonizing experience of a communication breakdown with friends and strangers. From this point of view the subject matter of sociology is already embedded in our everyday lives and without this fact we would be unable to conduct our lives in the company of others.

Although deeply immersed in our daily routines, informed by practical knowledge oriented to the social settings in which we interact, we often do not pause to think about the meaning of what we have gone through; even less frequently do we pause to compare our private experiences with the fate of others except, perhaps, to have private responses to social problems paraded for all to consume on television chat shows. Here, however, the privatization of social issues is reinforced, so relieving us of the burden of seeing the dynamics of social relations within what are instead viewed as individual reactions.

This is exactly what sociological thinking can do for us. As a mode of thought it will ask questions such as: 'How do our individual biographies intertwine with the history we share with other human beings?' At the same time, sociologists are part of that experience and so however hard they may try to stand aside from the objects of their study – life experiences as objects 'out there' – they cannot break off completely from the knowledge that they seek to comprehend. Nevertheless, this may be an advantage to the extent that they possess both an inside and outside view of the experiences they try to comprehend.

There is more to the special relationship between sociology and common sense. The objects of astronomy wait to be named, placed into an orderly whole and compared with other similar phenomena. There are few sociological equivalents of such clean and unused phenomena which have not been endowed with meaning before the sociologists appear with their questionnaires, fill up their notebooks or examine relevant documents. Those human actions and interactions that sociologists explore have been given names and considered by the actors themselves and so are objects of commonsensical knowledge. Families, organizations, kinship networks, neighbourhoods, cities and villages, nations and churches and any other groupings held together by regular human interaction have already been given meaning and significance by the actors. Each sociological term has already been laden with meanings given by commonsensical knowledge.

For these reasons sociology is intimately related to common sense. With fluid borders between sociological thinking and common sense, their security cannot be guaranteed in advance. As with the application of the genetic scientists' findings and their implications for social life, the sovereignty of sociology over social knowledge is likely to be contested. This is why drawing a boundary between sociological knowledge proper and the common sense is such an important matter for the identity of sociology as a cohesive body of knowledge. Not surprisingly, sociologists pay much attention to this issue and we can think of four ways in which these differences have been considered.

In the first place sociology, unlike common sense, makes an effort to subordinate itself to the rigorous rules of responsible speech. This is an attribute of science to be distinguished from other, reputedly more relaxed and less vigilantly self-controlled, forms of knowledge. In their practice sociologists are expected to take great care to distinguish – in a clear and visible fashion – between the statements corroborated by available evidence and those propositions that can claim the status only of provisional, untested ideas. The rules of responsible speech demand that one's 'workshop' – the whole procedure that has led to the final conclusions and is claimed to guarantee their credibility – be wide open to scrutiny. Responsible speech must also relate to other statements made on its topic and so it cannot dismiss or pass by in silence over other views that have been voiced, however inconvenient they may be to its argument. In this way the trustworthiness, reliability and eventually also the practical usefulness of the ensuing propositions will be greatly enhanced. After all, our belief in the credibility of science is grounded in the hope that scientists have followed the rules of responsible speech. As for the scientists themselves, they point to the virtue of responsible speech as an argument for the validity and reliability of the knowledge they produce.

Second, there is the size of the field from which the material for sociological thinking is drawn. For most of us in our daily routines this field is confined to our own life-worlds: that is, to the things we do, the people we meet, the purposes we set for our own pursuits and presuppose that other people set for theirs, as well as the times and places in which we routinely interact. Rarely do we find it necessary to lift ourselves above the level of our daily concerns to broaden the horizon of our experiences, for this would necessitate time and resources that many cannot afford, or are not inclined to embark upon. Yet given the tremendous variety of life conditions and experiences in the world, each experience is necessarily partial and possibly even one-sided. These issues can be examined only if we bring together and compare experiences drawn from a multitude of life-worlds. Only then will the bounded realities of individual experiences be revealed, as will the complex network of dependencies and interconnections in which they are entangled – a network which reaches far beyond the realm that may be accessed from the point of view of a singular biography. The overall result of such a broadening of horizons will be the discovery of the intimate link between individual biography and wide social processes. It is for this reason that the sociologists' pursuit of this wider perspective makes a great difference – not only quantitatively, but also in the quality and the uses of knowledge. For people like us, sociological knowledge has something to offer that common sense, for all its richness cannot, by itself, provide.

Third, sociology and common sense differ in the way that each makes sense of human reality in terms of how they understand and explain events and circumstances. We know from our experiences that we are 'the author' of our actions; we know that what we do is an effect of our intentions even though the outcomes may not be as we intended. We normally act to achieve a state of affairs, whether in order to possess an object, to receive praise, or to prevent something we do not like or help a friend. Quite naturally, the way we think of our actions serves as a model for making sense of other actions. To this extent the only way we can make sense of the human world around us is to draw our tools of explanation solely from within our respective *life-worlds*. We tend to perceive everything that happens in the world at large as an outcome of somebody's intentional action. We look for the persons responsible for what has occurred and once we have found them, we believe our inquiries to be complete. We assume that goodwill lies behind those events to which we are favourably predisposed and ill intentions lie behind those we dislike. In general, people find it difficult to accept that a situation was not an effect of the intended actions of an identifiable person.

Those who speak in the name of reality within the public realm – politicians, journalists, market researchers, commercial advertisers – tune in to the above tendencies and speak of the 'needs of the state' or the 'demands of the economy'. This is said as if the state or economies were made to the measure of individual persons like ourselves with specific needs and wants. Similarly, we read and hear of the complex problems of nations, states and economic systems as the effects of the thoughts and deeds of a select group of individuals who can be named, pictured and interviewed. Equally, governments often relieve themselves of responsibility by referring to those things outside of their control, or speaking of what 'the public demands' through the use of focus groups or opinion polls.

Sociology stands in opposition to the particularity of worldviews as if they can unproblematically speak in the name of a general state of affairs. Nor does it take-for-granted ways of understanding as if they constituted some natural way of explaining events that may be simply separated from historical change, or the social location from which they emerged. As it starts its survey from figurations (networks of dependencies) rather than from individual actors or single actions, it demonstrates that the common metaphor of the motivated individual as the key to understanding the human world – including our own, thoroughly personal and private, thoughts and deeds – is not an appropriate way to understand ourselves and others. To think sociologically is to *make sense* of the human condition via an analysis of the manifold webs of human interdependency – that toughest of realities to which we refer in order to explain our motives and the effects of their activation.

Finally, the power of common sense depends on its self-evident character: that is, not to question its precepts and to be self-confirming in practice. In its turn, this rests upon the routine, habitual character of daily life that informs our common sense while also being simultaneously informed by it. We need this in order to get on with our lives. When repeated often enough, things tend to become familiar and the familiar is seen as self-explanatory; it presents no problems and may arouse no curiosity. Questions are not asked if people are satisfied that 'things are as they are' for reasons that are not open to scrutiny. Fatalism may also play its role via the belief that one can do little to change the conditions in which we act.

From this point of view we could say that familiarity may be in tension with inquisitiveness and this can also inform the impetus to innovate and transform. In an encounter with that familiar world ruled by routines that have the power to reconfirm beliefs, sociology may appear as a meddlesome and irritating stranger. By examining that which is taken-for-granted, it has the potential to disturb the comfortable certitudes of life by asking questions no one can remember asking and those with vested interests resent even being asked. These questions render the evident a puzzle and may defamiliarize the familiar. With the daily ways of life and the social conditions in which they take place under scrutiny, they emerge as one of the possible ways, not *the* only way, of getting on in our lives and organizing relations between us.

Of course, this may not be to everybody's liking, particularly those for whom a state of affairs offers a great advantage. Equally, routines can have their place; here we may recall Kipling's centipede, who walked effortlessly on all her hundred legs until a sycophantic courtier began to praise her exquisite memory. It was this memory that allowed her never to put down the eighty-fifth leg before the thirty-seventh, or the fifty-second before the nineteenth. Having been made self-conscious, the poor centipede was no longer able to walk. Others may feel humiliated and even resentful that what they once knew and were proud of is devalued by virtue of being open to question. Yet however understandable the resentment that is generated, *defamiliarization* can have clear benefits. Most importantly, it may open up new and previously unsuspected possibilities of living one's life with others with more self-awareness, more comprehension of our surroundings in terms of greater self and social knowledge and perhaps also with more freedom and control.

To all those who think that living life in a more conscious way is worth the effort, sociology is a welcome guide. Although remaining in a constant and intimate conversation with common sense, it aims at overcoming its limitations by opening up the possibilities that can too easily become closed down. When addressing and challenging our shared knowledge, sociology prompts and encourages us to reassess our experience, to discover new possibilities and to become in the end more open and less reconciled to the idea that learning about ourselves and each other has an end point, rather than being an exciting and dynamic process whose aim is greater understanding.

To think sociologically can render us more sensitive and tolerant of diversity. It can sharpen our senses and open our eyes to new horizons beyond our immediate experiences in order that we can explore human conditions which, hitherto, have remained relatively invisible. Once we understand better how the apparently natural, inevitable, immutable, eternal aspects of our lives have been brought into being through the exercise of human power and resources, we shall find it much harder to accept that they are immune and impenetrable to subsequent actions, including our own. Sociological thinking, as an antifixating power, is therefore a power in its own right. It renders flexible what may have been the oppressive fixity of social relations and in so doing opens up a world of possibilities. The art of sociological thinking is to widen the scope and the practical effectiveness of freedom. When more of it has been learnt, the individual may well become just a little less subject to manipulation and more resilient to oppression and control. They are also likely to be more effective as social actors, for they can see the connections between their actions and social conditions and how those things which, by their fixity, claim to be irresistible to change, are open to transformation.

There is also that which lies beyond us as individuals. We have said that sociology thinks relationally to situate us within networks of social relations. Sociology thus stands in praise of the individual, but not individualism. Thus to think sociologically means to understand a little more fully the people around us in terms of their hopes and desires and their worries and concerns. In this way, we may better appreciate the human individual in them and perhaps learn to respect that which every civilized society must entitle them in order to sustain itself: their right to do what we do, so that they may choose and practise their ways of life according to their preferences. This means selecting their life-projects, defining themselves and defending their dignity as we might defend ours in the face of obstacles that we all encounter in differing degrees. Thinking sociologically thus has the potential to promote solidarity between us: that is, a solidarity grounded in mutual understanding and respect and in a joint resistance to suffering and a shared condemnation of the cruelties that are its causes. Ultimately, if this is achieved, the cause of freedom will be greatly enhanced through being elevated to the rank of a common cause.

Going back to what we were saying about the fluidity of that which appears inflexible, sociological insight into the inner logic and meaning of forms of life other than our own may well prompt us to think again about the boundaries that have been drawn between ourselves and others. A new understanding generated in this way may well allow our communications with 'others' to be easier and more likely to lead to mutual agreement. Fear and antagonism can be replaced by tolerance. There are no greater guarantees of individual freedom than the freedom of us all.

To note the connection between individual and collective freedom necessarily has a destabilizing effect on existing power relations or what are often called 'social orders'. It is for this reason that charges of 'political disloyalty' are all too often made against sociology by governments and other power-holders in control of the social order. This is very evident among those governments that seek to forge reality in their name by claiming to represent unproblematically the existing state of affairs as if it were natural, or by those who castigate contemporary conditions via nostalgic calls to a mythical bygone age in which all knew their place in society. When we witness yet another campaign against the 'subversive impact' of sociology, we can safely assume that another assault on the subjects' capacity to resist the coercive regulation of people's lives is in preparation by those who seek to govern by fiat. Such campaigns more often than not coincide with tough measures aimed at the extant forms of self-management and self-defence of collective rights; measures aimed at, in other words, the collective foundations of individual freedom.

Sometimes it is said that sociology is the power of the powerless. This is not always the case, particularly in those places where it is practised that find themselves under increasing pressures to conform to governmental expectations. There is no guarantee that having acquired sociological understanding, one can dissolve and disempower the 'tough realities' of life. Quite simply, the power of understanding is no match for the pressures of coercion allied with resigned and submissive common sense within prevailing political and economic conditions. Yet were it not for that understanding, the chance of the successful management of one's life and the collective management of shared life conditions would be slimmer still. It is a way of thinking whose value is often cherished only by those who cannot take-it-for-granted and when it comes to those who can, it is frequently undervalued.

▽

The Content of *Thinking Sociologically*

This book has been written with the aim of helping people to understand their experiences through and with others. In so doing, it shows how the apparently familiar aspects of life can be interpreted in novel and different ways. Each chapter addresses issues that are part of our daily lives, even if they may not be at the forefront of our everyday understandings.

They concern ways of seeing and the dilemmas and choices that we routinely encounter, but often have little time or opportunity to reflect upon. Our aim is thus to prompt thinking in these terms and not to 'correct' knowledge. We wish to expand horizons of understanding, but not to replace some notion of error with the idea of an unquestionable truth. In the process we hope to encourage a questioning attitude in which understanding others enables us better to understand ourselves *with* others.

This book differs from many others because it is organized according to the issues that inform daily life. There are topics that occupy professional sociologists in the course of their practice that are mentioned only briefly or omitted entirely: for example, social research methods for the study of social life. This book is a sociological commentary on matters that directly inform our daily experiences and is divided into parts and chapters with that in mind. In this guide our sociological narrative will not develop in a linear manner because there are some topics to which we shall return throughout the book. For instance, issues of social identity will appear in many different guises in the following chapters, for this is how the effort of understanding works in practice. After all, as we examine new topics, they will reveal new questions and so bring to light those issues we had not previously considered. As we noted earlier, this is part of a process in which we gain a better understanding – a task without end.

part one

ACTION, IDENTITY AND UNDERSTANDING IN EVERYDAY LIFE

chapter one

ONESELF WITH OTHERS

It is not an uncommon experience in our lives to resent being constrained by circumstances over which we feel we have no control. There are also times when we assert our freedom from such control by refusing to conform to the expectations of others, resist what we see as undue encroachments upon our freedom, and, as is evident throughout history and in contemporary times, rise up in revolt against oppression. Possessing feelings of being free and unfree at the same time is, therefore, a common part of our everyday experiences. It is also one of the most confusing issues that gives rise to feelings of ambivalence and frustration, as well as creativity and innovation.

We noted in the Introduction that we live in relations with others; how this relates to ideas of freedom within society has been the subject of a great deal of sociological thinking. At one level, we are free to choose and see our own choices to their end. You can get up now and make a cup of coffee before continuing to read this chapter. You can also choose to abandon the project of thinking sociologically and embark upon another course of study, or abandon the idea of study altogether. For you to continue to read on is a choice among the alternative courses of action that are currently available to you. Your ability to make conscious decisions in this way is an exercise of your freedom.

Choice, Freedom and Living with Others

Our choices are not, of course, always the product of conscious decisions. As we have already said, many of our actions are *habitual* and so not subject to deliberate and open choice. Nevertheless, others frequently remind us that our decisions leave us responsible for any consequences. You can hear it now: 'No one forced you to do so, you have only yourself to blame!' Similarly, if we break rules that are meant to guide people's conduct, then we may be punished. The act of punishment is intended as a confirmation that we are responsible for our actions. Rules, in this sense, orient not only our actions, but also their coordination with others who can, in their turn, anticipate how we are likely to act. Without this in place, communication and understanding in everyday life are inconceivable.

We often consider ourselves to be the authors of our destinies and so have the power to act in determining our conduct and controlling our lives. We thus have both the ability to monitor our actions *and* the capability to determine their outcomes. Yet is this really how life works? It might, for example, be claimed that being unemployed is entirely the fault of the individual concerned who, if they tried hard enough, could earn a living. People might retrain themselves and look for work, but the area in which they live has high unemployment, they cannot afford to move and so despite constantly seeking employment, there is none on offer. There are many such situations in which our freedom to act is limited by circumstances over which we have no control. It is, therefore, one thing to have the ability to change or modify our skills and quite another to possess the capability to reach the goals we seek. How does this manifest itself?

First, we can observe that in situations of scarcity, as well as how we are judged by others, limits our capabilities. People might seek the same goals, but not all reach them because the amount of available prizes is limited. In this case we compete with each other and the outcome may be only partially dependent on our efforts. We might seek a college place, only to find out that there are twenty candidates for every place available and that most of them have the qualifications required. In addition, the college may tend to favour candidates from certain social backgrounds. Our actions then become dependent upon the judgement of others over whom we exercise limited control. Such people can set the rules of the game and be, at the same time, the referees. Therefore, they are *positioned* by their institutions to exercise discretion and in so doing, draw the boundaries of our freedom. Factors such as these, over which we have little or no control, heavily influence the outcome of our efforts. We become dependent on others because it is they who pronounce the verdict as to whether our efforts are good enough and consider whether we exhibit the right characteristics to justify our admission.

Second, material factors inform our capability to reach our goals. While determination is very important, what if we lack the means to act upon our decisions? We might move to seek work in places where more jobs are available, only to discover that the cost of houses or of rents is far beyond our means. Similarly, we might wish to escape overcrowded and polluted conditions in order to move to a healthier location, yet find that it is those with more money who have already done so and therefore it is not affordable. In the process the wealthier people have inflated the price of houses and so left the populations who have been brought up in that area unable to afford to buy a house. We can say the same thing about education and health. Some areas have better equipped schools and hospitals, yet are too far away, while to opt for private education or health care would be beyond our incomes. What is being demonstrated here is that freedom of choice does not guarantee freedom to act on those choices, nor does it secure the freedom to attain our intended results. Further, that the exercise of our freedom may be to limit the freedom of others. To be able to act freely, we need more than *free will*.

Most commonly we think of being limited by the amount of money at our disposal, but we have also mentioned symbolic resources. In this case our freedom may not depend on what we do, but on who we are in terms of how others view us. We have used the example of a college, but we may also be refused entry to a club, or employment, because of the manner in which our qualities are judged, for example, on the grounds of race, sex, age, ethnicity or disability. Alternatively, access to the club may depend on past achievements – acquired skills, qualifications, length of service or the manner in which we have been brought up to speak. These are the lasting consequences of past choices which, when accumulated, have an effect on future actions. Our freedom to act in the present is thereby informed by our past circumstances and accumulated experiences.

Our accumulated experiences inform how we feel about the current situations into which we enter. We may find, going back to our college example, that a mode of speaking is expected, but it is one with which we are unfamiliar. Coming from a working-class family, we may feel uneasy among middle-class neighbours. Or being a Catholic who follows orthodoxy, we may not be able to accept divorce and abortion as facts of life. Perhaps it is the case that the groups we feel most at ease in actually limit our freedom by restricting the range of opinions that we can hold. Informal and formal groups are often constituted (as we shall discuss later on in the book) by the expectations that they place upon their members and in so doing exclude those who are presumed not to live up to those requirements. When these gaps in understanding occur between groups, they are frequently filled by stereotypical assumptions. Thus, the very fact that we may be adjusted to the conditions of action inside our group can be said to circumscribe our freedom by preventing us from exploring poorly charted and unimagined experiences that lie beyond the confines of that group. Having being trained in the ways and means of our groups, we are thereby enabled to practise our freedom, but the price can be to limit us to particular ideas and territories.

We are both enabled and constrained in the everyday practices of freedom. At one level we are taught that there are types of desires that are acceptable and achievable within the group. Appropriate ways to act, talk, dress and conduct ourselves generally provide for the orientation that is needed to get us through life within the groups to which we belong. We then judge ourselves according to those expectations and our self-esteem is given accordingly. With all that, however, these advantages may so easily become problems when we venture beyond those expectations and find ourselves in an environment where different desires are promoted. Here, alternative ways of conducting ourselves may be deemed appropriate and so the connections between other people's conduct and their intentions are not familiar, but appear alien. The same understanding that allowed us to conduct ourselves now appears as a limitation upon the horizons of our understanding. The French sociologist Pierre Bourdieu, in his wide-ranging studies of social life, referred to the disjuncture which occurs between our sense of ourselves and the fields of action within which we find ourselves as the 'Don Quixote' effect.

When disjunctures occur between our expectations and experiences, we may reflect upon the possibility that the groups to which we belong are not ones we have opted for out of free choice. Quite simply, we can be members of a group because we are born into them. The group that defines us, assists us to orient our behaviour and is seen to provide for our freedom, may not be one that we have consciously chosen and so may become an uninvited guest. When we first joined it was not an act of freedom, but a manifestation of dependence. We do not decide to be French, Spanish, African Caribbean, white or middle class. We can accept this fate with equanimity or resignation, or we can transform it into our destiny in an enthusiastic embrace with group identity - being proud of what we are and the expectations placed upon us as a result. If we want to transform ourselves, however, it will require a great deal of effort against the taken-for-granted expectations of those who surround us. Self-sacrifice, determination and endurance will take the place of conformity to the values and norms of the group. The contrast is one between swimming with the tide and against the current. This is how, despite not always being conscious of it, we are dependent upon others: even though we may swim against the current, we do so in a direction that is oriented or informed by the expectations or actions of those who lie outside of the familiar group.

How we act and see ourselves is informed by the expectations of the groups to which we belong. This is manifested in several ways. First, there are the *ends* or goals that we assign with particular significance and so consider worth pursuing. These vary according to such factors as class, ethnicity and gender. Most of the work of caring for others, for instance, is provided by women and so there is a clear tendency to gravitate to particular occupations in which caring for others is rewarded, for example, nursing, teaching and social work. This is based on largely unexamined assumptions about the division of labour between men and women in terms of the types of characteristics that each is supposed to exhibit.

Second, how we are expected to achieve these ends is influenced by another manifestation of group expectations: the accepted *means* employed in the pursuit of ends. We are concerned here with the forms of conduct that are taken to be appropriate in everyday life. How we dress, use our bodies, talk, display our enthusiasm and even hold our knives and forks when eating are just part of the ways in which groups inform our conduct in the pursuit of ends.

Third we have noted, groups also seek to identify themselves through acts that distinguish them from those outside of their formal and informal networks of relations. We call this manifestation the *criteria of relevance*. Here we are taught to distinguish between those objects or people who are relevant and irrelevant to the life-projects we embark upon. Identifying allies, enemies, rivals, who to listen to and who to disregard is part of this process. Thus, we owe the ends which we pursue, the means employed in their pursuit and how to distinguish between those who may and may not assist us in the process, to the groups to which we belong. An enormous amount of practical knowledge is thereby gained without which we would be unable to conduct our daily activities and orient ourselves to particular life-projects.

In most cases this is tacit knowledge for it orients our conduct without us necessarily being able to express how and why it operates in particular ways. If asked, for example, what codes we use to communicate with others and how we decipher the meaning of actions, we may not even understand the meaning of the question. How do we explain the codes, such as the rules of grammar that provide for communication, when we take them for granted in our fluency and competency? Yet that knowledge is required to inform our daily tasks and even if we cannot recite the rules that enable us to act, we can routinely display the practical skills that rely upon their existence. Indeed, the American sociologist Harold Garfinkel founded a branch of sociology known as ethnomethodology. This form of sociology studies the minutiae of everyday interactions and provides for fascinating insights into just those things that we take-for-granted: for example, turn-taking in conversations, how we begin and end sentences and how we attribute characteristics to people on the basis of their mode of dress and bodily deportment in everyday, routine gestures.

It is thanks to the background knowledge that ethnomethodologists take as their object of study that we feel secure in our actions. This relies upon our forgetting the origins of the very knowledge that has such a powerful grip upon us. It comes in the form of a *natural attitude* that suspends the sort of questioning that micro-sociologists turn into objects of investigation. When we consult the sociological literature on social knowledge and everyday life, it opens up a fascinating area of interest that enables us to understand more about our interactions with each other. In so doing, what appeared as self-evident is revealed to be a collection of beliefs that vary according to group characteristics, time, place, space and power. In the next section we shall examine some of these insights in terms of how we become ourselves *with* others.

Oneself with Another: Sociological Perspectives

One of the central figures who provided much insight into how we internalize group understandings was the American social psychologist and philosopher George Herbert Mead. For Mead, who we are, our 'selves', is not an attribute that we are born with, but one acquired over time through interaction with others. In order to understand how this occurs, Mead divided our sense of self into two parts: the 'I' and the 'Me'. Mead held that our minds seek an 'adjustive relationship' with the world in which we find ourselves. However, that does not mean we simply reflect the expectations of our groups because (as we have seen) we can also act on the world. To understand this process, Mead argued that we can come to know ourselves through others only via symbolic communication.

Language is the medium not only through which we speak, but also through which we hear ourselves and evaluate our actions and utterances according to the responses of others. In this way the 'I' may best be thought of as a 'conversation' that takes place within ourselves where language acts as a medium that allows this process to take place and to think of ourselves as a 'whole'. The 'Me', on the other hand, refers to how we organize the expectations of groups within our actions. We then respond to others in terms of how we see ourselves and that is constantly modified according to the different social settings we routinely inhabit.

The above process takes place via three stages in our development. First, there is the *preparatory stage*. Here our sense of self is passive in that it is made up of the attitudes that others display towards us. Awareness then rapidly builds up and we respond to others with the symbols of the group, enabling us to define our conduct in terms that are deemed appropriate to the setting. In other words, a growing awareness of ourselves is derived via the responses of others. At this stage we cannot experience ourselves directly, only through the responses of others, but this commences the process of being able to judge our performances in interaction with others.

Second, as children in the *play stage*, we act out different 'others' in roles. However, these are not connected and lack overall organization. Learning language and attaching feelings to particular roles are central at this stage; the responses of others are, again, of importance in understanding what is appropriate play. Third, the organization of the attitudes of the group then begins to be consolidated in the *game stage*. Roles are learnt along with their relations to one another. Although a variety of 'parts' are played, the rules that govern the game become more apparent. Our reflexive character is then built up by treating ourselves as objects of our own actions as they are understood through the responses of others to our performance.

Mead's idea of the self is not a passive one. Activity and initiative mark both sides of the interaction. After all, one of the first skills that a child learns is to discriminate and select, which cannot be acquired unless supported by the ability to resist and withstand pressure; in other words, to take a stand and act against external forces. Because of the contradictory signals from various significant others, the 'I' must stand aside, at a distance, looking at the external pressures *internalized* in the 'Me'. The stronger the 'I', the more autonomous becomes the character of the child. The strength of the 'I' expresses itself in the person's ability and readiness to put the social pressures internalized in the 'Me' to the test, checking their true powers and their limits, and so challenging them and bearing the consequences.

In the course of this acquisition, we ask questions of ourselves and the first reflexive question of selfhood is, as the French philosopher Paul Ricoeur put it, 'Who am I?' Here we experience the contradiction between freedom and dependence as an inner conflict between what we desire and what we feel obliged to do because of the presence of significant others and their expectations of us. There are, therefore, images of acceptable behaviour that are placed upon our predispositions.

At this point we meet the interactions between the biological and the social. A great deal of money is being spent on trying to determine the genetic bases of different aspects of human behaviour. However, interpretations among those scholars influenced by Darwin's theory of evolution differ on whether, for example, we are competitive or cooperative by nature, while we know that actions and how they are evaluated differ between cultures. As Steve Jones, a geneticist, put it, the most problematic word in genetics is 'for' – as if finding a gene meant that it then stood *for* a particular form of behaviour.

Despite these arguments and the vast sums of money that are being poured into genetic research, with pharmaceutical companies busying themselves for potential profits, most scholars would support the claim of a society to set and enforce standards of acceptable behaviour. Societies and groups develop, over time, ways of controlling their populations. Sigmund Freud, the founder of psychoanalysis, suggested that the whole process of self-development and the social organization of human groups may be interpreted in the light of the need and the practical effort required, to tame sexual and aggressive instincts. Freud suggested that these instincts are never tamed, but 'repressed' and driven into our subconscious. Thus, they are kept in limbo by the superego as the internalized knowledge of demands and pressures exerted by the group. It is for this reason that Freud described the superego as a 'garrison left in a conquered city' by the victorious army of society. The ego itself is then permanently suspended between two powers: the instincts that have been driven into the subconscious yet remain potent and rebellious, and the superego which presses the ego to keep the drives subconscious and prevent their escape from confinement.

Nancy Chodorow, the American feminist sociologist and psychoanalyst, modified such insights utilizing object relations theory in order to examine gendered differences in emotional attachment. Despite a son exhibiting a 'primary love' for his mother, that desire is then repressed. As a result, he moves out of the relationship into a realm in which a tie with his mother is severed and that love then repressed. The son then becomes the 'other' and his autonomy is achieved via a repression of desire. A daughter, on the other hand, experiences an alignment and so her sense of self is not formed through a process of distinction from her mother. This is where we find a gendered emphasis upon empathy and less of a concern among women to differentiate themselves from the worlds of which they are a fundamental part.

Other sociologists have followed up Freud's hypotheses. Norbert Elias, who fused these insights with comprehensive historical research, suggested that the experience of the self we possess arises from a double pressure to which we are all exposed. Our previously mentioned ambiguous attitude towards our selves is the result of the ambivalent position in which the two pressures, acting in opposite directions, cast us. Therefore, the fact that all societies control the predispositions of their members, and strain to contain a range of permissible interactions, is beyond question. However, as far as we know, there is no conclusive evidence that human beings are naturally aggressive and so must be bridled and tamed. What tends to be interpreted as the outburst of natural aggression is more often than not an outcome of callousness or hatred – both attitudes traceable to their social rather than genetic origin. In other words, although it is true that groups train and control the conduct of their members, it does not necessarily follow that they make such conduct more humane and moral. It means only that as a result of this surveillance and correction, the conduct better conforms to the patterns recognized as acceptable within a given kind of social group.

Socialization, Significance and Action

The process of how our selves are formed and how instincts may or may not be suppressed is often given the name *socialization*. We are socialized – transformed into a being capable of living in society – by the internalization of social pressures. We are fit to live and act in a group when we have acquired the skills to behave in an acceptable manner and are then regarded as being free to bear the responsibility for our actions. Yet who are those significant people with whom we interact who socialize us in this way? We have seen that the force which truly operates in the development of the self is the child's image of the intentions and expectations of significant others. True, the child's freedom to select from these expectations is not complete, for some may force their views into the child's perception more effectively than others within their worlds. Nevertheless, the child can hardly avoid choosing, even if the demands of others are contradictory and cannot be met at the same time. After all, some of them must be paid more attention than others and so assigned greater significance in their lives.

A need to assign differential significance to expectations is not confined to children. We experience this as a matter of routine in our daily lives. We risk the displeasure of some friends whom we cherish and respect in order to placate others who we like equally strongly. Whenever we express political views, there will be those we care about who do not like them and who may even bear a grudge against us for expressing them. Assigning relevance in this way means, unavoidably, assigning less importance and even irrelevance to other views. The risk itself will grow to the degree that the environments we inhabit are heterogeneous, that is, characterized by different views, values and interests.

Making a selection from our environments means choosing *reference groups*. Here we find a group against which we measure our actions and provide the standards to which we aspire. How we dress, talk, feel and act in different circumstances are all informed by our reference groups. The Canadian-born American sociologist, Erving Goffman, a wonderful observer of everyday life whose books provide a fascinating insight into our actions, wrote of the importance of 'face work'. 'Face' is defined as the value that a person attaches to their action in terms of the attributes they display. In turn, those they seek to identify themselves with value those attributes. A good 'professional' performance is one instance in which a person's self-esteem and standing among their group may be enhanced as a result.

These processes are not always conscious, nor is there any necessary link between our intentions and the outcome of our actions. As we have said in respect to communication, what we intend and what actually occurs may not be aligned and this leads to frustration and misunderstanding. Alternatively, groups may be unaware of our efforts to imitate their modes of conduct. Some of the groups are normative reference groups in that they set the norms for our conduct without being present at each and every interaction. Particularly prominent among these are family, friends, teachers and bosses at work. Yet even when these people are in a position to respond to our actions, it does not follow that they then become reference groups. They do so only when we assign them with significance. Disobedience at work may occur when we disregard the normative pressures placed upon us by bosses and choose to follow standards that they might condemn. We might also 'play it cool' when the group calls for deep involvement and passion. Thus, in order to exercise their influence, a degree of consent is required to become a reference group.

Another instance of influence beyond the immediate contexts of our actions is comparative reference groups. These are groups to which we do not belong, because either we are beyond their reach or they are beyond our reach. We therefore 'see' the group without being seen by them. Assigning significance in this case is one-sided. Because of the distance between us and them, they are incapable of evaluating our actions and so can neither correct deviations, nor lavish praise upon us. Over recent times we have increasingly moved towards a situation in which we gain, via the mass media, increasing amounts of knowledge through description rather than acquaintance with others. As a result, the role of comparative reference groups in shaping our contemporary sense of self is more pronounced. The mass media transmit information about the latest fashions and styles with ever greater speed and reach the most distant parts of the world. In the process an authority may be vested upon the very lifestyles they make visually accessible, all of which can lead to imitation and the aspiration to belong to such groups.

▽

Summary

Socialization never ends in our lives. For this reason sociologists distinguish between stages of socialization (primary, secondary and tertiary). These bring with them changing and complex forms of interaction between freedom and dependence. In some instances those brought up in small rural communities may find themselves lost in a strange city in which the indifference of strangers leads to feelings of helplessness, all of which is exacerbated by the volume of traffic, rushing crowds and architecture. Risk and trust then mix in different degrees to enable or undermine what the sociologist Anthony Giddens called 'ontological security'. Equally, there are those at home in the city whose anonymity provides for easy movement and whose diversity may be the source of their identity. Yet there are also those situations over which individuals have no control. What sociologists refer to as these macro-structural conditions can have dramatic consequences for us all. Sudden economic depression, the onset of mass unemployment, the outbreak of war, destruction of life savings by rampant inflation and a loss of security through withdrawal of the right to a benefit in times of hardship are just some examples. These changes have the potential to place into doubt and even undermine the achievements of our patterns of socialization and so require a radical restructuring of our actions and the norms that orient our conduct.

In a less spectacular mode, each of us confronts problems on a daily basis that call for readjustment or question our expectations: for example, when we change schools or jobs, go to university, change from being a single to a married person, acquire a home of our own, move house, become parents or turn into senior citizens. Therefore, it is better to think of the relations between freedom and dependence as a continuing process of change and negotiation in which their complex interactions start at birth and end only with death.

Our freedom is also never complete. Our present actions are informed and even constrained by our past actions; we find ourselves routinely faced with choices that, however attractive, are unattainable. Freedom has a cost that varies with circumstances and while we look for new opportunities and things to which we aspire, the feasibility and the likelihood of a 'new break' becomes increasingly remote beyond a certain age. At the same time, freedom for some may be bought at the cost of greater dependence for others. We have spoken of the role that material and symbolic resources play in making choice a viable, realistic proposition and that not all people can enjoy access to those resources. Thus, while all people are free and cannot but be free – they are bound to take responsibility for whatever they do – some are more free than others because their horizons and choices for action are wider and that, in turn, may depend on restricting the horizons of others.

We can say that the ratio between freedom and dependence is an indicator of the relative position a person, or a whole category of persons, occupies in a society. What we call privilege appears, under closer scrutiny, to be a higher degree of freedom and a lesser degree of dependence. This manifests itself in different ways and for different reasons, while societies and groups seek to justify this state of affairs in order to legitimize their respective positions. Nevertheless, when gaps in our knowledge of others are left, they are frequently filled by prejudice. How sociologists look at these issues is a subject to which we shall turn in chapter 2.

chapter two

VIEWING AND SUSTAINING OUR LIVES

We have discussed issues of group belonging and how these relate to the conception we have of ourselves in interaction with others. How these groups influence our conduct and how we interact with others, and what groups we belong to and exclude as a result, are all part of everyday life. These outcomes, whether intended or not, contribute to the form and content of the social relations that characterize our societies. In this chapter we consider these issues in more detail and examine the consequences that these processes have for how we see others and ourselves.

▽

Sustaining our Lives: Interaction, Understanding and Social Distance

Let us think of all those people whose actions are indispensable to our everyday lives. Who puts the coffee in the cup? Who provides the electricity, gas and water upon which we might rely? At the same time, who are those people who make decisions about how, where and when to move the $1.5 trillion that circulates in the global financial markets every day with consequences for the prosperity and development of individual countries? They are part of the unknown multitudes who enable and constrain our freedom to select the lives of our liking, much like those manufacturers who find robots more profitable than living employees and hence trim the chances of finding employment. Also, there are those who, in a preoccupation with their own ends, produce foul air and industrial wastes with long-term consequences for the quality of our lives, the environment and wildlife in general.

Compare these people with those who you have met, recognize and can name. Now consider that among all the people who influence how you conduct your life and what choices you can and cannot make, the people you actually know are a very small proportion of those persons – even those who we actually encounter in our lives appear to us in different capacities. Some people we meet often and know what we can and cannot expect of them and so we talk to each other, share our knowledge and discuss matters of common interest. Others are casual acquaintances, or those we meet on just one occasion. There are also the places in which we meet in what Erving Goffman called the 'interaction order'. Here we are concerned with those 'spaces' that are not 'personal' as such, but the regions and social situations in which we interact with others. The content of the interactions within these places may be functional, for example, when obtaining money from a bank, seeing a dentist or buying groceries in a shop. Relations then take place that are driven by our purpose and we are often not interested in the people we meet except in terms of their ability to perform those functions. Intimate inquiries are out of place in such circumstances and often regarded as an unwarranted intrusion into what, in relation to the encounter, we see as our privacy. Should an intrusion occur, we might resist it as a breach of the unwritten expectations of the relationship – a relationship that is, after all, concerned with an exchange of services.

Although proximity informs an episode of social interaction, that tells us nothing of the experience of its quality among the participants. Some will claim that their 'net friends' – those with whom they communicate over the internet – are just as much their 'friends' as those whom they have physically met. Alfred Schutz, a German American sociologist, suggested that from any individual point of view all other members of the human race may be plotted against an imaginary line – a continuum measured by social distance – which grows as social intercourse shrinks in its volume and intensity. This ranges from a personalized knowledge to knowledge limited to an ability to assign people to types: the rich, football hooligans, soldiers, bureaucrats, politicians, journalists and others. The more distant from ourselves, the more typified is our awareness of the people who occupy the point on the continuum, as well as our reactions to them.

Aside from those who are our contemporaries, there are those who fall within our mental maps as predecessors and successors. Our communications with them are one-sided and incomplete. Yet, at the same time, such communication, perhaps handed down in the form of myths, can assist in seeking to solve contemporary contradictions over our identities. As social anthropologists have shown, we can relate in this way to particular traditions preserved by historical memory in the form of ceremonies or an adherence to particular interpretations of the past. With successors, it is different, for we leave imprints of our existence for them, but do not expect them to answer back. We might project imaginary futures, but cannot 'know' them. However, it is not unknown for modern-day scientists to be motivated by the genre of science fiction and contemporary actions to imagine the possibilities they hold for the future. The idea of managers 're-engineering' organizations, for example, is about the projection of a future ideal onto existing reality. These have the possibility of relieving their authors of their responsibility in the present because the effects of their decisions are contained within an imagined future. However, whether talking about the influence of the past or imagining possible futures in the present, they are not fixed over time. People change locations, move from one category to another, travel towards and away from our point on the continuum and shift from being contemporaries to predecessors. In the process our capacity for empathy – the ability and willingness to put oneself in another person's position – also changes. Thus, our self-identity is bound up with the social identities that we portray to others and those we encounter in our everyday existence.

'Us' within the 'Other'

Our ability to make distinctions and divisions within the world also includes that between 'us' and 'them'. One stands for the group to which we feel we belong and understand. The other, on the contrary, stands for a group which we cannot access or do not wish to belong. Our vision of this is vague, fragmentary and due to poor comprehension, even frightening. Further, we may be assured in our beliefs by suspecting that 'they' feel the same reservations and anxieties about 'us'.

The distinction between 'us' and 'them' is sometimes presented in sociology as one between an in-group and out-group. These opposites are inseparable, for there cannot be one without the other. They sediment, as it were, in our map of the world on the two poles of an antagonistic relationship and this makes the two groups 'real' to their respective members and provides for the inner unity and coherence they are imagined to possess. Given that our self-identities are bound up with the groups to which we belong, some scholars, notably the French historian and philosopher Michel Foucault and the French philosopher Jacques Derrida, have argued that we possess an 'essence' to what we are only by the exclusion of negatives, in this case the assumed characteristics of 'them'. Therefore, self-identification is enabled by the resources that we draw from our environment and there is no fixed 'core' to our identities. As such, oppositions become tools that we draw upon to chart the world. Examples of this process include the distinctions made between the 'deserving' and 'undeserving' poor, 'respectable' citizens and the 'rabble' who defy all rules and are characterized as disliking all order. In each case our respective traits, as well as investments of feeling, derive from this mutual antagonism.

From these observations, we can draw the following conclusion: an out-group is precisely that imaginary opposition to itself that the in-group needs for its self-identity, for its cohesiveness, for its inner solidarity and emotional security. A readiness to cooperate within the confines of the group thereby requires, as its prop, a refusal to cooperate with an adversary. It is as if we needed the fear of wilderness in order to feel security. The ideals that sustain this include solidarity, mutual confidence and what might be termed, following the French sociologist Emile Durkheim, a 'togetherness' or 'common bond'. This is how one would expect the members of an ideal family to behave towards each other, and parents towards their children in terms of their patterns of love and care.

If we listen to the rhetoric of those who wish to evoke a mutual loyalty in their audience, we often hear the metaphors of 'sisterhood', 'brotherhood' and all being in one 'family'. Expressions of national solidarity and a readiness to sacrifice oneself for a greater good are peppered with references to a nation as 'our mother' or 'the fatherland'. Mutual help, protection and friendship therefore become the imaginary rules of in-group life, all of which make us perceive of relationships in this context as emotionally warm, suffused with mutual sympathy and the potential to inspire loyalty, as well as the determination required for the defence of the group's interests. Thus, there is a feeling of community as a pleasant place to be which precedes all argument and reflection. In this place times may be difficult, but one can always find a solution in the end. People may seem harsh and selfish, but one can count on their help if the need arises. Above all, one can understand them and be certain of being understood by them.

As we have discussed, we do not necessarily have to be in the physical presence of those persons with whom we identify in order to evoke these feelings and engage in activities and beliefs that link us to them. There are face-to-face groups, as well as those which are large and widespread to which we can relate. Class, gender and nation are typical examples of this second category of in-group. Though we often consider them as if they were like the small, intimate groups we are familiar with, they are imaginary communities. While they are often characterized by similar language and customs, they are also divided in their beliefs and practices. These cracks, however, are thinly plastered by a 'we' image that appeals to a sense of unity. Indeed, the speeches of nationalist leaders so often refer to the burying of differences in a spirit of commonality that is oriented towards a collectively held goal.

There is work to do in making classes, genders, ethnicities and nations in-groups by themselves because they lack the social cement of groups that are familiar to us in everyday interactions. One consequence of this process may to be to suppress or dismiss evidence that runs counter to their ideal image as being false or irrelevant. The process of purification demands a disciplined and resourceful body of activists whose practices add to plausibility of the imaginary unity of interests and beliefs. Given this, the actions of a body – political party, trade union, government of a national state – precede the formation of large-scale in-groups. Nationalism thus precedes the emergence of unified national units.

Despite the work that goes into the image of unity, the hold on reality remains fragile. Why? Because it lacks the substance that can derive from networks' daily interaction and so no effort to induce loyalty in large groups stands a chance of success if there is not an accompanying practice of hostility towards an out-group. Here we find the image of an enemy who is lurid and frightening and possesses the characteristics of cunning and scheming. Vigilance becomes a constant necessity where images are informed by prejudice. Prejudice – as the refusal to admit any virtues that the enemies may possess and an inclination to magnify their real and imaginary vices – prevents one from accepting the possibility that their intentions may be honest. Prejudice also manifests itself in double moral standards. What the members of an in-group argue that they deserve as entitlement will be an act of grace and benevolence if granted to those of the out-group. Most importantly, one's own atrocity against out-group members does not seem to clash with moral conscience, while severe condemnation is demanded in cases where much milder acts have been perpetrated by the enemy. Prejudice thereby prompts people to approve of the means used in the promotion of their own cause, means that would never be justified if employed by the out-group in pursuit of their own purposes. Identical actions are thus called different names: for example, one group's freedom fighter is another group's terrorist.

Dispositions towards prejudice are not uniformly distributed. They can manifest themselves in racist attitudes and actions or, more generally, in xenophobia as the hatred of everything 'foreign'. People who entertain high levels of prejudice are ill prepared to endure any deviation from strict rules of conduct and hence favour a strong power capable of keeping people 'in line'. Such people were characterized by the German social theorist, philosopher and cultural critic, Theodor Adorno, as having 'authoritarian personalities'. These are closely related to expressions of insecurity generated by drastic changes in habitual conditions. What people have learned as effective ways to go about their daily lives suddenly becomes less reliable. The result can induce feelings of losing control of the situation and so the change may be resented and/or resisted.

The result of these transformations in social conditions may be the need to defend 'the old ways' against newcomers who represent the 'new ways' and so become the subjects of resentment. Pierre Bourdieu wrote of this process within what he called 'fields' of social relations in terms of people pursuing strategies of 'orthodoxy' or 'heresy'. The stakes are the conservation or subversion of established relations and so the set of pre-reflexive or taken-for-granted assumptions that inform everyday actions are forced to awake from their slumbers to defend the status quo against intrusion.

Norbert Elias also presented a theory of these situations in terms of what he called the 'established' and the 'outsiders'. An influx of outsiders always presents a challenge to the way of life of the established population, whatever the objective difference between the newcomers and the old inhabitants. Tensions then arise out of the necessity to make space and so recognize the newcomers. Resulting anxieties become hostile feelings, but the established inhabitants tend to possess better resources to act upon their prejudices. They can also invoke the rights they have acquired by their sheer length of habitation as encapsulated in such phrases as 'this is the land of our forebears'.

The complex relationship between the established and the outsiders goes a long way towards explaining a large variety of the conflicts between in-groups and out-groups. The birth of modern anti-Semitism in nineteenth-century Europe and its wide reception can be understood as the result of a coincidence between the high speed of change in a rapidly industrializing society and the emancipation of the Jews, who emerged from the ghettos or separate Jewish quarters and closed communities to mix with the Gentile population of the cities and enter 'ordinary' occupations. Similarly, changes in the industrial landscape of post-war Britain generated widespread anxiety which was subsequently focused on the newcomers from the Caribbean countries or Pakistan, while male resistance to women's claims of equal rights in employment and in competition for positions of social influence is another example. Calls by feminists for equality still spark a prejudice that is thinly disguised by allusions to a 'natural' state of affairs. Underlying this is an assertion that women should know their place within an order of social relations that tends to grant men privileges over women.

Gregory Bateson, an American anthropologist, suggested the term 'schismogenesis' for the chain of actions and reactions that follows the above processes. Each action calls for a stronger reaction, and control over the situation is gradually lost. He distinguishes between two types of schismogenesis. First, there is 'symmetrical schismogenesis', in which each side reacts to the signs of strength in the adversary. Whenever the adversary shows power and determination, a still stronger manifestation of power and resolve is sought in reaction. What both sides fear most of all is to be seen as weak or hesitant. Think of the slogans 'deterrence must be credible' or 'the aggressor must be shown that aggression does not pay'. Symmetrical schismogenesis breeds self-assertiveness on both sides and contributes to a destruction of the possibility of rational agreement.

Neither side remembers the original reason for the conflict and instead becomes incensed by the bitterness of their present fight.

The second characteristic is 'complementary schismogenesis'. This develops from exactly opposite assumptions, but leads to identical results, that is, the breakdown of the relationship. The schismogenetic sequence of actions is complementary when one side strengthens its resolve at the sign of weakness in the other side, while the other side weakens its resistance when confronted with manifestations of growing strength in the opposite side. Typically, this is the tendency for any interaction between a dominant and a more submissive partner. The self-assurance and self-confidence of one partner feed on symptoms of timidity and submissiveness in the other. Cases of complementary schismogenesis are as varied in their content as they are numerous.

On one extreme we can think of a gang terrorizing an entire neighbourhood into unconditional submission and then, convinced of its own omnipotence via an absence of resistance, raises its demands beyond the capacity of its victims to pay. Victims are then driven to desperation, or they will ignite their rebellion, or they may be forced to move out of the gang's territory. On the other extreme, one can think of the patron–client relationship. The dominant majority (national, racial, cultural and religious) may accept the presence of a minority on condition that the latter studiously demonstrates an acceptance of the dominant values and an eagerness to live by their rules. The minority would be keen to please and thereby to curry favour, but may discover that the necessary concessions tend to grow with the dominant group's confidence. The minority will be driven either to escape into its own ghetto, or to change its strategy to one modelled on symmetrical schismogenesis. Whatever the choice, the breakdown of the relationship is the likely outcome.

There is, thankfully, a third type of framework in which interaction takes place. This form – reciprocity – combines features of both symmetrical and complementary schismogenesis, but does it in a way that neutralizes their self-destructive tendencies. In a reciprocal relationship, each single case of interaction is asymmetrical, yet over long periods the actions of both sides balance each other, because each has to offer something that the other side needs; for instance, the resented and discriminated minority may possess skills that are lacking among the population as a whole. Arguably, some form of reciprocity characterizes most frameworks of interaction. It ought to be noted, however, that no reciprocal framework is fully immune against the danger of sliding into a symmetrical or complementary relationship and thereby triggering off the process of schismogenesis.

We have seen that we are 'us', as long as there is 'them', makes sense only together, in their opposition to each other. In addition, they belong together and form a group only because each and every one of them shares the same characteristic: none of them is 'one of us'. Both concepts derive their meaning from the dividing line they service. Without such a division, without the possibility of opposing ourselves to 'them', we would be hard put to make sense of our identities.

Viewing and Living Lives: Boundaries and Outsiders

'Strangers' defy the above divisions. Indeed, what they oppose is the opposition itself: that is, divisions of any kind in terms of the boundaries that guard them and thus the clarity of the social world which results from these practices. Herein lie their significance, their meaning and the role they play in social life. By their sheer presence, which does not fit easily into any established categories, the strangers deny the very validity of the accepted oppositions. They expose the apparent 'natural' character of oppositions and so lay bare their fragility. Divisions are then seen for what they are: imaginary lines that can be crossed or redrawn. After all, they come into our field of vision and social spaces – uninvited. Whether we desire it or not, these people sit firmly inside the world that we occupy and show no signs of leaving. We note their presence because it simply cannot be ignored and because of this we find it difficult to make sense of them. They are, as it were, neither close nor distant and we do not know exactly what to expect of them and ourselves.

In these cases, constructing boundaries that are as exact, precise and unambiguous as possible is a central feature of the human-made world. All our acquired skills and knowledge would be rendered questionable, useless, harmful and even suicidal, were it not for the fact that well-marked boundaries send us signals as to what to expect and how to conduct ourselves in particular contexts. Yet those on the other side of these boundaries do not differ so sharply from us in a way that relieves us from mistaken classifications. Because of this, a constant effort is needed to maintain divisions in a reality that knows of no sharp, unmistakable contours.

The understanding of others and ourselves now becomes the effort of understanding why these barriers exist and how they are maintained. The anthropologist Anthony Cohen argued that the idea of boundaries is central to the effort of comprehending the limits to our self-consciousness in and through the task of understanding those who fall outside of symbolic demarcation points. Here we can see how if people differ in one respect, they may be similar in others. Most traits can be shown to vary in a gradual, smooth and often imperceptible way in the manner that Alfred Schutz's continuous line suggests. Because of overlap, there are ambiguous areas in which people are not immediately recognizable as belonging to one or other of opposing groups. As we have said, for some this is a source of threat, rather than an opportunity to know more of ourselves through knowing more of others.

Among human preoccupations, a crucial role is played by the never-ending task of making the human-made order 'stick'. As the anthropologist Mary Douglas noted in her work *Purity and Danger*, boundaries are not simply negative, but also positive because rituals enact forms of social relations that enable people to know their societies. To achieve this purpose, however, ambiguity which serves to blur boundaries needs to be suppressed. Consider some examples of this process. What makes some plants into 'weeds', which we poison and uproot, is their horrifying tendency to obliterate the boundary between our garden and wilderness. They are often quite nice looking, fragrant and pleasing, but their 'fault' is that they have come, uninvited, to a place that demands neatness, even if that means using numerous chemicals to achieve the desired result. The same may be said about 'dirt' in houses. It has been found that some chemical companies had to put two clearly distinct labels onto packages containing identical detergents. Why? Because they learned from research that those who were proud of their housekeeping would not dream of confusing the difference between a bathroom and kitchen by using the same detergent in both places. Such concerns can manifest themselves in obsessive behaviour that is devoted to the purity and cleanliness of local environments. Products are sold with this in mind, but the result can lead to an reduction in the ability of our immune systems to cope with infections. Therefore, the desire to make the world orderly in the face of the permanent threat of ambiguity and disorder has a cost not only for ourselves, but also for those people and things that are seen to disturb that harmony.

The boundary of a group can be threatened from both outside *and* inside. Within the group there are those ambivalent people who have been branded as deserters, detractors of values, enemies of unity and turncoats. It can also be attacked and eventually pierced from the outside by people who demand parity and who move about in spaces where they are not so easily identifiable. In so doing, the boundaries which were assumed to be safe are exposed as flimsy. Those who have lifted themselves from their old place and passed to our own, accomplish a feat which makes us suspect they possess some power we cannot resist and so we do not feel confident in their presence. 'Neophyte' (someone who converted to our faith), 'nouveau riche' (someone poor yesterday, who made a sudden fortune and today has joined the rich and powerful) and 'upstart' (someone of low social standing quickly promoted to a position of power) are just some of the terms that signify reprobation, loathing and contempt in such situations.

Such people arouse anxiety for other reasons. They ask questions which we do not know how to answer because we have had no occasion and saw no reason to ask them ourselves: 'Why do you do it this way? Does it make sense? Have you tried to do it differently?' The ways we have lived, the kind of life that gave us security and made us feel comfortable, now find themselves open to what we view as a challenge and we are called upon to explain and justify our actions.

A resulting loss of security is not something we would forgive lightly. It is often viewed as a threat and, on the whole, we are not inclined to forgive. Hence such questions are viewed as offences and subversions. Ranks can be closed in defence of established ways of life and what were previously a disparate group of people become united against a common foe. They are the strangers whom we hold responsible for a crisis of confidence. Discomfort may descend into anger against those now castigated as 'troublemakers'.

Even if the newcomers refrain from asking awkward questions, the way they go about their daily business will still raise issues. Those who have come from other places and are determined to stay will wish to learn ways of life, imitate them and try to become 'like us'. However hard they try to mimic, they cannot help making mistakes in the beginning because the assumptions upon which the way of life are built need to be learnt over time. Thus, their attempts look unconvincing and their behaviour looks clumsy and awkward and appears like a caricature of our own conduct, which forces us to ask what the 'real' thing is like. We disown their inept imitations by ridiculing them and composing and telling jokes which 'caricature the caricature'. However, there is bitterness in laughter when anxiety masks itself as hilarity.

Members of the group have been forced, by the newcomers' presence, to examine their own habits and expectations with a heavy dose of irony. Although never having been open to explicit questioning, their comforts have been disrupted and resistance will result. In terms of possible responses to such situations, the first is towards a restoration of the status quo. Boundaries require a return to what was seen as an unproblematic clarity. They can be sent back to where they are presupposed to have originated from – even though such a place may not exist! Life is therefore made uncomfortable for them by, for example, turning humour into ridicule and denying them recognition in terms of the rights that are granted to existing members of the group. However, even if they leave, when a group is based upon such fragility, new targets will need to be discovered in order to sustain themselves.

At a national level, the form of this process changes and attempts may be made to force them to emigrate, or to make their lives so miserable that they themselves would treat exodus as a lesser evil. If such a move is resisted, the stakes are raised and genocide may follow; thus cruel physical destruction is charged with the task that attempts at physical removal failed to fulfil. Of course, genocide is the most extreme and abhorrent method of 'restoring order'. Yet recent history has proved in a most grue-some way that the danger of genocide does not go away so easily – despite condemnation and widespread resentment.

Although genocide is an extreme form, less odious and radical solutions may be chosen, with one of the most common being separation. This may be territorial, spiritual or a combination of both. Its territorial expression may be found in ghettos or ethnic reserves: that is, parts of cities or areas of the country reserved for the habitation of people with whom the more powerful elements of population refuse to mix. Sometimes walls and/or legally enforced prohibitions surround the allocated land. Alternatively, movements to and from these spaces is not punishable and nominally free, but in practice its residents cannot or will not escape their confinement because the conditions 'outside' have been made intolerable for them, or because the standard of living in their own, often derelict, areas is the only one they can afford.

In cases where territorial separation is incomplete or becomes altogether impracticable, spiritual separation grows in importance. Intercourse with the strangers is reduced to strictly business exchanges; social contacts are avoided. Every effort, conscious and otherwise, is made to prevent or reduce physical proximity from turning into a spiritual one. Resentment or overt hostility is the most obvious among such preventive efforts. Barriers of prejudice may be built that prove far more effective than the thickest of walls. Active avoidance of contact is constantly boosted by the fear of contamination from those who 'serve' but are not like 'us'. Resentment spills over into everything one can associate with the strangers: their ways of talking, their ways of dressing, their rituals, the way they organize their family life and even the smell of the food they like to cook. Layered upon this is their apparent refusal to engage in the natural order of social relations and so they do not accept responsibility, as 'we' have to do, for their actions. The order that produced this state of affairs is not questioned, but instead it is their 'personal' failure to adhere to its apparent logic.

Segregation and Movement in the City

So far we have assumed a separation between groups, although we have noted the ambivalence and ambiguities which surround such barriers. Who belongs to each group has not been in dispute. It is easy to see, however, that this kind of simple situation and the clear-cut task it tends to generate is hardly ever met in our type of society. The societies in which most of us live are urban: that is, people live together in great density, travel continuously and in the course of their daily business they enter diverse areas inhabited by diverse people. In most cases, we cannot be sure that people we meet uphold our standards. Almost constantly we are struck by new sights and sounds that we do not fully comprehend and, perhaps unfortunately, hardly ever have the time to pause, reflect and make an honest attempt to understand these people and places. We live among strangers, among whom we are strangers ourselves. In such a world, strangers cannot be confined or kept at bay.

Despite these interactions within the city, the practices described earlier are not completely abandoned. Practices of *segregation* take place in, for example, the wearing of salient, easily visible marks of group membership. Law may enforce such a group-ascribed appearance, so that 'passing for someone else' will be punished. Nevertheless, it is often achieved without necessarily resorting to the law for enforcement. Those who have more disposable income than others can afford to dress in particular ways and these act as codes for classifying persons by the splendour, misery or oddity of their appearance. However, relatively cheap copies of admired and highly praised statements of fashion are now produced in mass quantities, rendering such distinctions more blurred. The result is that they may hide, rather than disclose, the territorial origin and mobility of their owners and wearers. This does not mean that appearance does not set the wearers apart, for they are public statements concerning the reference groups they have chosen. Equally, we may disguise our origins by dressing in different ways in order to subvert or disrupt the socially imposed classification. As such, the informative value that comes with the appearance of others may be diminished.

If appearance has, over time, become more problematic, this is not so for segregation by space. The territory of shared urban spaces is divided into areas in which one kind of person is more likely to be found than others. The value that segregated areas provide in orienting our conduct and expectations is attained by routine practices of exclusion: that is, by selective and limited admission. Exclusive residential areas, policed by private security companies, are but one example of this phenomenon, in which those with financial means exclude those who do not enjoy the possibilities that are derived from their income and wealth.

It is not only security guards at the gates of exclusive residences who symbolize practices of exclusion, but also those in large shopping areas where time is to be lost in conspicuous acts of consumption – ably assisted by the relative absence of clocks. There are also box offices and receptionists; in each the criteria of selection employed will vary. In the case of the box office, money is the most important criterion, though a ticket may still be refused to a person who does not meet some other requirement, for instance, their clothes or skin colour. The tests of entitlement set a situation in which the entry is denied to all as long as they remain total strangers. These ritual acts of identification transform a faceless member of the grey, indiscriminate category of strangers into a 'concrete person' who is recognized as being entitled to enter. The uncertainty entailed in being in the presence of persons 'who can be anybody' has now, though only locally and temporarily, been reduced for those who identify themselves with such places.

The power to refuse entry, and so to demarcate boundaries according to the acceptable characteristics of their entrants, is deployed to secure a relative homogeneity. These practices seek a reduced ambivalence in selected spaces within the densely populated and anonymous world of urban living. This power is practised on a small scale whenever we take care in controlling those spaces identified as being private. We trust, however, that other people will use their powers to do a similar job for us on a grander scale in the enclosures between which we move as a matter of routine. On the whole, we try to minimize the time spent in intermediary areas by, for example, travelling from one closely guarded space to another. One clear example of this is to travel in the isolation of the hermetically sealed shell of a private car while, perhaps, complaining about the increased road congestion.

When moving within these areas and the gaze of strangers who have the potential to disrupt our self-identities, the most we can do is to try to remain inconspicuous, or at any rate to avoid attracting attention. Erving Goffman found that such *civil inattention* is paramount among the techniques that make life in a city, among strangers, possible. Characterized by elaborate modes of pretending that we do not look and do not listen, or assuming a posture that suggests that we do not see and do not hear, or even care, what the others around us are doing, civil inattention is routinized. It is manifested in the avoidance of eye-contact which, culturally speaking, can serve as an invitation to open up a conversation between strangers. Anonymity is thereby assumed to be given up in the most mundane of gestures. Yet total avoidance is not possible, for a simple passage in crowded areas requires a degree of monitoring in order to avoid collision with others. Therefore, we must be attentive, while also pretending that we are not looking or being seen.

Newcomers not used to the urban context are often struck by such routines. For them, they might signify a peculiar callousness and cold indifference on the part of the population. People are tantalizingly close in a physical sense, but spiritually appear remote from one another. Lost in the crowd, there is a feeling of abandonment to our own resources leading, in turn, to loneliness. Loneliness then appears as the price of privacy. Living with strangers becomes an art whose value is as ambiguous as the strangers themselves. Yet there is another side to this experience.

Anonymity can mean emancipation from the noxious and vexing surveillance and interference of the others, who in smaller and more personalized contexts would feel entitled to be curious and to meddle in our lives. The city provides for the possibility of remaining in a public place while keeping our privacy intact. An invisibility, enabled by the application of civil inattention, offers a scope for freedom that is unthinkable under different conditions. This is fertile soil for the intellect and, as the great German sociologist Georg Simmel pointed out, urban life and abstract thinking are resonant and develop together. After all, abstract thought is boosted by the awesome richness of an urban experience which cannot be grasped in all its qualitative diversity, while the capacity for operating general concepts and categories is the skill without which survival in an urban environment is inconceivable.

So there are two sides to this experience and there appears to be no gain without loss. Together with the cumbersome curiosity of others, their sympathetic interest and willingness to help may disappear. With the exhilarating bustle of urban life, there comes cool human indifference fuelled by many interactions that are driven by exchange of goods and services. What is lost in the process is the ethical character of human relationships. A wide range of human intercourse which is devoid of significance and consequences now becomes possible, because so much routine conduct appears free from evaluation and judgement by some standards of morality.

A human relationship is moral when a feeling of responsibility arises within us for the welfare and well-being of the 'other'. This does not derive from a fear of being punished, nor from a calculation that is made from the point of view of personal gain, or even the obligations that are contained within a contract we have signed and are legally bound to fulfil. Neither is it conditional on what the other person is doing or what sort of person they may be. Our responsibility is moral as long as it is totally selfless and unconditional. We are responsible for other people simply because they are persons and so command our responsibility. Our responsibility is also moral in so far as we see it to be ours alone. It is, therefore, not negotiable and cannot be passed on to another human being. Responsibility for other human beings arises simply because they are human beings and the moral impulse to give help that follows from this, requires no argument, legitimation or proof beyond that.

As we have seen, physical proximity may be cleansed of its moral aspect. People who live close to one another and affect each other's conditions and well-being may well not experience moral proximity. In this way they remain oblivious to the moral significance of their actions. What follows may be to refrain from actions that moral responsibility would have prompted and to engage in actions that moral responsibility would have prevented. Thanks to the rules of civil inattention, strangers are not treated as enemies and most of the time escape the fate that tends to befall the enemy; they are not targets of hostility and aggression. Yet not unlike the enemies, the strangers of which we are all, at some time, a part, are deprived of the protection that moral proximity offers. Therefore, it is but a short step from civil inattention to moral indifference, heartlessness and disregard for the needs of others.

Summary

We have spoken about the roles of social distance, boundaries and space in our everyday lives. These boundaries are both symbolic and physical, but they interact in complex ways. We are all bound up with the routines, decisions and consequences which provide for the knowledge and conditions that enable us not only to monitor our actions, but also to have the capability to act. While there are clear differences in the access that people have to the means to pursue their ends, we are all implicated, at different levels and with different effects, in the processes we have described in this chapter. They provide us with not only our social identities, but also our self-identities and ways of viewing others, with each of these being intimately bound up with each other. In chapter 3 we shall continue this exploration by examining such social phenomena as communities, groups and organizations and their roles in our lives.

chapter three

THE BONDS THAT UNITE: SPEAKING OF 'WE'

In this chapter we shall examine the processes through which each of us, as individual subjects, are brought together within larger configurations of people. How does this occur, under what circumstances and with what effects? These are just some of the issues we wish to consider. Such issues are brought to our attention every day through the use of such terms as 'all of us', 'we demand' and 'we would agree' that we find written in our newspapers and expressed by business people, religious leaders and politicians through the media. Who is this 'we' that is supposed to be based on mutual understanding and how is it constituted?

Communities: Forging Consensus and Dealing with Conflict

A collection of people, who are not clearly defined or circumscribed, but who agree to something that other people reject and bestow an authority upon those beliefs, may be referred to as a *community*. While we may try to justify or explain this 'togetherness', it is a spiritual unity that is foremost in its characterization. Without this in place, there is no community. Agreement, or at least the readiness and potential to agree, is assumed to be the primary underpinning for all community members. As such, the unifying factors are taken to be stronger and more important than anything which may divide it, while the differences between members are secondary in comparison to their similarities. In this way community is thought of as a natural unity.

The power of such bonds should not be underestimated. They relieve people of the need to explain and convince one another of 'who' they are and enable shared views to be constituted as truth and deserved of belief and respect. Belonging to a community is at its strongest and most secure when we believe that we have not chosen it on purpose and that we have done nothing to make it exist, and so can do nothing to transform it through our actions. For the sake of effectiveness, their images and postulates, as implied by phrases such as 'we all agree', are never given in detail or come into question; they are never written down in a formal code or turned into objects of conscious effort aimed at *demarcation* and *maintenance*. Their hold is stronger when they stay silent as taken-for-granted orders and so remain unchallenged. The common bond that unites is at its fullest among isolated people who conduct all their lives, from birth to death, in the same company and who never venture into other places and are not visited by members of other groups. With these conditions in place, they may have no occasion to reflect upon their own ways and means and to see them in need of explanation and justification.

Situations such as these hardly ever exist. Instead, community is a postulate, an expression of desire and a call to mobilize and close ranks, rather than a reality. In the memorable words of the Welsh critic and novelist Raymond Williams, 'the remarkable thing about community is that it always has been'. Even assuming that it had existed, it does not exist any more and its moment has passed. Yet the unshakeable powers of 'natural' unity are often evoked when people confront the practical task of creating unity, or rescuing through conscious effort its ideal – an ideal which, in fact, may be no more than a crumbling edifice of the past.

Any reference to a natural state within the idea of community is itself a factor in rendering appeals to unity effective. Most powerful are those assumed to be beyond human interpretation and control in allusions to such things as 'common blood', hereditary character and a timeless link with the 'land'. These bind people to a common past and common destiny over which they have little or no control. Common religions and the unity of nations are appealed to in terms of the objective 'facts of the case' that may effectively hide the elements of arbitrariness that are involved in the choice and interpretation of selected events and characteristics. Those who go against such interpretations are seen to commit acts that betray their own nature. From this they may be labelled as renegades, fools and being so wrapped up in self-serving arrogance that they challenge decisions already decreed by historical inevitability.

Allusions to those things that are beyond our control arrive with increasing possibilities for greater control over our destinies. Speaking of genetic similarities for the purposes of creating unity does not relieve the speaker of the burden of choice in their translations. Why? Because aside from difference in opinion, when it comes to understanding the relations between genes and human behaviour, such assumed inevitability in an age in which genetic engineering is a reality is highly problematic. As the feminist psychologist and social theorist Lynne Segal put it, we face a choice. On the one hand, we can look backwards in order to examine the 'constraints in our genetic heritage that determine our fate'. On the other hand, we can look forward by putting our faith in the 'new Genetic Gods' and the freedoms that may be provided through rendering our natures 'infinitely malleable'.

In the face of such possibilities, any reference to natural states that unify is limited. Instead, another route is to be open in intention to create a community of beliefs or faith by converting (proselytizing) people to new ideas. The aim here is to create a community of the faithful among those who are unified in their attachment to a cause that is revealed to them by a saintly founder or a perceptive, far-sighted, political leader. In this kind of exercise, the language employed is not that of sacred traditions or historical fate, but one of the good news that comes with being 'born again' and above all, of living according to *the* Truth. Appeals are not made to situations in which people have no choice but, on the contrary, to the noble act of embracing the true faith by rejecting superstition, illusion or ideological distortion through any doubt. Overt acts of joining are seen as acts of liberation and the beginning of new lives. This is not fate at work, but an act of free will that is read as the first true manifestation of a new-found freedom. What is concealed at this time, however, are the pressures that will be exerted on converts to remain obedient to the newly embraced faith and subsequently to surrender their freedom to what the cause may demand. Therefore, the demands upon their adherents may be no less excessive than from those who invoke historical tradition or genetic predisposition to legitimize their practices.

Communities of faith cannot limit themselves to the preaching of a new creed intended to unite future devotees. Devotion would never be secure unless supported by ritual: that is, a series of regular events – patriotic festivals, party meetings, church services – in which the faithful are called to participate as actors so that their common membership and fate may be reasserted and devotion reinforced. However, there will be variations in the stringency and volume of demands that are made upon members. Most political parties – with the important exception of those right and left-wing parties that pursue radical or reactionary ends and treat their members as fighters and so demand loyalty and subordination – seek no more unity of thought than is necessary to secure regular electoral support. After this time the army of volunteers may be forgotten until, of course, they are needed again. In other words, they will leave the rest of the members' lives to their own discretion and would refrain from legislating about, say, the nature of their family life or their choice of occupation.

Religious sects, on the other hand, tend to be more demanding. They are unlikely to settle for participation in periodic cult rituals because the whole of their members' lives will come into their domain of concern. As sects are, by definition, minorities exposed to outside pressures a complete reform of the way in which the faithful conduct their daily business in all its aspects will be monitored. Through making the whole of life into a profession of faith and a manifestation of *loyalty*, sectarian communities will attempt to defend their members' commitment against the scepticism or outright hostility of the environment. In extreme cases, attempts will be made to cut off the community altogether from the 'ordinary' flow of social life with 'normal' society being censured for its sinfulness or temptations.

Which of the many possible charges against the 'outside' that may be invoked depends upon the life that the community wishes to promote. Members may be invited to run away from the abominations of mundane life to a solitary existence, or they may be enjoined to opt out of a 'rat race' and enter into relations that are based solely on mutual intimacy, sincerity and trust. Members are normally also asked to turn their backs on the attractions of consumerism and reconcile themselves to a life of modesty and austerity. Communities of this type, often described as communes, confront their members with the task of belonging without legally enforced contractual obligations, these being a second line of defence if animosities or a lack of consensus threatens. All dissent, therefore, constitutes a threat and the more comprehensive that communities are, the more oppressive they tend to become.

Communities differ in terms of the uniformity that they demand of their members. In most cases, however, stipulations tend to be diffuse, ill defined and impossible to determine in advance. Even if the advocates of unity declare neutrality regarding non-spiritual aspects of members' lives, they still claim priority for the beliefs they advocate. Potentially, such a claim may lead to interference in matters that were previously regarded as neutral if they subsequently appear at odds with the shared creed.

Calculation, Rationalization and Group Life

Aside from the above there are communities that bring people together solely for the aim of pursuing defined tasks. As the purpose of such groups is limited, so may be the claims on their members' time, attention and discipline. By and large, such groups are clear in their orientations. Thus, it is in terms of the overall purpose, or specific task to be performed, that the discipline and commitment of members are claimed. In this sense we can speak of purpose groups, or organizations. A deliberate and openly declared self-limitation is perhaps the most salient and distinctive feature of organizations.

Most organizations have written statutes that detail the organizational *rules* to which members must adhere. This, by default, implies that those areas of members' lives that are not covered by such rules remain free from organizational interference. Note that if the presence or absence of self-limitation, rather than of consensus of beliefs, is taken as the main difference between communities and organizations, then some of the communities discussed above ought to be, contrary to their own claims, counted among organizations.

We may characterize the partial nature of members' involvements in organizational activity in terms of the playing of roles. 'Role' is a word drawn from the language of the theatre. This is a reason why the work of Erving Goffman, who assigned particular significance to performance in interactions, is often characterized as 'dramaturgical'. After all, a stage play, with its plot decided in advance and written up in the scenario, which assigns different lines to every actor in the cast, offers a pattern through which the organization may run its life. The theatre is also a prototype in another respect: stage actors do not 'exhaust' themselves in the roles they have been assigned, while they 'enter' the prescribed character only for the duration of the performance and are free and expected to leave afterwards.

Organizations are specialized according to the tasks they perform and so, therefore, are their members, who are recruited according to skills and attributes that they possess in terms of fulfilling the organization's goals. Each member's role is not only set apart, but also related to, the other roles played by members of the same organization. Matters of *coordination* and *communication* within the organization are paramount. Yet these skills and attributes are also different from those that are demanded by the other roles we play in different contexts. For instance, we could be voluntary members of a charitable society, a local branch of a political party or an ad-hoc committee set up to oppose a motorway development. In many instances, fellow members of these different groups will not be interested in the other roles we perform in everyday life, for each will wish us to identify fully with the role in their particular activity and contribute to the task in hand.

Let us repeat: unlike the community, which we think of as a group to which its members belong (or ought to belong) 'body and soul', the organization seems to absorb only part of the persons involved. People involved in an organization are expected to embrace their roles in order to dedicate themselves to their performance while working in and for the organization. At the same time, there is also an expectation of distance in order that they can not only reflect upon their performance in order to improve it, but also not confuse the rights and duties attached to a particular role with those belonging to another activity or place. To this extent, there must also be a relative stability in organizational roles in order that people can identify the expectations made of them; furthermore, while the incumbents may come and go, the roles themselves remain the same. People join and leave the organization, are hired and fired, admitted and expelled, yet the organization persists. People become interchangeable and disposable, and what counts is not them as whole persons, but the particular skills they possess to perform the job.

What we see here are concerns on the part of the organization with calculability and predictability in the pursuit of formal goals. The German sociologist Max Weber, a central figure in the history of sociology, regarded the proliferation of organizations in contemporary society as a sign of the continuous rationalization of everyday life. Rational action, as distinct from traditional and affective action – those triggered by habit, custom and momentary emotion perpetrated without due consideration of the consequences, respectively – is oriented towards clearly stated ends. Actors are then enjoined to concentrate their thoughts and efforts on selecting suitably effective, efficient and economical means towards those ends.

For Weber, the characteristics of organization, or more specifically what he called 'bureaucracy', represent the supreme adaptation to the requirements of rational action. The methods of bureaucracy represent the most effective means to pursue ends in a rational way. Indeed, Weber listed the principles which must be observed in members' actions and in relations between them in order that an organization could be an instrument of rationality.

According to this analysis, it is important that all those within the organization must act solely in terms of their 'official capacity' as given by the rules attaching to the roles they perform. Other aspects of their social identities, such as family connections, business interests, private sympathies and antipathies, should not be allowed to interfere with what they do, how they do it and with the way others judge their actions. To achieve this a truly rational organization must split tasks into simple and elementary activities, so that each participant in a common effort becomes an expert in doing his or her own job. In addition, each person must be responsible for every element of the overall task, so that no part remains unattended. This means that in all aspects of the task it must be clear who is in charge, thereby ensuring that competencies do not overlap; hence ambiguity, which would detract from the rational pursuit of ends, is avoided.

Weber added further characteristics of bureaucracy to those above. In the actual performance of their respective roles, the officials ought to be guided by abstract rules in order that there is no regard to personal peculiarities. The officials themselves should be appointed to their offices and promoted or demoted solely according to a criterion of merit considered in terms of the 'fit' of their skills and attributes to those required by the office. Any considerations that fall outside of this judgement such as being of noble or plebeian origin, political or religious beliefs, race, sex and so on, must not interfere with this policy. The individual role incumbent is therefore able to orient their actions according to clear roles and expectations and match their abilities and skills to the tasks that are accorded to the position. The organization, on the other hand, is bound to adhere to a set of rational rules in the selection of such persons and be bound by the precedents – decisions made in the past in its name – that were made by them in those positions, even if they have left or moved on to other roles within the organization. The history of the organization is then made up of its files and is, therefore, independent of personal memories or the loyalties of individual officials.

To ensure the rational coordination of activity, the roles must be arranged in a hierarchy that corresponds to an internal division of labour oriented towards the pursuit of the overall goal of the organization. The further down one moves in the hierarchy, the more specialized, partial and focused are the tasks, while the higher up one moves, the wider becomes the vision and more of the overall purpose comes into view. To achieve this situation, the flow of information must be from the lower to the higher rungs of the hierarchical ladder and commands must flow from the top to the bottom becoming, as they do so, more specific and unequivocal. Control from the top needs to be reciprocated by discipline from the bottom; thus power, as the capability to influence conduct throughout the organization, is also *hierarchical*.

Returning to our theme of the unity of groups, the key factor here is the postulate that everybody's decisions and behavioural choices must be subordinated to the overall goals of the organization. The organization as a whole should surround itself with thick and impenetrable walls with just two gates being left open: the 'inputs', through which the goals and subsequent tasks the organization has to perform in pursuit of those are fed in, and the 'outputs', which provide for the results of that organizational processing. Between the feeding in of the tasks and the production of results in terms of goods and/or services, all outside influences ought to be barred from intervening with the strict application of organizational rules and the selection of the most effective, efficient and economical means in the pursuit of the declared end.

In deriving these characteristics of rational organizations, Weber was not suggesting that all organizations were, in practice, like this. However, he was proposing with these 'ideal-types' that increasing aspects of our lives are subject to rules and procedures aimed at calculability and predictability via routinization. It is this process that the American sociologist George Ritzer called the 'McDonaldization' of society. In Weber's work we find that actions which are informed by absolute values, without due regard to the possibility of their success in these terms, form an increasingly smaller part of our lives in the unfolding of history, all of which led Weber to write of 'disenchantment' with the forward march of modernity.

Although there are organizations that proximate Weber's ideal model with consequent effects on their employees and customers, the model remains, by and large, unfulfilled. The question is, can it ever be fulfilled? A person reduced in their orientations to just one role, or to a single task unaffected by other concerns, is a fiction that no reality can match. This, however, is not to suggest that idealizations of efficiency, effectiveness and economy in the pursuit of goals do not inform the strategic management of organizations. Indeed, we might reasonably characterize the practice of management as the continual attempt to marry the formal and informal aspects of organizational life in pursuit of what are set as organizational imperatives. Therefore, managerial practices move according to trends in pursuit of solutions to this issue; ably assisted by the armies of organizational consultants and so-called management 'gurus'. In this process we see the continual invention of ideas as solutions to the issue of orienting the actions of individual members towards collective ends: for example, 'total quality management', 'business process re-engineering', 'human resource management', management by 'objectives' and a concern with getting the 'right culture' in an organization.

In terms of the informal aspects of organizations, as opposed to the rules and procedures that make up the formal dimension, members of organizations are naturally concerned with their own, as well as the well-being of significant others, which may be adversely affected by the risks involved in certain forms of decision-making. A tendency to avoid taking decisions on dubious and/or controversial matters may then arise: for example, the idea of the 'hot potato' as a popular name for eluding responsibility by shifting an urgent file or matter for decision onto somebody else's desk. So, relieved of the burden, it becomes someone else's problem. A member of an organization may also find that a command received from superiors cannot be squared with her or his moral beliefs, leaving a choice between organizational obedience and loyalty to moral principles. Other members may believe that the requirement of secrecy put to them by superiors may endanger public welfare or some other cause they believe to be equally valid or even more important than organizational efficiency. In such cases we have witnessed the practice of 'whistle-blowing'. Here a person or group within an organization takes matters into the public arena in the hope that such attention may stop what they see as dubious organizational practices.

The reasons for resistance to managerial edicts may also lie in the imbalance of power that comes with hierarchical structures. For Michel Foucault, because power is always enacted on free persons, resistance is bound to result. Therefore, we can say that managerial intentions in implementing organizational policies will not always correspond to their actual effects on practices. In addition, we might also observe that organizational members bring into their work the prejudices they hold in their daily lives. A man, for instance, may find it difficult to accept commands coming from a woman and despite widespread denials that 'glass ceilings' do not exist in organizations, women are still disproportionately under-represented in managerial positions. From this point of view, the idea of 'merit' is routinely undermined in organizations by the mirroring of prejudices that are found in societies in general.

From this last observation we can question the idea that the boundaries between an organization and its environment are fixed. Instead, they are fluid and constructed according not only to the strategies of those in positions of power, but also to the pressures and influences coming from places ostensibly unrelated to its tasks and hence denied authority in organizational decision-making. There may, for example, be an anticipatory concern with public image which places limits on taking courses of actions that are calculated in technical terms alone, or which lead to obsessive secrecy, thereby placing limitations upon the flow of communications. These can be concerned with matters that might arouse public concern and anger, or that are related to preventing a rival learning of new technological developments.

These are just some of the practical limitations of the model. Let us both suppose, however, that the conditions for its implementation have been met. Here we find that the persons involved in the organizational division of tasks have been reduced to the roles they have been assigned, while the organization as a whole has been effectively fenced off from all concerns and influences irrelevant to its declared purpose. Regardless of how improbable these conditions might be, would they guarantee the rationality of organizational activity if put in practice? Would an organization that fully conforms to the ideal model behave as rationally as Weber suggested it would? There are strong arguments that this would not happen because this ideal recipe would produce numerous obstacles to the realization of such a form of rationality.

For a start, equal weight is ascribed in the model to the authority of the office and that of the relevant technical skill. Would these two differently grounded authorities coincide and remain in harmony? In fact, it is more than likely that the two will tend to clash, or at least be in tension. One may, for example, place a professionally trained person, such as a doctor, in a position in which there is an expectation that costs are uppermost in their decision-making. What if they are then faced with a patient who is very ill and there are drugs available, at some cost, which would cure the condition? There is a clear clash here between their ethical duty as a doctor and their accountability for budgetary matters.

Another tension arises in the model concerning the minute division of labour that is calculated according to tasks. Allegedly, this is a factor that boosts efficiency but, in fact, tends to produce a 'trained incapacity'. Having acquired expertise in the quick and efficient performance of narrowly circumscribed tasks, members can gradually lose sight of the wider ramifications of their job. Therefore, they will fail to note the adverse consequences of their activities, which have become mechanical routines, for both their overall performance, those with whom they work and the organizational goals in general (this is a frequent criticism that strategic managers make of their operational counterparts who, in turn, accuse them of failing to understand the technicalities of their work). Because of the narrowness of their skills, members can also be ill prepared to adjust their routines to changing circumstances and to react to unfamiliar situations with the necessary speed and flexibility. In other words, the organization as a whole falls prey to the pursuit of perfect rationality. It becomes stiff and inflexible and its methods of work fail to adapt quickly enough to changing circumstances. Sooner or later, it may well turn into a factory of increasingly irrational decisions.

From an internal viewpoint the ideal model is also subject to *goal displacement*. For the sake of their effectiveness, all organizations ought to reproduce their capacity to act. In other words, come what may, an organization must be continuously ready to make decisions and take actions. Such reproduction calls for an effective mechanism of self-perpetuation that is immune to outside interference. The problem here is that the goal itself may fall among these outside interferences. There is nothing in the model to prevent that mechanism from outliving the task that the organization had been called to fulfil in the first place. On the contrary, everything points to the likelihood, and even desirability, that the concern for self-preservation will prompt the endless expansion of organizational activities and the scope of its authority. It may happen, in effect, that the task originally seen as the reason to establish the organization is relegated to a secondary position by the all-powerful interest of the organization in pursuit of self-perpetuation and self-aggrandizement. The survival of the organization then becomes a purpose in its own right and so a new end against which it will tend to measure the rationality of its performance.

There is another trend that we can identify from those above. We have spoken about the partial demands of organizations in terms of role expectations and performance. This presupposed that social and self-identity are, in some senses, separate from organizational existence. In situations tending towards total embrace, the organization would exhibit the characteristics of the kinds of communities we described as being of religious origin: that is, they demand of their members an allegiance in all aspects of their lives. As organizations respond to the increasingly rapid nature of change, complacency and an unwillingness to change are taken as signs of an absence of competitive advantage. Therefore, that employees should be flexible, dynamic and innovative is taken to be of paramount importance. Organizations have thus become more interested in the whole person in terms of their temperament, attributes, dispositions, skills, knowledge and motivations. A series of quasi-scientific practices and concerns with areas hitherto regarded as being of little interest to organizations, have now fallen under their routine gaze.

In this process we have seen a questioning of the ideal model and its ideas of rationality as being the bracketing of the emotional aspects of our lives. Now, the idea of unlocking something called 'emotional intelligence', the psychometric testing of candidates and concerns with the aesthetics of office design may fall within the gaze of organizations. Depending upon the sector about which we are speaking and the nature of the role within the organization, a greater concern with what were, hitherto, private aspects of employees' lives is more commonplace. This even extends to the routine surveillance of organizational members.

In his book *Surveillance Society*, David Lyon noted how organizations utilize computer software to monitor emails and to inform them if an employee violates company policy; how active badges alert a central computer where someone is located in a building in order to enable them to locate the nearest phone and screen for their 'convenience'; how routine drug testing is employed and private detectives are used to research all aspects of a person's identity to ensure they are of good character. In the process, the way in which identities are constructed also changes. Yet there is also resistance to the routine surveillance of space and time and what may be seen as impositions into areas that are not applicable to work activities.

Because of such things as resistance to the demands placed upon people, both models of human groupings are wanting. Neither the image of community, nor the model of organization, adequately describes the practice of human interaction. The two models sketch artificially separated, polar models of action, with separate and often opposite motives and expectations. Real human actions, under real circumstances, resent such a radical division and so manifest a tension in the expectations that are routinely placed upon people's actions. By representing and seeking to impose a representation on its members, communities and organizations display an inherent tendency to streamline complex and convoluted actions. The response may then be to seek to purify the action further, but our interactions are torn between two gravitational forces, each pulling in an opposite direction.

Routine interactions are, unlike the extreme models, mixed: they are *heterogeneous* by being subject to tensions. For instance, the family often does not meet with the idealizations that many have of it and there are tasks to be performed as in any other group of cooperating people. Therefore, it too exhibits some of the criteria of performance that comes with organizations. On the other hand, in every organization the members can hardly avoid developing personal links with people with whom they join forces for a protracted period. Sooner or later, informal patterns of interaction will emerge which may or may not overlap with the official chart of formal relationships of command and subordination. Sociologists have long recognized these relations and how they develop and coincide or lie in tension with the formal requirement of the organization.

Contrary to what the ideal model would suggest, it is found in practice that the task-oriented performance may considerably benefit if the interaction is not reduced to specialized roles. Companies set about soliciting the deeper commitment of their employees through bringing more of their concerns and interests within the orbit of the organization. The people in command of the organization may utilize the fusing of the formal and informal aspects of organization. This strategy has witnessed the 'cultural turn' in management theory with its emphasis upon values, commitment, motivation, teamwork and mission statements. Organizations now offer, for example, recreation and entertainment facilities, shopping services, reading groups and even living accommodation. None of these extra services is logically related to the explicit task of the organization, but all of them together are hoped to generate 'community feelings' and to prompt members to identify themselves with the company. Such emotions, apparently alien to the organizational spirit, are deemed to boost the members' dedication to the ends of the organizations and thus neutralize the adverse effects of the purely impersonal setting suggested by the criteria of rationality.

Communities and organizations often act as if freedom was presupposed in their members, even if their practices do not live up to their own expectations. Members may then, of course, leave or act in ways contrary to dominant expectations. However, there is one case when the organization explicitly denies freedom to leave and the people are kept under its jurisdiction by force. They are what Erving Goffman called 'total institutions'. Total institutions are enforced communities in which the totality of members' lives is subjected to scrupulous regulation, with their needs being defined and catered for by the organization. Actions are then explicitly sanctioned by organizational rules. Boarding schools, army barracks, prisons and mental hospitals all approximate, in varying degrees, the model of total institutions. Their inmates are kept under routine surveillance at all times so that deviations from the rules are visible and then subject to prevention or punishment. Neither spiritual dedication nor the hope of material gains can be appealed to in order to elicit desirable behaviour and secure the members' will to stay together and cooperate. Hence we find another feature of total institutions: the strict divide between those who set the rules and those who are bound by them. The effectiveness of coercion, as the only substitute for commitment and calculation, depends on the gap between the two sides of the division remaining unbridgeable. That said, personal relationships do develop inside total institutions and often span the gap between the supervisors and the inmates.

Summary

Manuel Castells writes, in the conclusion to the second of his three-volume study on *The Information Age*, that we are witnessing the growth of networks, markets and organizations that are increasingly governed by 'rational expectations'. Yet if this is the summary of a dominant trend in contemporary western societies, in our survey of the bonds that unite, what is most striking is also the diversity of human groupings. They are all forms of human interaction in which the group exists by virtue of being a persistent network of the interdependent actions of its members. The assertion that 'there is a college' refers to the fact that a number of people come together to engage in a routine called a lecture: that is, a communicative encounter whose purpose is learning and which is temporally and spatially structured in such a way that one person speaks while others, facing that person, listen and take notes. In their interactions, group members are guided by an image of what is the right conduct that is specific to the setting.

These images are never complete and so their power to provide an unambiguous prescription for any situation that may arise in the course of interaction, is correspondingly diminished. The ideal framework for interaction is constantly being interpreted and reinterpreted and in the process it provides for new orientations and expectations. Interpretation cannot but feed back on the image itself and so practices and the expectations inherent in the ideal framework continually inform and transform each other.

part two

LIVING OUR LIVES: CHALLENGES, CHOICES AND CONSTRAINTS

chapter four

DECISIONS AND ACTIONS: POWER, CHOICE AND MORAL DUTY

There is no shortage of questions that arise within our daily activities. Some may occur fairly regularly and not preoccupy us for very long, while others may be prompted by abrupt changes in our circumstances and lead to further and deeper reflection. These types of questions concern matters that do not, ordinarily, preoccupy us, but which still inform issues about who we are and how we make sense of the world around us. Sometimes these inquiries will raise questions about why something happened? When we ask this we are engaging in a habit that we all share and which, at the same time, characterizes scientific activity. This is the habit of explaining events as 'effects of a cause'. How these issues relate to and inform our decisions and actions in everyday life is the subject of this chapter.

$$\bigtriangledown$$

Making Decisions

When it comes to seeking explanations as the result of a cause, our curiosity is, by and large, satisfied when we conclude that the event was inevitable or, at the very least, highly probable. Why was there an explosion in the house down the road? Because there was a leak in the gas pipes and, gas being an inflammable substance, a spark was sufficient to ignite it. Why did no one hear the burglar breaking the window? Because everybody was asleep and people do not normally hear sounds when they are asleep. Our search for the explanation grinds to a halt once we have found either that one event is always followed by another, or that it follows in most cases. With the former we can speak of 'laws' because there are no exceptions, whereas in the latter case, we are dealing with a 'norm' because it happens in most, but not all, cases. With both types, however, there is no possibility of choices intervening because one event is *necessarily* followed by another.

This form of explanation becomes problematic when applied to the realm of human conduct. After all, we are dealing with events brought about by the actions of people who are faced with choices in their conduct. Because there were potentially different ways of acting, the events cannot be deemed inevitable. Given this, there are no set of general propositions from which it could be deduced with any degree of certainty and it was not, therefore, predictable. We can try to comprehend this event retrospectively: that is, with the benefit of hindsight, we can interpret the action in terms of certain rules, or dispositions within that context, that they must have followed to perform the action in the first place. However, there still seems to be something missing, for we know from our own experiences that people undertake activities with a purpose. As such, they have 'motives' in creating or responding to a situation which, for one reason or another, seems to them preferable. We can say, therefore, that we have the capacity to choose between courses of action. Of course, driving a car and stopping at a red traffic light may be observed to be a regular form of behaviour, but that is still a demonstration of a preference informed by a reason – in this case the avoidance of accidents.

Human actions may still vary under similar conditions with shared motivations. Quite simply, people may draw different conclusions from their surroundings, or motives may be discarded and circumstances ignored. We know well that this woman or man could have behaved differently in objectively identical circumstances. If we wish to know why this rather than that form of action has been selected, we might now turn our attention to the person's decision-making process. Although attractive as a solution, this is still not adequate, for it assumed that such decisions are formulated according to conscious choices towards explicitly stated ends. We thus come up against actions that are unreflective and of these there are two main types.

First, as we discussed earlier, there are *habitual* actions. We get up, clean our teeth and perform a morning routine while still half asleep, but do not recall making conscious decisions to follow that routine and may even be thinking of something else during its performance. So, too, we eat at regular times and develop all sorts of habits that become part of our actions without any conscious planning. However, in cases where such routines are broken by unexpected interruptions, we then have to make decisions because habit has suddenly become a poor guide. Habitual conduct thus represents the sediment of past learning. It also, thanks to regular repetition, relieves us from the need to think, calculate and make decisions in many of our actions just as long as the circumstances we encounter appear in a regular pattern. Indeed, so habitualized are our actions that it would be difficult to describe how they occur and the reasons for their existence. As noted, they come into our attention when things go wrong, that is, when the regularity and orderliness of the environments in which our actions occur break down.

The second type of unreflective actions is those that arise out of strong emotions. *Affective* actions are characterized by a suspension of the rational calculations that inform the purposes and possible consequences of action. Such actions are compulsive and deaf to the voice of reason. However, with the passage of time, passions may cool down and deliberation interrupts the act. These forms of action may result in hurting those we love and cherish, but if the act were premeditated it would not be affective because it was the outcome of a calculated decision. We can now say that an action is affective in so far as it remains unreflective, spontaneous, unpremeditated and is embarked upon prior to any weighing of arguments or contemplation of consequences.

Habitual and affective actions are frequently described as 'irrational'. This does not imply that they are foolish, ineffective, wrong or damaging. Nor does it suggest any evaluation of the utility of the act, for many habitualized routines may be effective and useful. Indeed, they enable us to accomplish the practical activities that make up our everyday lives, as well as sparing us what would be the burden of having to contemplate all our actions before undertaking them. Similarly, an outburst of anger without due regard for consequences may be helpful in getting people to understand how we feel about an event, action or issue. From this point of view, an irrational action can be more effective than a rational one.

A *rational* action is characterized by a conscious choice being made from among several alternative courses of action that are oriented towards the achievement of an end. In this 'instrumental-rational' view of action, the *means* are selected according to the requirements of the given *end*. Another form of rational action will also necessitate the choice of means towards ends, but in this case those ends are considered to be more valuable than others. 'Value-rational' action is thus motivated by considerations such as what is 'dear to one's heart', attractive, desirable and most closely connected to the felt need of the moment. What they share are a choice of means measured against given ends and that the fit between these is the ultimate criterion in the choice between a right and wrong decision. Furthermore, that the act of choosing is voluntary in so far as the actor has exercised a free choice without being goaded, pulled, pushed or bullied into it, nor did it arise habitually or via a momentary outburst of passion.

In choosing our courses of action through conscious and rational deliberation, we also anticipate their probable outcomes. This necessitates taking stock of the current situation in which the action will take place and the effects we expect to attain as a result. Here we would normally consider both available resources and the values that inform our conduct. Pierre Bourdieu divides the forms of capital that are employed in our actions into the following: symbolic, cultural and economic capital. Symbolic capital refers to the power to confer meaning upon objects, attributes and characteristics, cultural capital is the skills and knowledge that we possess and can draw upon in our actions and economic capital refers to our access to wealth and material resources. These resources can be turned to many uses and they differ from each other by carrying different degrees of attractiveness and being attractive for different reasons. Symbolic capital will confer meaning upon objects and attributes and so produce an assessment of what is valuable and for what reasons. We may then chose to apply our skills in the pursuit of those things that promise to be most useful, or which may increase the volume of resources at our disposal and so enhance our range of future freedoms. Ultimately, it is our values that preside over the decision to spend extra cash on a new compact disc player, a holiday or purchasing sociology books. Taking stock of our resources and values shows us the degrees of freedom we enjoy: that is, what we can do and what is out of the question.

$$\triangledown$$

Values, Power and Action

Talking about what we can do refers to our capability to act which, along with our ability to monitor our actions, comprise the two dimensions of social action. We may possess the ability to monitor our actions, but the range of freedoms that we enjoy in order to be capable of action is differentially distributed. Quite simply, different people have different degrees of freedom. The fact that people differ in their freedom of choice refers to social inequality; a more recent term that has been employed in a broader context is 'social exclusion'. Some people enjoy a wider range of choice due to their access to more resources and we can refer to this in terms of *power*.

Power is best understood as pursuing freely chosen ends towards which our actions are oriented and of then commanding the necessary means towards the pursuit of those ends. Power, therefore, is an enabling capacity. The more power that people have, the wider is their range of choices and the broader the scope of the outcomes that they may realistically pursue. Being less powerful, or even powerless, means that it may be necessary to moderate and even curtail the realistic hopes that are held for the outcome of actions. Thus, to have power is to be able to act more freely, while being relatively less powerful, or powerless, means having the freedom of choice limited by the decisions made by others via their capability to determine our actions. One person exercising their autonomy can result in the experience of heteronomy by another. The devaluation of the freedom of others in pursuit of the enhancement of freedom may be achieved by two methods.

The first method is *coercion*. Coercion comprises the manipulation of actions in such a way that the resources of other people, however large they may seem in other contexts, become inadequate or ineffective in that context. An entirely new game is created by the manipulation of a situation in such a way that those doing the manipulating can then assume the advantage: for example, whether the victim of a mugger is a rich banker or a powerful politician, their respective resources, which assure them a large degree of freedom in other contexts, lose their 'enabling' capacity once they are confronted in a dark and deserted street with a knife, or the sheer physical power of an assailant. Similarly, to force a reconsideration of cherished values may result in people feeling that their practices are now more subject to evaluation and questioning by those whose authority they do not recognize. Other values then come to predominate in reaction to this situation. In the extreme conditions of concentration camps, for instance, the value of self-preservation and survival may well overshadow all other choices.

The second method consists of the strategy of *enlisting* the desires of others towards one's own ends. What characterizes this form is a manipulation of the situation in such a manner that other people may attain the values they pursue only if they follow the rules set by the power-holder. Thus, the zeal and efficiency with which the enemies are killed is rewarded by enhancing the social standing of the brave soldier with medals and honourable citations. Factory workers may secure improved living standards (wage rises) provided they work with more dedication and intensity and comply, without question, to managerial edicts. The values of subordinates then become the resources of their superordinates. They are not valued as ends in themselves, but as means to be deployed in the service of ends set by power-holders. Yet for those subject to such manipulations, they have no other choice but to surrender a considerable part of their freedom.

The actions of others affect the values that inform the ends we seek and our evaluation of how realistic it is that we shall attain these ends. What we call 'realistic' and what we call 'dreams' are all given by the relations we have with others and the resources we can hope to deploy in our actions. However, where do these values come from in the first place? After all, why do we place a particular premium upon some ends and disregard or downgrade others? Are the values that inform our orientations matters of free choice? These questions are fundamental to understanding ourselves, the contexts in which we interact and the influences upon our conduct. Consider the following example.

We intend to go to university straight from school. Our friends, however, have decided otherwise and in arguing about our respective choices, they convince us that more fun will result from starting work immediately rather than being condemned to three years of self-sacrifice, semi-starvation and subsequent debt. We then change our minds and seek work for an instant income and for a while, enjoy the benefits that this provides. However, management then announce that they are going to reorganize the office and make people redundant, but our job will be secure and the prospects for promotion promising. As members of a union, our colleagues vote for strike action and the management respond by announcing that in the event of a strike, important orders will be lost with the result that everyone will be made redundant. Understandably, we seek to avoid such a prospect, but most of our colleagues in voting for such action have appeared to place solidarity above the security of their own jobs. In reflecting upon our position, we recognize that our interests are bound up with our colleagues and so we vote for a strike. The consequence is now the possibility that the job will be lost along with the freedoms that the income enabled us to enjoy.

What is happening here? The values that people adopt in orienting and justifying their actions transform in the course of social interaction within different contexts. People are influenced in particular ways; this manifests itself through an alteration in the hierarchy of importance that people attach to certain values. This means that they select, consciously or by default, some ends above others. Either way, the consequence is that the ends that have been assigned priority may be justified in terms of being more satisfying, dignified and morally elevating. In this way we become attuned to the sense we have of what is proper and improper conduct in our lives.

As noted, not all values are consciously chosen, for many of our actions are habitual and routine. As long as the actions remain habitual, we seldom pause to ask about the values they serve. Habitual action does not need justification as long as we are not called to account by others or by abrupt changes in the circumstances in which we act. These discursive justifications – those *about* our actions – may be difficult to embark upon. If pressed, we might answer with something like 'This is the way things have always been done', or 'This is how it is'. What we are doing here is to suggest that the length of time in which these habits have persisted lends them an authority which is not normally the object of questioning. Let us remember, however, that these are 'enforced' explanations because they are prompted by questioning.

What we are witnessing here is that action remains habitual as long as it is not called upon to legitimize itself: that is, it does not require reference to the values and purposes it is supposed to serve. It goes on repeating itself, by and large according to the same pattern, on the strength of the habit alone. The values that inform these actions are sedimented at the subconscious level and we become aware of their influence only when it comes to the making of deliberate choices: for example, in situations where the values we obey are challenged, defied and questioned in terms of being called to legitimize themselves. At this point, the authority of those values is called into question.

Those who occupy positions of command over others, where those positions are circumscribed by rules, may be said to exercise authority. Clearly, this has an influence upon conduct, but the particular form of this relationship is given by the rules that surround the relations that exist between the subordinate and superordinate. Thus, returning to our discussion on bureaucracy, we can see how the rules that surround a hierarchical division of labour in organizations, provide for its authority. To be accepted as legitimate, however, requires not only that the relationship conforms to particular rules, but also that it is justified by the beliefs that all those who are subject to them share and that they willingly consent to that relationship. To have all three conditions in place – rules, justifications and consent – means that someone submits themselves to the authority and the values that underpin its existence.

To become an authority for us, a person or an organization must produce a legitimation, or an argument, which demonstrates why their advice ought to be followed in preference to another. One such legitimation we have already met in the form of tradition in terms of being time-honoured and time-tested. History, we are told, binds its heirs and what it brought together, no human presumption should set apart. However, rather than values being revered because of their old age, those who seek popular acceptance for the values they preach will go to some lengths to dig out genuine, or putative, historical evidence of their antiquity. The image of the historical past is always selective and the deference that people feel for it may be enlisted in the service of contemporary contests over values. Once it has been accepted that certain values were held by our ancestors, they are less vulnerable to contemporary criticism. The *traditionalist legitimation* becomes particularly attractive in times of rapid change which cannot but generate uneasiness and anxiety and so it seems to offer a relatively safe, less agonizing set of choices.

The alternative would be to defend new values as a type of revelation. This kind of argument is associated with *charismatic legitimation*. Charisma was the quality first noted in the study of the deep and unchallenged influences exerted by the Church upon the faithful. The concept of charisma in this instance refers to the conviction of the faithful that the Church is endowed with a privileged access to truth. Charisma, however, need not be confined to religious beliefs and institutions. We can speak of charisma whenever the acceptance of certain values is motivated by the belief that the preacher of values is endowed with privileged powers and that these guarantee the truth of their vision and the propriety of their choice. Therefore, the reason of ordinary people possesses no means of evaluating these claims and so no right to doubt the power of their perception. The stronger the charisma of the leaders, the more difficult it is to question their commands and the more comforting it is for people to follow their orders when exposed to situations of uncertainty.

We are said to live increasingly in an age of anxiety in which the relations between trust and risk are ever changing. Anthony Giddens argued that the control over lives associated with traditional societies has passed to external agencies with resulting increases in feelings of powerlessness. As we learn more about our environment, in the sense that aspects of scientific findings are filtered via the mass media into everyday consciousness, the more people are aware that previous forms of authority are not as invulnerable as they once thought. Ulrich Beck, the German sociologist, wrote about these trends in modern society under the theme of 'risk society'. We might observe that this can be accompanied by a demand for charismatic solutions to these shifting problems of value, with some political parties and social movements stepping in to provide a substitute service. Those organizations can then turn themselves into collective carriers of charismatic authority, and place influence on an altogether new, more stable basis which in principle may outlive the charismatic leader.

The centre of charismatic authority seems to have shifted away from the religious and the political arena, although that is not to suggest that there is not still a strong pull by the former with occasional examples of sects routinely demanding the mass suicide of their members as ultimate acts of faith. The advent of mass media has a role in this shift, with the effects of this situation proving to be shattering. The sheer mass exposure of television personalities, or TV-assisted public personalities, seems to be a powerful influence in this trend. Much like the charismatic leaders of old, they can be credited with a capacity for superior judgement exemplified in terms of becoming the trendsetters of particular lifestyles. The significant number of people who look to public personalities for guidance and advice on their own choices reinforces this power and adds strength to the validity of such sources.

The two legitimations that we have considered so far – the traditionalist and the charismatic – share one feature: they both imply the surrender of our right to make value choices and can be associated with the surrender of responsibility. Others have made the choices for us and so may be held responsible for the consequences of our actions. There is a third type, however, to which we have already alluded: the *legal–rational*. This implies that some organizations, and the persons who are positioned to speak on their behalf, have the right to tell us what sort of action ought to be undertaken, while it is our duty to obey without further argument. If this is the case, the very question of the wisdom or moral quality of the advice seems to have lost its importance. It may now become the law and it is lawful command that selects for us the authority that determines our action. The legal–rational legitimation separates action from value choice and hence appears to render it value-free. The executors of a command need not scrutinize the morality of the action they have been ordered to perform, nor do they need to feel responsible if the action fails a moral test. Self-righteously, they would react with indignation to any reproach on this account with the justification that 'I was only carrying out the orders I received from my legal superiors'.

Legal–rational legitimation is pregnant with potentially sinister consequences because of its tendency to absolve the actors from their responsibility for value choice. The mass murder and genocide of the Second World War and a number of wars since that time provide the most conspicuous, though by no means unique and exceptional, examples of such consequences. Those who have perpetrated murder refuse to accept moral responsibility, pointing instead to the legal determination of their obedience to command. In so doing they reject the charge that their decision to obey was, in fact, a moral choice on their part.

Removing the values which the actions serve from the sight of the actors by the simple expedient of extending the chain of command beyond the vision of the executors renders the action apparently value-free and exempt from moral judgement. The actors are offered, so to speak, escape from the burden of their freedom, which always comes complete with the responsibility for one's actions. In this way moral duty mixes in a tension with a desire for self-preservation that is derived from membership of a group. This group identity (as we have seen) may be achieved with disastrous consequences for those who are defined as the other. These issues, in their turn, vary according to the situations in which we find ourselves and what are regarded as the values to which we aspire. To consider this further, we now turn to matters of competition, exclusion and ownership.

$$\triangledown$$

The Motivation to Act

Most, but not all, of our actions are motivated by our needs. We have basic needs, in terms of survival, and another set of needs that relates to the meaningful constitution of social reality that provides for a degree of satisfaction. The fulfilment of those needs, as we have suggested, is dependent upon the autonomy of our actions and that, in turn, on our ability to monitor, understand and reflect upon our actions, as well as the capability to act. How often, however, do we say about some object 'I need it. I must have it'?

Whether such utterances occur in situations in which relative affluence or poverty is manifest is of prime significance. In the western world, lifestyle now seems bound up with the ability to consume, the purpose of which is rarely reflected upon and when considered, may be justified according to the satisfaction of unmet needs. However, note that in the above utterance a movement has taken place with the second sentence placing a greater emphasis on the point being made in the first. With this act of clarification comes a shift from the satisfaction of an expressed need, to its absence leading to a state of deprivation that will undermine self-preservation and even survival! Without it, the person's life would be flawed, intolerable and even place their existence in danger.

It is the quality of being needed for survival or self-preservation that makes the object that is desired into a 'good'. As Gilles Deleuze, the French philosopher, and Félix Guattari, a psychonalalyst, have written, as soon as desire and acquisition become one, we feel that there is a significant 'lack' in our lives. We fill this gap with the desire to acquire something: for example, commodities that one can buy in a shop in exchange for money, silence in the street at night and clean air or uncontaminated water, which cannot be attained without the concerted effort of many others. Our needs cannot be satisfied unless we gain access to the goods in question, either through being allowed to use them, or through becoming their owners. Yet this always involves other people and their actions. However self-concerned our motivations, our ties with other people are required and, even if not acknowledged, we are rendered more dependent upon other people's actions and the motives which orient them.

This situation is not evident upon first glance. On the contrary, the idea of holding goods in terms of ownership is widely accepted as a 'private' matter. It seems that the object (the property) is somehow invisibly connected to its owner; it is in such a connection that we suppose the essence of ownership rests. If one is the owner of something, then at the same time there is a right as to its use determined by the will of its owner. Of course, that right is circumscribed in particular ways. Thus, trees in our garden subjected to preservation orders may not be felled without official permission and neither can we set fire to our houses without the risk of being prosecuted. Nevertheless, the fact that a special law is needed to forbid us to dispose of our property in such a manner only bolsters the general principle that self-determination and property are inextricably linked. However, problematic issues arise at this point in our discussion.

First, ideas of property, labour and entitlement to its use and disposal are not free from influence in relation to gender, ethnicity and class. We have long equated the entitlement to our property through the labour we exert in its acquisition. This goes back a long way and is apparent in the work of the seventeenth-century philosopher John Locke. Here we find ideas of property rights being laid down by the first labourer who appropriated them and then being handed down through subsequent generations – a principle that survives to this day. However, based upon particular views of human motivation, Locke argued for a 'social contract' so that order could be brought to what would otherwise be a chaotic social and political world. In his argument he then made a leap. As women were held to be 'emotional' and exhibit a 'natural dependence' upon men, he argued that they do not then possess such rights. Marriage was a contract that women entered into so that they could produce sons who inherited the property. The contract of marriage thus ensures that property rights are stable within society and men have sons in order to perpetuate their lineage. Aside from assuming that the ability to be rational inheres in the individual man prior to his membership of a society (and we have seen how groups form our social identities in contrast to a position that removes people from the societies of which they are a part), this same ability was then denied to half the human race on the basis of a prejudice that exists to this day: women are emotional and men are rational. The result is to exclude women from the social contract.

The issue of the exclusion of women brings us on to another problematic issue. Popular descriptions of the property relation leave out a central aspect of its exercise. It is, more than anything else, a relation of *exclusion*. Whenever we say 'This is mine', we are also implying that it is *not* somebody else's. Ownership is not a private quality; it is a social affair that conveys a special relation between an object and its owner and at the same time, a special relation between the owner and other people. Owning a thing means denying others access to it. At one level, therefore, ownership establishes a mutual dependence, but it does not connect us with things and others as much as it divides us from people. The fact of ownership sets apart, in a relation of mutual antagonism, those who own the object from those who do not. The first can use and abuse (unless specifically constrained by the law) the object in question, while the second are denied such a right. It may also (remember our discussions of power) make the relationship between people asymmetrical: that is, those who are denied access to the object of ownership must obey the conditions set by the owner whenever they need or want to use it. Therefore, their need and their willingness to satisfy that need put them in a position of dependence on the owner.

All ownership divides and distinguishes people. Ownership, however, confers power only if the needs of the excluded require the use of the objects owned. For instance, ownership of the tools of work, of raw materials to be processed by human labour, of technology and the sites on which such processing can take place, offers such power. This is not so with the ownership of goods to be consumed by the owner. Owning a car or a video-recorder or a washing machine may make our lives easier or more enjoyable and may even add to our prestige, but they do not necessarily give us power over other people. Unless, of course, other people wish to use these things for their own comfort or enjoyment, in which case we might set the conditions of use to which they must conform. Most things we own do not offer power, but independence from the power of others by removing the need to utilize their possessions. The larger the part of our needs that we can meet in this way, the less we have to conform to the rules and conditions set by other people. In this sense, ownership is an enabling condition because it can extend autonomy, action and choice, thus ownership and freedom are often taken to be fused together.

Returning to our earlier discussions, the principle underlying all ownership is that the rights of others are the limits of our own rights and therefore the promotion of our freedom requires that others are restricted in the exercise of their freedom. By this principle, the enabling condition of property always comes together with varying degrees of constraint. The principle assumes an irreparable conflict of interests in terms of being a zero-sum game. Thus, nothing is assumed to be gained by sharing and cooperation. In a situation in which the capability to act depends on control over resources, to act reasonably will mean to follow the commandment 'everyone for themselves'. This is how the task of self-preservation appears to us.

Pierre Bourdieu wrote of what he called 'doxic acceptance'. He used this phrase to indicate how there are many categories of thought that we routinely employ in our understandings, but rarely reflect upon in our practice. One of the most powerful, if not *the* most, is the idea of self-preservation based upon competition. Competitors are moved by the desire to exclude their actual or potential rivals from using the resources they control, hope to control or dream of controlling. The goods for which the rivals compete are perceived as scarce: it is believed that there are not enough of them to satisfy everybody and that some rivals must be forced to settle for less than they would wish to possess. It is an essential part of the idea of competition, and a basic assumption of competitive action, that some desires are bound to be frustrated and hence the relations between the winners and the defeated must be permanently marked with mutual dislike or enmity. For the same reason no competitive gains are considered secure unless actively and vigilantly defended against challenge and contest. Competitive struggle never ends; its results are never final and irreversible. From this, a number of consequences follow.

First, all competition contains within it a tendency towards monopoly. Large corporations are now becoming even larger through mergers involving vast sums of money. In the process, the winning side tends to make its gains secure and permanent by seeking to deny the losers the right to challenge their gains. The ultimate, though elusive and unattainable, purpose of the competitors is to abolish the competition itself with the result that competitive relations have an in-built tendency to self-annihilation. If left to themselves, they would eventually lead to a sharp polarization of chances. Resources would cluster and tend to become ever more abundant on one side of the relationship, while becoming increasingly scarce on the other. More often than not, such a polarization of resources would give the winning side the ability to dictate the rules of all further interaction and leave the losers in no position to contest the rules. Gains in such a case would be transformed into a monopoly and so attract more gains still and further deepen the gap between the sides. It is for reasons such as these that the leading economist, John Kenneth Galbraith, wrote in his book *The Culture of Contentment* that government action is necessary to prevent the 'self destructive tendencies of the economic system'.

Second, the polarization of chances brought about by monopolistic activity tends to lead in the long run to the differential treatment of winners and losers. Sooner or later winners and losers solidify into 'permanent' categories. The winners blame the failure of the losers on the latter's inherent inferiority and so the losers are declared responsible for their own misfortune. This is a triumph of the type of thinking that believes social problems have individual, biographical solutions. These people are then described as inept, wicked, fickle, depraved, improvident or morally contemptible: that is, lacking the very qualities that are assumed to be necessary for the competition that contributed to this state of affairs in the first place. Then, so defined, the losers are denied a legitimacy for their grievances. The poor become defiled as lazy, slovenly and negligent, as *depraved* rather than deprived. Assumed to be lacking in character, shirking hard labour and inclined to delinquency and law-breaking, they can be seen as having 'chosen' their own fate. Similarly, in male-dominated societies women are blamed for their oppressed state, leaving their confinement to what are assumed to be less prestigious and desirable functions to be explained by an 'inborn' inferiority manifested in excessive emotionality and a lack of competitive spirit.

Morality and Action

In contemporary times, defamation of the victims of competition is one of the most powerful means of silencing an alternative motive for human conduct: moral duty. Moral motives clash with those of gain because moral action requires solidarity, disinterested help, willingness to assist the neighbour in need without asking for, or expecting, remuneration. A moral attitude finds its expression in consideration for the need of others and more often than not would result in self-restraint and a voluntary renunciation of personal gain.

Max Weber noted that the separation of business from the household is one of the most conspicuous characteristics of modern societies. The overall effect is to isolate the spheres in which gain and moral duty are, respectively, the dominant considerations. When engaged in a business activity, we are prised from the network of family bonds. We are freed, in other words, from the pressures of moral duties. Considerations of gain may therefore be given the sole attention that successful business activity demands while, ideally, family life and those communal forms which are patterned after the family, ought to be free from the motivations of gain. Equally ideally, business activities should not be affected by the motives prompted by moral feelings and so instrumental-rational action prevails. After all, we have noted that the idea of an organization is the attempt to adjust human action to the ideal requirements of rationality. We see again that such an attempt must involve, more than anything else, the silencing of moral considerations via every task being reduced to a simple choice of obeying or refusing to obey a command. It is also reduced to a small part of the overall purpose pursued by the organization as a whole, so that the wider consequences of the act are not necessarily visible to the actor. Most importantly, the organization puts discipline in place of moral responsibility and as long as a member of an organization strictly follows the rules and the commands of superiors, that person is offered freedom from moral doubts. A morally reprehensible action, unthinkable under different conditions, can suddenly become a real possibility.

The potency of organizational discipline to silence or suspend moral reservations was dramatically demonstrated in the notorious experiments of the American psychologist Stanley Milgram. In these experiments, conducted in the 1960s, a number of volunteers were instructed to deliver painful electric shocks to the objects of a fake 'scientific research'. Most volunteers, convinced of the noble scientific purpose of their cruelty and relying on the admittedly superior judgement of the scientists in charge of the research project, followed the instructions faithfully – undaunted by the cries of anguish of their victims. What the experiment revealed on a small scale and in laboratory conditions had been demonstrated in breathtaking dimensions by the practice of genocide during the Second World War and thereafter. The murder of millions of Jews initiated and supervised by a few thousand top Nazi leaders and officials was a gigantic bureaucratic operation that involved the cooperation of millions of 'ordinary' people. They drove the trains which carried the victims to gas chambers and worked in the factories that produced the poisonous gases or crematoria appliances. The final results were so remote from the simple tasks which preoccupied them on a daily basis that the connections could escape their attention or be barred from consciousness.

Even if the functionaries of a complex organization are aware of the ultimate effect of the joint activity of which they are a part, that effect is often too remote to worry them. Remoteness may be a matter of mental rather than geographical distance. Because of the vertical and horizontal division of labour, the actions of any single person are, as a rule, mediated by the actions of many others. In the end, our own contribution pales into insignificance and its influence on the final result seems too small to be seriously considered as a moral problem. These 'techniques of neutralization', as the American sociologist David Matza termed them, enable perpetrators to relieve themselves of the responsibility for their actions. After all, they could have been doing things as innocuous and harmless as drawing blueprints, composing reports, filing documents or switching on and off the machine which mixed two chemical compounds. In this case they would not easily recognize the charred bodies in an exotic country as being in any way connected with their own actions.

Bureaucracy employed in the service of inhuman ends has ably demonstrated its ability to silence moral motivations not only in its employees, but also well beyond the boundaries of the bureaucratic organization itself. It achieved this by appealing to the motive of self-preservation, while the bureaucratic management of genocide secured the cooperation of many of its victims and the moral indifference of most of the bystanders. Prospective victims had been transformed into 'psychological captives' and so were bewitched by the illusory prospects of benign treatment as a reward for compliance. They hoped against hope that something might still be saved, some dangers averted, if only the oppressors were not unduly aggrieved and so their cooperation would be rewarded. In many cases this anticipatory compliance appeared in the sense that the victims went out of their way to please the oppressors by guessing their intention in advance and implementing it with zestful passion. Not until the last moment were they faced with the unavoidability of their fate. The managers of genocide thereby attained their ends with the minimum of disorder and few guards were needed to supervise the long, obedient march to the gas chambers.

As for the bystanders, their compliance, or at least their silence accompanied by inactivity, was secured through setting a high price for any expression of solidarity with the victims. Choosing morally correct behaviour would have meant inviting an awesome punishment. Once the stakes were raised in this way, the interests of self-preservation may have pushed aside moral duty and techniques of rationalization were left to perform their purpose: for example, 'I could not help the victims without jeopardizing my own and my family's lives; I would have saved one person at best, yet if I failed, ten would die.' Such rationalizations were assisted by those scientists who, in separating the means and ends of their inquiries, provided the dominant ideology with scientific evidence for the inferiority of those persons subject to such horrific crimes. Subjects were transformed into inferior 'objects' whose manipulation and destruction became not a moral matter, but one of the technical know-how of experts whose authority was assumed to alleviate the perpetrators of any responsibility for inflicting suffering upon other human beings.

Admittedly, the above is an extreme illustration of the opposition between self-preservation and moral duty, but such 'ethnic cleansing' is still with us. However, this opposition leaves its imprint on the everyday human condition, albeit in a less extreme form. After all, extinguishing moral obligations may be facilitated by the statistical treatment of human actions. Viewed as numbers, human objects can lose their individuality and so be deprived of their separate existence as bearers of human rights and moral obligations. What then matters is the category to which they have been officially designated. The classification itself can then sharpen the focus on selected shared attributes of the individuals in which the organization has expressed its interest. At the same time, this may license a neglect for all the other attributes of the person and thus for those very characteristics that form them as moral subjects and unique and irreplaceable human beings.

For Michel Foucault, as populations grew and social life became more complicated, so the care of its citizens became a central concern of the state. A new regime then arose in the art of government, with everyday life becoming an object of intervention in the desire to predict and control populations, all of which was ably assisted by developments in statistical reasoning. People then became regulated and disciplined according to the strategies that were pursued with these ends in sight. The productivity of labour was very important in these rationalizations. What were once houses of confinement became hospitals in which those who were unable to work for physical or non-physical reasons became the objects of medical intervention. It was here that the idea of 'psychiatry' was born. However, we must ask that if such means were employed, then for what purpose and with what consequence? Not only governments, but also large corporations, including marketing and insurance services, classify populations for the purpose of collecting information. We have seen that business matters are in tensions with moral purpose. Why? Because people are treated as means to the pursuit of those interests and not ends in their own right. Yet this may equally occur in situations not informed by such interests, as we saw in our earlier examples.

There is another silencer of morality: the crowd. It has been noted that people who find themselves tightly packed together in confined spaces with great numbers of other people whom they do not know – who they have not met under other circumstances, have not interacted with before and with whom they are 'united' at present only by a temporary, accidental interest – are prone to behave in a way they would not deem acceptable in 'normal' conditions. The wildest of behaviour may suddenly spread through the crowd in a fashion which can be compared only with a forest fire, wind blast or contagion. In an accidental crowd, for instance in a congested marketplace or in a theatre in the grip of panic, people overwhelmed with the desire for self-preservation may trample over their fellow humans, push others into the fire, just to secure a breathing-space for themselves or to get out of danger. In a crowd people may be able to commit deeds no single perpetrator would be morally capable of committing left to themselves. If the crowd may commit acts that its individual members might abhor, it is because of its 'facelessness'; individuals lose their individuality and 'dissolve' into the anonymous gathering. The crowd may disappear as quickly as it gathers and its collective action, however coordinated it may appear, neither follows nor generates interaction of any degree of permanence. It is precisely the momentary and inconsequential character of the crowd action which makes possible the purely affective conduct of its individual members. For a fleeting moment, inhibitions may be removed, obligations rendered void and rules suspended.

At first glance the orderly, rational conduct of the bureaucratic organization and the riotous eruptions of a crowd's anger may seem poles apart. Nevertheless, they both tend towards 'depersonalization' and so may reduce the propensity for moral action in their faceless anonymity. After all, people remain moral subjects as long as they are acknowledged as *humans*: that is, as beings eligible for the treatment reserved for fellow human beings alone and considered appropriate for every human being. This assumes that the partners to our interactions possess their own unique needs and that these needs are as valid and important as our own and so ought to be paid similar attention and respect. Whenever certain persons or categories of people are denied the right to our moral responsibility, they are treated as 'lesser humans', 'flawed humans', 'not fully human', or downright 'non-human'. To guard against this, as the French philosopher and novelist Simone de Beauvoir put it, this necessitates not treating someone we meet as a member of a class, nation or some other collectivity, but as an individual who is an end in their own right.

In the universe of moral obligations not all members of the human species may be included. Many 'primitive' tribes gave themselves names which meant 'human beings'. An accompanying refusal to accept the humanity of strange tribes and their members lingered on in slave-owning societies in which slaves had been assigned the status of 'talking tools' and considered solely in the light of their usefulness to the accredited task. The status of limited humanity meant in practice that the essential requirement of a moral attitude – respect for another person's needs that includes, first and foremost, the recognition of their integrity and sanctity of their life – was not seen as binding in relation to the bearers of such status. It looks as if history consisted of a gradual, yet relentless extension of the idea of humanity – with a pronounced tendency of the universe of obligations to become ever more inclusive and in the end co-terminous with the totality of the human species.

This process has not been straightforward. The twentieth century was notorious for the appearance of highly influential worldviews that called for the exclusion of whole categories of the population – classes, nations, races, religions – from the universe of obligations. The perfection of the bureaucratically organized action, on the other hand, has reached a point where moral inhibitions cannot effectively interfere with considerations of efficiency any more. The combination of both factors – the possibility of suspending moral responsibility offered by the bureaucratic technology of management and the presence of worldviews ready and willing to deploy such a possibility – resulted on many occasions in the successful confinement of the universe of obligations. This, in its turn, opened the way to such diverse consequences as the mass terror practised in communist societies against the members of hostile classes and persons classified as their helpers; persistent discrimination of racial and ethnic minorities in countries otherwise proud of their human-rights record, many of whom practised overt or surreptitious apartheid systems; the sale of arms to those countries which were subsequently castigated for their lack of morality and who may then have been subject to a declaration of war only to be shot at by those same weapons; the numerous cases of genocide, moving from the massacre of Armenians in Turkey, through the annihilation of millions of Jews, gypsies and Slavs by Nazi Germany, to the gassing of Kurds or the mass murders in Cambodia, the former Yugoslavia and Rwanda. The boundaries of the universe of obligations remain to this day a contentious issue.

Inside the universe of obligations, the authority of other people's needs is recognized. Everything possible ought to be done to secure their welfare, expand their life-chances and open their access to the amenities that society has to offer. Their poverty, ill health and dreariness of daily life constitute a challenge and an admonition to all other members of the same universe of obligations. Faced with such a challenge, we feel obliged to excuse ourselves – to supply a convincing explanation of why so little has been done to alleviate their lot and why not much more can be done; we also feel obliged to prove that everything that could be done has been done. Not that the explanations provided must of necessity be true. We hear, for instance, that the health service offered to the population at large cannot be improved because 'money cannot be spent until it is earned'. What such an explanation conceals, however, is that the profits made by private medicine used by well-off patients are classified as 'earnings', while the services provided for those who cannot afford private fees are counted among 'expenditures'. Such explanations conceal a differential treatment of needs depending on the ability to pay. The very fact that the explanation is thought to be needed at all, however, testifies to the recognition that the people whose health needs are neglected remain, to some degree, inside the universe of obligations.

Summary

Self-preservation and moral duty often stand in tension. Neither can claim to be more 'natural' than the other; that is, better attuned to the inherent predisposition of human nature. If one gains an upper hand over the other and it becomes a dominant motive of human action, the cause of the imbalance can usually be traced back to the social context of interaction. Self-interested and moral motives become prevalent depending on the circumstances over which the people who are guided by them may have only a limited control. It has been observed, however, that two persons may act differently when faced with the same circumstances. Thus, the power of circumstances is never absolute and the choice between the two contradictory motives remains open even under the most extreme conditions, while (as we have seen) our individual actions are bound up with the actions of others upon whom we are dependent. A moral predisposition in our actions towards others thus also becomes a precondition for self-esteem and self-respect.

chapter five

MAKING IT HAPPEN: GIFTS, EXCHANGE AND INTIMACY IN RELATIONSHIPS

In our discussions on action, power and choice, we examined some of those issues that inform our daily lives and the decisions that we routinely face in our interactions with others. Many of these interactions are informed by the ideas of gift and exchange and which bring form and content to our lives. In this chapter we shall continue our journey over the challenges, choices and constraints that we all routinely face by examining the issues that surround and inform these transactions.

The Personal and Impersonal: The Gift and Exchange

For some, debt is an occasional visitor about which it is possible to seek remedies without unduly altering the material and symbolic aspects that make up the routines and exceptions that inform their lifestyles. For others, debt is a routine feature of life that requires daily attention in order to fulfil obligations to children, family and friends. It is not a visitor, but a permanent resident that requires continual attention and activity in seeking to ameliorate its worse effects. Consider the following scenario.

Reminders from creditors flood into the places where we live (we do not use the term 'home' here because that signifies some permanence and security). We sort through them and prioritize as best we can. After all, some may be urgent because the creditors are threatening to remove a valued piece of furniture or possession in order to recover some of the debt. What can be done? We could go to a close relative and ask them for a loan – if they have the means to help us. We could then explain the situation and promise to pay the money back as soon as circumstances improve. They might grumble a little and inform us of the virtues of foresight, prudence and planning and not living above our means but, if able, might reach into their pockets.

There is another option open to us. We could go to a bank manager or credit agency. Nevertheless, would they be interested in how we are suffering as a result of our situation? Would they care? The only questions they might ask would refer to the guarantees that could be offered in order to ensure the loan would be repaid. They will inquire about income and expenditure in order to ascertain whether the capital repayments and interest on the loan can be met. Supporting documentation will be required and if satisfied that we are not an excessive risk and that the loan is likely to be duly repaid – with the interest that ensures good profits – we may then be lent the money.

Depending on to whom and where we turn to solve our financial problems, we can expect two very different kinds of treatment. Different sets of questions will relate to different conceptions of our rights to receive assistance. Our close relative may not inquire about matters relating to solvency for the loan is not a choice between good and bad business. What counts is that we are in need and so have a claim to help. A bank manager, on the other hand, is not positioned within their organization to be concerned with such matters, they simply want to know whether the loan is likely to be a sensible, profitable business transaction. In no way is there an obligation, morally or otherwise, to lend us the money.

In this case we see human interaction being influenced by two principles: equivalent *exchange* and *gift*. In the former case, self-interest rules supreme. Although the person who has the need for the loan may be recognized as an autonomous person with legitimate needs and rights, those are subservient to the satisfaction of the potential lender's own interests or the organization they represent. Above all, the lender is guided by technical preoccupations with the risks involved in making the loan, how much will be paid back and what material benefits may be derived from the transaction. These and similar issues will be asked of the prospective action in order to evaluate its desirability and to establish the order of preference between alternative choices. Parties to these interactions will bargain about the meaning of equivalence and deploy all the resources at hand in order to obtain the best possible deal and so tilt the transaction in their favour.

As the French anthropologist Marcel Mauss recognized in the 1920s, the idea of the gift is another matter. In this case an obligation motivates the exchange of gifts in terms of the needs and the rights of others. These gifts have symbolic value for the group to which the parties to the interaction belong and take place within belief systems in which reciprocity is praised. Thus, in the act of giving, we are also giving something of ourselves and this is prized above the instrumental calculations that inform the impersonality of the equivalent exchange relationship. Rewards, even if they come in the end, are not a factor in the calculation of desirability of action. The goods are given away with the services being extended merely because the other person needs them and, being the person they are, they have a right to their needs being respected.

The idea of the 'gift' is a common name for a wide range of acts that differ in their purity. 'Pure' gift is, as it were, a liminal concept – a sort of benchmark against which all practical cases are measured. Such practical cases depart from the ideal in various degrees. In the purest of forms, the gift would be totally disinterested and offered without regard to the quality of the recipient. Disinterestedness means a lack of remuneration in any shape or form. Judged by the ordinary standards of ownership and exchange, the pure gift is a pure loss. After all, it is a gain solely in moral terms and this is a basis for action that its logic cannot recognize.

The moral value of the gift is not measured by the market price of the goods or services offered, but precisely by the subjective loss they constitute for the donor. The disregard for the quality of the recipient means that the only qualification considered when the gift is offered is that the recipient belongs to the category of people in need. For this reason, generosity towards members of one's own kin or close friends, which we discussed earlier, does not in fact meet the requirements of the pure gift: it sets apart the recipients as special people selected for special treatment. Being special, the recipients have the right to expect such generosity from others with whom they are bound by a network of special relationships. In its pure form, the gift is offered to anyone who may need it simply because and only because, they need it. The pure gift is thus the recognition of the humanity of the other. Aside from this they remain anonymous and are allocated to no particular division in the donor's cognitive map.

As noted, gifts offer the donor that elusive, yet deeply gratifying, reward of moral satisfaction in which the act of giving is also an act of giving something of themselves: that is, the experience of selflessness, of self-sacrifice for the sake of another human being. In a sharp contrast to the context of exchange or gain seeking, such moral satisfaction grows in proportion to the painfulness of self-sacrifice and the resulting loss. The philosopher, social critic and social policy analyst Richard Titmuss wrote, for example, about the British context of giving blood to the National Health Service for no reward except that inspired by *altruistic* motives. He spoke of the gift of blood having attributes that distinguished it from other forms of giving in that it was 'a voluntary, altruistic act'. To replace such altruism with a system that legitimizes such giving in terms of being a consumption good would, he argued, undermine its fundamental basis which relates to the values that are accorded to strangers and not what people expect to obtain from society.

Research conducted on human behaviour under extreme conditions – war and foreign occupation – has shown that the most heroic cases of gift-giving, in terms of sacrificing one's own life in order to save another whose life was threatened, were on the whole performed by people whose motives came very close to the ideal of pure gift. They simply considered helping other human beings as, purely and simply, their moral duty and one that did not call for any justification, as it is natural, self-evident and elementary. One of the most remarkable findings of this research is that the most selfless among the helpers found it difficult to understand the unique heroism of their actions. They tended to play down the courage such conduct required and the moral virtue it demonstrated.

The two kinds of treatment, which we discussed at the beginning of this chapter, offer an example of the daily manifestations of the gift – exchange choice. As a first approximation, we may call the relationship with the relative *personal* and the relationship with the bank manager *impersonal*. What happens in the framework of a personal relationship depends almost entirely on the quality of the partners to the interaction and not on their performance. In an impersonal relationship, this is not the case. It is only performance which counts, not the quality. It does not matter who the people are, only what they are likely to do. The partner who is positioned to make the loan will be interested in past records as a basis on which to judge the likelihood of future behaviour, all of which takes place under the terms and conditions of a formal agreement.

A highly influential American post-Second World War sociologist, Talcott Parsons, considered the opposition between quality and performance as one of the four major oppositions among conceivable patterns of human relationship that he gave the name 'pattern variables'. A second pair of opposite options to choose between is that of 'universalism' and 'particularism'. Under the gift situation, people are not seen as part of a category, but a particular individual in need. With the bank manager, on the other hand, a client is just a member of a large category of past, current and prospective borrowers. Having dealt with so many 'like-others' before, the bank manager will assess the person on the basis of general criteria that are applied to similar cases. The outcome of a case then depends on the application of general rules to particular cases.

The third pattern variable also sets the two cases under consideration in opposition to each other. The relationship with the family member is 'diffuse', while the relationship with the bank manager is 'specific'. The generosity of the relative was not just a one-off whim; it was not an attitude improvised specifically for the distress that was reported during a conversation. Their predisposition towards the person in need spills over into everything which concerns that person regarding their life. Thus, there is a willingness to assist in this particular case because they are generally well disposed towards the person in need and interested in all aspects of their life. The bank manager's conduct is not geared to the specific application and their reactions to the application and their final decision are based upon the facts of the case, not to other aspects of the person's life. According to the logic of the situation, those things important to the applicant are, rightly from the point of view of the bank manager in terms of being positioned by their institution to dispense loans, irrelevant to the application and so ruled out of consideration.

The fourth pattern of human relationships for Talcott Parsons is one that might be argued to underlie all the others. It is that between 'affectivity' and 'affective neutrality'. Some interactions are infused with emotions – compassion, sympathy or love – while others are detached and unemotional. Impersonal relations do not arouse in the actors any feelings other than a passionate urge to achieve a successful transaction. The actors themselves are not objects of emotions in terms of being either liked or disliked. If they strike a hard bargain, try to cheat, prevaricate or avoid commitments, some of the impatience with the unduly slow progress of the transaction may rub off on the attitude towards them, or they may be regarded as someone with whom it was 'a pleasure to do business'. By and large, however, emotions are not viewed as an indispensable part of impersonal interactions, while they are the very factors which make personal interaction plausible.

In terms of the loan by a close relative, there is a probability that the parties empathize with each other and share a sense of belonging in which each person puts themselves in the other's position in order to understand each other's predicament. The American psychologist Carole Gilligan identified what she called a tendency for women to adopt an 'ethic of care' (she did not rule out men having such a predisposition) in which concern is given over to others and a concern for oneself is considered 'selfish'. Such an ethic is about a responsibility in which the parties do not see themselves as autonomous in terms of being governed by abstract rules, but as 'connected' with others in binding relationships. This is hardly the case with the bank manager. A person seeking a loan might seek to avoid making them angry and even flatter them, but otherwise such concerns will be regarded as interfering with their judgement for they detract from the calculation of risk in terms of profit and loss.

Perhaps the most crucial distinction between personal and impersonal contexts of interaction lies in the factors on which the actors rely for the success of their action. We all depend on the actions of so many people of whom we are likely to know very little. With so little knowledge of the type of people upon whom we rely at our disposal, a transaction would be impossible were it not for the opportunity to settle the issue in an impersonal manner. Under conditions of limited personal knowledge, appealing to rules seems to be the only way to make communication possible. Imagine what an incredibly large, unwieldy volume of knowledge you would need to amass if all your transactions with others were based solely on your properly researched estimate of their personal qualities. The much more realistic alternative is to get hold of the few general rules that guide the interchange. This is one of the justifications for the existence of the market mechanism that governs so much of our lives. However, there is also implied in this a *trust* that the partner to the interaction will observe the same rules.

Many things in life are organized so as to enable partners to interact without any or with little personal information about each other. It would be quite impossible for many of us, for example, to assess, in advance, the healing ability and dedication of the medical practitioners to whom we may turn in times of illness. Such professionalism is not only about knowledge and competence as certified by professional bodies after lengthy periods of training and examinations, but also about trust. We often have no choice but to submit ourselves to their care and hope that in exchange, we receive the care that our case warrants and requires. In this and similar cases people, personally unknown to us, took it upon themselves to endorse the competency of people whose credentials they then endorsed. By so doing and through upholding standards in terms of a set of professional ethics, they have made it possible for us to accept the services of such people on trust. Anthony Giddens, along with the German sociologists Ulrich Beck and Niklas Luhmann, have all examined the relations between trust and risk. Anthony Giddens defines risk as a 'confidence in the reliability of a person or system' in terms of given events or outcomes, 'where that confidence expresses a faith in the probity or love of another, or in the correctness of abstract principles (technical knowledge)'.

It is precisely because so many of our transactions are performed in an impersonal context that the need for personal relationships becomes so poignant and acute. Trust is a social relationship that if overly subjected to the impersonality and commodification of the market, which is often assumed to be the epitome of impersonality, will be undermined. It is not surprising, therefore, that in their different ways the German philosopher and sociologist Jürgen Habermas, the American social commentator Francis Fukuyama and the Hungarian financier and philanthropist George Soros have all noted how the success of such a mechanism is dependent upon a cultural basis of community and commitment. If permitted to reign unchecked, therefore, the market will tend to undermine the basis upon which its existence relies.

We have noted on numerous occasions that the more we depend on people of whom we have but vague and superficial knowledge and the more perfunctory and fleeting our encounters are, the stronger is the tendency to expand the realm of personal relations. The result of this is to force the expectations that fit only personal transactions onto interactions that are best performed in an impersonal fashion. Thus, resentment of the indifference of an impersonal world is likely to be felt most strongly by those who move, in an abrupt fashion, between two worlds. Young people, for instance, who are just about to leave what may be the relatively caring world of the family and youthful friendships, find themselves entering the emotionally cool world of employment and occupational practice.

For such reasons we witness attempts to opt out of a callous and heartless world where people appear to serve only as the means to some ends which bear little relation to their own needs and happiness. Some escapees try to establish commune-like, self-enclosed and self-contained little enclaves, inside which only relations of a personal type are allowed. Such attempts, however, may lead to disenchantment and bitterness. It transpires that the unrelenting effort needed to maintain a high intensity of feelings over a long period of time and to absorb frustrations arising from the constant clashes between affections and the considerations of effectiveness, can generate more misery than that experienced by the indifference of the alternative.

In Pursuit of Ourselves: Love, Intimacy, Caring and Commodities

If the personal context cannot accommodate the whole business of life, it still remains an indispensable ingredient. Our craving for 'deep and wholesome' personal relationships grows in intensity the wider and less penetrable is the network of impersonal dependencies in which we are entangled. If we have jobs, we find ourselves being employees at one moment and then at another moment some of the following: customers in shops; passengers on buses, plains or trains; spectators at sporting events or in theatres; voters for political parties; patients in doctors' and dentists' surgeries and numerous other activities in different places. Everywhere we may feel that only a small section of our selves is present. In each context we may have to remind ourselves about appropriate forms of behaviour within these contexts and so judge those that are acceptable and unacceptable accordingly. Nowhere do we feel at home in terms of being truly 'ourselves'. So, who in the end is the real 'I'?

Most of us would fall shy of settling for an image of ourselves as a mere patchwork of different roles. Nevertheless, sooner or later we grow to reconcile ourselves to a plurality of 'Me's' and even to some lack of coordination between them. As the unity is evidently missing in the world 'out there', split as it is into a multitude of partial transactions, it must be supplied instead by our cohesive selves. As Georg Simmel observed in the early twentieth century, in the densely populated, variegated world we inhabit, individuals tend to fall back upon themselves in the never-ending search for sense and unity. Once focused on us rather than on the world outside, this overwhelming thirst for unity and coherence is articulated as the search for self-identity. This tension between adjustment and autonomy is a recurrent feature of the human condition and is demonstrated by the popularity of books that pick up on these very themes, for example, David Reisman's post-Second World War study on the changing nature of the American character entitled *The Lonely Crowd*.

None of the many impersonal exchanges in which we are involved will suffice to supply the identity we seek because it lies beyond any of those exchanges. No impersonal context can accommodate it in full. In each single context we are, so to speak, somewhat displaced: our real selves, we feel, are located somewhere outside the context of the interaction now taking place. Only in a personal context, with its diffuseness, particularity, emphasis on quality and the mutual affection which saturates it, can we hope to find what we are looking for and even then, we may be frustrated in our attempts. Perhaps it is in the actions we perform in its pursuit that our self lies, rather than some end-state in which autonomy and unity may be presupposed without question?

Niklas Luhmann presented the search for self-identity in terms of our overwhelming need for love – of loving and being loved. Being loved means being treated by the other person as unique, as unlike any other; it means that the loving person accepts that the loved ones need not invoke universal rules in order to justify the images they hold of themselves or their demands; it means that the loving person accepts and confirms the sovereignty of their partner and their right to decide for themselves and to choose on their own authority. It means, in essence, that they agree with the emphatic and stubborn statement of their partner: 'Here is what I am, what I do, and where I stand.'

Being loved also means being understood in the sense in which we use it whenever we say, 'I want you to understand me!', or ask with anguish, 'Do you understand me? Do you really *understand* me?' This craving for being understood is a desperate call to someone to put themselves in our shoes, to see things from our point of view and to accept without further proof that we have a point of view that ought to be respected for the simple reason that it is ours. What we are pursuing in these situations is a confirmation of our own, private experiences: that is, inner motives; images of ideal life, of ourselves and our miseries and joys. It concerns the *validation* of our self-portrayal. Such validation is sought through a partner's willingness to listen seriously and with sympathy when talking about ourselves. This means that the partner, in Luhmann's words, should 'lower the threshold of relevances' and accept everything that is said as relevant and worth listening to and thinking about.

There is a paradox here. On one hand, we find a desire for the unique whole of the self as opposed to a collection of roles. Thus, there is an assertion and desire for uniqueness and not to be just a cog in the impersonal machine of life. On the other hand, there is awareness that nothing exists just because it is imagined to be so. The difference between fantasy and reality is thereby necessary and so whatever truly exists must exist for others as much as it does for ourselves. Therefore, the more people feel they succeed in developing a truly unique self – in making their experiences unique – the more they require social confirmation of those experiences. It seems, at first sight, that such confirmation is possible only through love. In our complex society in which most human needs are attended to in an impersonal way, the need we have for a loving relationship appears deeper than at any other time. As a result, the burden that love carries in our existence is formidable. The private consequences of our public troubles, as feminist researchers have found, lead to ever greater pressures, tensions and obstacles that lovers must encounter and seek to overcome with differing degrees of success.

What makes a love relationship particularly vulnerable and fragile is the need for reciprocity. If we seek love then, in all probability, our partners will ask us to reciprocate – to respond with love. This means (as we have said) that we act in such a way as to confirm the reality of our partner's experience: to understand at the same time we are seeking to be understood. Ideally, each partner will strive to find meaning in the other partner's world. However, the two realities will not be identical. When two people meet for the first time, both have behind them biographies which are not shared with the other. Two distinct biographies would in all probability have produced two fairly distinct sets of experiences and expectations. Now they must be renegotiated. At least in some respects the two sets are likely to be mutually contradictory. It is improbable that both partners will regard each as real and acceptable without the need for correction and compromise. One set, or even both, will have to give way for the sake of a lasting relationship. Yet surrender defies the very purpose of love and the very need that love is expected to satisfy. If renegotiations do take place, if both partners see it through, the rewards are great. Nevertheless, the road to the happy end is thorny and much patience and understanding are needed to travel it unscathed. Many succeed, but the gap between the ideal and the actual can lead to frustrations and tensions with some of its manifestations resulting in divorce, separation and even domestic violence.

Richard Sennett coined the term 'destructive Gemeinschaft' for a relationship in which both partners obsessively pursue the right to intimacy. This is to open oneself up to a partner and share the whole, most private truth about one's inner life via absolutely sincerity. In this way nothing is hidden from view, however upsetting the information may be for the partner. The result is to place an enormous burden on the latter's shoulders as the partner is asked to give agreement to things which do not necessarily arouse enthusiasm and to be equally sincere and honest in reply. Richard Sennett does not believe that a lasting relationship – particularly a lasting *loving* relationship – can be erected on the wobbly ground of mutual intimacy. The odds are overwhelming that partners will make demands of each other which they cannot meet (or, rather, do not wish to meet, considering the price). In the process they will suffer and feel tormented and frustrated. More often than not, they will decide to call it a day by stopping the attempt and withdrawing. One or other of the partners will choose to opt out and seek to satisfy their need for self-confirmation elsewhere.

We can say from these discussions that the requirements of reciprocity in a loving relationship are double-edged. Strange as it may seem, the least vulnerable is love as a gift: there is a preparedness to accept a beloved's world, to put ourselves in that world and try to comprehend it from inside – without expecting a similar service in exchange. We need no negotiation, agreement or contract. Once aimed in both directions, however, intimacy makes negotiation and compromise inevitable. At this point it is precisely the negotiation and compromise which one or both partners may be too impatient, or too self-concerned, to bear lightly. With love being such a difficult and costly achievement, it is no wonder one finds demand for a substitute for love: that is, for someone who would perform the function of love without demanding reciprocity in exchange. Herein lies the secret of the astounding success and popularity of psychoanalytic sessions, counselling, marriage guidance, and so on. For the right to open oneself up, make one's innermost feelings known to another person and in the end receive the longed-for approval of one's identity, one need only to pay money for a service.

Love and care, as Lynn Jamieson reminds us in her study of intimacy in modern society, are not necessarily the same. While paid carers meet practical needs, they do not love, while 'some associates feel a deep affection for each other that they call love but yet do little caring'. Monetary payment transforms the analyst's or the therapist's relation to their patients or clients into an impersonal one. One can be concerned with oneself and have the concerns shared, without giving a single thought to the people whose services have been bought and who have therefore taken upon themselves the obligation of sharing as a part of a business transaction. The patient thereby purchases the illusion of being loved. However, as this relationship is in sharp disagreement with the socially accepted model of love, psychoanalytical exercises tends to be plagued with transference. This may be defined as the patient's tendency to mistake the 'as if' conduct of the analyst for an expression of love and to respond with a behaviour which steps beyond the strictly business-like, impersonal terms of the agreement. Such occurrences may be interpreted as a powerful confirmation of therapy as a love substitute.

The Commodification of Identity

The consumer market precisely, for the function of identity approval, offers another, perhaps less vulnerable substitute for love in putting on a wide range of 'identities' from which a consumer can select. Commercial advertisements take pains to show the commodities they try to sell as a part of a particular lifestyle, so that prospective customers can consciously purchase symbols of such self-identity as they would wish to possess. The market offers identity-making tools that can be used to produce results which differ somewhat from each other and are in this way personalized. Through the market we can put together various elements of the complete identikit of a do-it-yourself (DIY) customized self. We can learn how to express ourselves as a modern, liberated, carefree woman, a thoughtful, reasonable, caring housewife, an aspiring, self-confident tycoon, an easy-going, likeable fellow, an outdoor, physically fit, macho man, a romantic, dreamy and love-hungry creature, or any mixture of all these! The advantage of market-promoted identities is that they come complete with elements of social approval – introduced as they are by using means of advertising that people seem to approve of – and so the agony of seeking confirmation is spared. Social approval does not need to be negotiated for it has been, so to speak, built into the marketed product from the start.

For some, such as the French social commentator Jean Baudrillard, the pursuit of the authentic self in the market is nothing more than an illusion. Appearance is all we have and that reveals no deeper, underlying, reality in terms of who we *really* are. Appearances are manufactured and taken on and off in the seduction that comes with continual consumption. With so many alternatives that are widely available and growing in popularity, the effort required by the drive to solve the self-identity problem through reciprocal love has an ever smaller chance of success. Asked in one interview about whether there was such a thing as love, Baudrillard replied that there was 'acting-out', but he does not have 'a great deal to say about love'. Nevertheless, if he is correct then the implications of his analysis seem to place ever greater burdens upon the need for reciprocity and recognition within loving relationships as people may retreat to seek what they feel are more authentic experiences in the face of the alternative.

As we have seen before, negotiating approval is a tormenting experience for the partners in love. Success is not possible without long and dedicated effort. It needs self-sacrifice on both sides. The effort and the sacrifice would perhaps be made more frequently and with greater zeal were it not for the availability of 'easy' substitutes. With the substitutes being easy to obtain – the only sacrifice being, if one has the means, to part with a quantity of money – and aggressively peddled by the sellers there is less motivation for a laborious, time consuming and frequently frustrating effort. Resilience may wither when confronted with alluringly 'foolproof' and less demanding marketed alternatives. Often the first hurdle, the first setback in the developing and vulnerable love partnership would be enough for one or both partners to wish to slow down, or to leave the track altogether. Often the substitutes are first sought with the intention to 'complement' and hence to strengthen or resuscitate, the failing love relationship. Sooner or later, however, the substitutes may unload that relationship of its original function and drain off the energy which prompted the partners to seek its resurrection in the first place.

One of the manifestations of such a devaluation of love, which has been discussed by Richard Sennett, is the tendency of *eroticism* to be ousted and supplanted by sexuality. Eroticism means the deployment of sexual desire and ultimately of sexual intercourse itself, as a hub around which a lasting love relationship is built and maintained: a social partnership of a stable kind, bearing all the features previously ascribed to multi-sided, personal relations. Sexuality means the reduction of sexual intercourse to one function only: the satisfaction of sexual desire. Such a reduction is often supplemented by special precautions aimed at preventing the sexual relationship from giving rise to mutual sympathy and obligation and thus from growing into a fully fledged personal partnership. Prised from love, sex is reduced to an unloading of tension, in which the partner is used as an essentially replaceable means to an end. Another consequence, however, is that the emancipation of sexuality from the context of eroticism leaves the love relationship considerably weakened. It now lacks (or has to share) one of the most powerful of its resources, and finds its stability still more difficult to defend.

A loving relationship is thus exposed to a twofold danger. It may collapse under the pressure of inner tensions, or it may retreat into a type of relationship that bears many or all the marks of an impersonal relationship – one of exchange. We have observed a typical form of exchange relationship when considering bank customers' transactions with the bank manager. We have noted that the only thing which counted there was the passing of a particular object, or a service, from one side of the transaction to the other – an object was changing hands. The living persons involved in the transactions did not do much more than play the role of carriers or mediators in that they prompted and facilitated the circulation of goods. Although their gaze was fixed on their respective partners, they assigned relevance solely to the object of exchange, while granting the other party a secondary, derivative importance in terms of being holders or gatekeepers of the goods they wanted. They saw 'through' their partners, straight into the goods themselves. The last thing the partners might consider would be the tender feelings or spiritual cravings of their counterparts. The supreme motive of their action was to give away as little as possible and to get as much as possible and so both pursued their own self-interest, concentrating their thought solely on the task at hand. We may say that in transactions of impersonal exchange, the interests of the actors are in conflict.

Nothing in an exchange transaction is done simply for the sake of the other. In this sense there is a tendency to experience an accompanying fear of being cheated and a need to remain wide awake, wary and vigilant. They want protection against the selfishness of the other side. There is no reason to expect the other party to act selflessly, but there may be an insistence upon a fair deal. Hence the exchange relationship calls for a binding rule and an authority entrusted with the task of adjudicating the fairness of the transaction. This authority must be capable of imposing its decisions in cases of transgression. Various consumer associations, watchdogs and ombudspersons are established out of this urge for protection. Such bodies are charged with the difficult task of monitoring the fairness of exchange and lobby the authorities for laws which would restrain the freedom of the stronger side to exploit the ignorance, or naivety, of the weaker one.

Seldom are the two counterparts of a transaction in a truly equal position. After all, those who produce or sell the goods know much more of the quality of their product than the buyers and users are ever likely to learn, regardless of the number of guarantees of quality that are made. They may well push the product to gullible customers under false pretences, unless constrained by law. The more complex and technically sophisticated the goods, the less their buyers are able to judge their true quality and value. To avoid being deceived, the prospective buyers have to resort to the help of independent authorities. It is precisely because the partners enter exchange relationships only as functions of exchange, as conveyers of the goods and so remain 'invisible' to each other, that they feel much less intimate than in the case of love relationships. They do not take upon themselves duties, or obligations, other than the promise to abide by the terms of the transaction. Aspects of their selves which are not relevant to the transaction at hand are unaffected and retain their autonomy – depending upon which side of the transaction they fall!

Is this really the case? There is a mode of thought, often taken-for-granted in economic and political reasoning, that human labour is a commodity like others and so can be treated as an object of exchange. Yet unlike exchangeable goods, labour cannot be detached from the labourer. Selling our labour means agreeing that our actions as a person – the whole of the person for a specific period of time – will from now on be subordinated to the will and decisions of others. The totality of the labourer's self, and not just a detachable object in their possession, is parted with and transferred to somebody else's control. The apparently impersonal contract thus reaches far beyond the limits proper for transactions of exchange. The promise to repay a debt, enforced by law, also involves an undertaking to work to make the repayments with, of course, handsome interest.

$$\bigtriangledown$$

Summary

Love and exchange are two extremes of a continuous line along which all human relations may be plotted. In the form we have described them, they seldom appear in our experience. We have discussed them in pure forms, as models. Most relationships are 'impure' and mix them in varying proportions. There are now ethical banks and investment funds whose purpose is to contribute to ends that are social and environmental and so not governed solely by instrumental calculations aimed at control and profitability for its own sake. Similarly, loving relationships will contain elements of business-like bargaining for the fair rate of exchange in the 'I'll do this if you do that' style. Except for a chance encounter or one-off transaction, the actors in exchange relationships may not remain indifferent to each other for long and sooner or later more may be involved than just money and goods. We are routinely told that market transactions are always impersonal, but as the discipline of socio-economics makes clear, they are based upon networks of interdependencies in which cultural factors such as norms, values and accompanying evaluative judgements are routine features of interactions.

Despite these qualifications, each model retains its relative identity even if submerged in a mixed relationship. Each carries its own set of expectations and idealizations and hence orients the conduct of the actors in its own specific direction. Much of the ambiguity of the relationships we enter into with other people can be accounted for by reference to the tensions and contradictions between the two extreme, complementary yet incompatible, sets of expectations. The model-like, pure relationships seldom appear in life, where the ambivalence of human relationships is the rule. That ambivalence (as we have suggested) creates tensions within personal relationships that are a response to an impersonal world. Those tensions, in turn, can lead to the creation of a new set of impersonal services such as counselling, based upon exchange, in response to this situation.

Our dreams and cravings appear in tension between two needs which are difficult to gratify at the same time, yet equally difficult to satisfy when pursued separately. These are the needs of *belonging* and of *individuality*, to which we must add the capability to act in terms of being *positioned* in different ways within social relationships. Belonging prompts us to seek strong and secure ties with others. We express this need whenever we speak or think of togetherness or of community. Individuality sways us towards privacy as a state in which we are immune to pressures and free from demands to do whatever we think is worth doing. Both needs are pressing and powerful. On the other hand, the nearer one comes to the satisfaction of one need, the more painful may be the neglect of the other. We find out that community without privacy may feel more like oppression than belonging, while privacy without community can be more like loneliness than 'being oneself'. Perhaps, therefore, we can say we are ourselves with others, in differing degrees, with all the accompanying joys, pleasures, hopes, wishes and frustrations and constraints that accompany our states of being. Thus, to be a friend to ourselves means that we must have already entered into a friendship with others.

chapter six

CARE OF OUR SELVES: THE BODY, HEALTH AND SEXUALITY

We mentioned in chapter 5 the potential tension between eroticism and sex. These matters, like the health and well-being of our bodies, are fundamental features of our everyday lives. We find ourselves routinely subject to adverts about dieting, exercise and holidays. In this process people can oscillate between wanting to be with others and wanting to be left alone, being concerned with their bodies and rejecting the call to be healthy with binges of eating and drinking, and expressing the desire to be close to those with whom they feel comfortable and at the same time, 'getting away from it all' by travelling to places where few people will bother them. These all express feelings of wanting to break or suspend a relation that is thought to be cumbersome, unwieldy, constraining, irritating or just too demanding for comfort. As we may oscillate between the desires for intimacy and solitude, so too we construct a relation with our bodies that is a fundamental part of our everyday existence.

▽

In Search of Security

We have already noticed how vexing and enjoyable are our relations with other people. More often than not, they are complex and confusing, send contradictory signals and call for actions that are not easy to reconcile. Therefore, others not only provide security for our well-being, but also cause anxiety and this is not a pleasant condition – no wonder so many of us create strategies to avoid such situations. Having found confusion difficult to resolve and difficult to endure, we may feel an urge to cut the strings which attach us to its source and wish to withdraw. However, where do we go? Where can we find the secure shelter we seek?

In answering these questions, let us think of the world around us – the places and people we know and believe we understand – as a series of concentric circles, each one being larger than the next. The circumference of the largest circle is blurred in our cognitive map: it is a misty, far away place. That circle contains the 'great unknown', lands that have never been visited and would not be without the assistance of a reliable guide, armed with a phrase-book and maps and supplied with insurance against the risks that such an adventure might entail. The smaller circles are safer and more familiar; the smaller they become, the safer they feel. There is, first, a place that is our country, where each passer-by is assumed to be able to speak the language we understand, obey the same rules and behave in a manner that is understood in such a way that we might know how to respond to their gestures and conversation.

A smaller circle may be called our 'neighbourhood'. Here we know people by face, but mostly also by name and perhaps not simply by name, but also their habits. Knowing people's habits reduces the uncertainty that comes with unfamiliarity and so we can know what we might expect from each person. Then last, but by no means least, there is an 'inner circle', quite small by comparison, that we might call 'home'. Ideally, this is the place where all those differences between people, however deep they are, do not count for much, because we know that we can count on them all come what may; that they will stand by us through thick and thin and will not let us down. Here is the place where there is no need to prove anything, show a 'true face' and hide nothing. Home is often seen in these terms and regarded as a place of safety, warmth and security, where we can be sure of our place and our rights without fighting or keeping watch.

As with all neat definitions and presuppositions concerning clear boundaries that demarcate spaces and places, this is fine if it exists in the first place and then only as long as it continues to exist. Homelessness, family break-ups, the struggles between youth and older generations representing different cultural traditions and beliefs, appear not to exist as long as the boundaries between the circles are assumed to be clearly demarcated. If so, we know who we are, who are others, what are the expectations made of us and so where we stand in the order of things. We know what we may reasonably expect in each situation and which expectations would be illegitimate and presumptuous. However, what if the distinctions between the circles become blurred or even break down entirely? What if the rules which are in their right place in one circle leak into another, or are changing too fast and are too hazy to rely upon and to follow? Feelings of confusion and uncertainty, through to resentment and hostility, are the result. Where once clarity existed, ambivalence enters and with a lack of certainty, fear can knock at the door, as equally can a reactionary attitude born of a lack of willingness to engage and understand.

Many have compared the past to the present in these terms. A nostalgia for tradition is one in which people knew their place and the expectations correspondingly placed upon them. Historical research has questioned the existence of these comfortable certitudes, but they persist via an appropriation of these imagined communities of bygone eras as a response to contemporary conditions. The world that was meant to be familiar and secure appears no more. The speed of change now appears to govern the conditions in which we live with people moving around quickly; those who were once intimately known disappear from view and new people enter, of whom little is known. The feeling is that if we could have once defined who we were in terms of where we lived and in what era, those resources have evaporated with changes that are driven by frenetic desires apparently devoid of meaning and purpose. Then, if rules seem to be changing rapidly and without notice, they no longer possess the legitimacy that must underpin their existence. Little can be taken-for-granted and what has been achieved, cannot be assumed to last long unless constantly refreshed by continuous effort. Careers for life become fleeting moments in the struggle for recognition that comes with every job application and interview. Even in the innermost, most homely of circles, vigilance is required. As these processes govern more of our lives, commodification can so easily turn that home of security into a house that is no more an object of exchange as with any other.

Of course, we exaggerate somewhat to illustrate. Yet there is much we assume which affords our security that many do not possess, nor have the means to acquire. At the same time, these processes affect relationships despite the prevalent belief that they are hermetically sealed off from social, political and economic influences. Take, for example, the most intimate of relations: the family or love partnership. Anthony Giddens coined the term 'confluent love' to describe the sentiments which hold the partnership together and 'pure relationships' to characterize the kind of partnership that is built on this foundation. Confluent love simply means that at one particular moment partners love each other, are attracted to each other and wish to stay together. For them, their partnership is pleasurable, satisfying and desirable. Nevertheless, there is no promise or guarantee that this agreeable condition will last 'till death us do part'. Those things that flow together may also flow apart. If this occurs, the partnership itself, deprived of the basis that bound it together – it was, after all, a 'pure' relationship – will crumble. Confluent love, however, needs two, but to start drifting apart it is enough that the feelings of one begin to fade. Pure relationship, held together by confluent emotions, is therefore a brittle and vulnerable construction. Neither of the partners can be really sure of the other, who may declare tomorrow that they do not feel like sharing lives and staying together. They need 'more space' and would rather seek that elsewhere. Partnerships that have no other basis never stop being on a 'trial period', with a series of daily tests without end. Such partnerships offer freedom of manoeuvre, for they do not bind the partners by timeless commitments, nor do they 'mortgage the future' of either. That said, the price to be paid for what some would call this 'freedom' is high – perpetual uncertainty and so a lack of security.

All this cannot help but influence the status of the family – an institution regarded as a source of stability and security. After all, the family is seen as a bridge between the personal and impersonal and between the mortality of its individual members and its immortality. Sooner or later a member may die, but their family, kin and lineage will outlive them; their legacy is to have perpetuated that lineage in some way. Nowadays, many families split up and then rearrange themselves in different contexts, or simply dissolve into other relationships. Nothing, therefore, is given and so more things become tasks that have to be performed in order to sustain them. Lynn Jamieson called this process *disclosing intimacy* in which what was once assumed becomes something that needs to be rendered explicit in order that the bonds that unite are routinely sustained within relationships.

At one level we can say that the place where we might feel secure is shrinking; few people, if any, enter it and stay long enough to elicit trust and confidence. At the same time, however, there are numerous ways in which the circles we have suggested are sustained within everyday life, with differing consequences for the partners within a relationship. The practices of 'segmentation' and 'integration' between home and work within relationships, for example, have been examined by Christena Nippert-Eng. While paid work was a place assumed to be separate from the home, new technologies have opened up possibilities in terms of the use of space and time. That, however, requires facing new pressures within relationships in order that space and time within the home is demarcated to enable the work in the first place. If the other partner does not recognize that and adjustments made accordingly, then conflicts are likely to be heightened. We should, therefore, be cautious in our embrace of the supposed new-found freedoms that the information revolution is supposed to provide. Household structures and the gendered divisions of labour within them can be, as Christine Delphy and Diana Leonard demonstrated in their study of marriage, extraordinarily resistant to change.

There is another issue. When we have spoken about the call that people make for their 'own space', what does this mean? If they get it, what is left? After all, if others are left outside and so they are apparently free of those who 'get on their nerves' and make 'unreasonable demands', what is left of the person who seeks such a place and what is the basis of this demand? As we have argued throughout this book, we know ourselves through others and so, what is it to know ourselves and to what are we alluding when we make such a claim? One answer may lie in our *embodied selves*: that is, with reference to us as a 'body'.

Embodied Selves: Perfection and Satisfaction

Let us pause here and reflect. This book is about the difference that living in society makes to what we do, how we see ourselves, objects and others, and what happens as a result. Yet our bodies are something we have 'inherited', fully made up by genes and thus not a 'product' of society. A belief in such immutability, however, is an error. Like anything else about us, the circumstance of living in society makes an enormous amount of difference to our bodies. Even if quite a lot in the size and form of our bodies and its other features has been determined by genes and so not by our own choices and intentional actions – by nature, not culture – societal pressures are such that we do all we can to bring our bodies to a condition that is recognized as being right and proper.

This process is dependent on the kind of society in which we live and whether we are at peace with our body. We may view our bodies as a task – something to work on which requires daily care and attention. Once working on our body has been formed into a duty, society sets the standards for a desirable and so approved shape, for what every body ought to do in order to proximate those standards. Failure to comply can induce feelings of shame, while those not meeting such requirements may find themselves subjected to routine discrimination: for example, prejudicial attitudes towards disabled people as manifest in the very design of buildings. However bizarre it may seem at first glance, our bodies are the objects of social conditioning. Therefore, their place in a book dedicated to 'thinking sociologically' is entirely legitimate.

Michel Foucault became interested in what he called 'technologies of the self' and how our relation to ourselves, and so our bodies, has changed over time. How we act upon our bodies and care for ourselves is not, of course, a matter that takes place within a social vacuum. Thus, as far as the care for the body is concerned, our society happens to be particularly demanding. Given the large volume of risk and uncertainty in the 'world out there', the body emerges as what we hope to be the last line in a set of defensible trenches. The body can become a trustworthy shelter because it is a site that we can control and so feel secure, unvexed and unharassed. Given the habit of the allegedly most stable and durable parts of the world 'out there' to hold all sorts of surprises in store – to vanish without trace or change beyond recognition – the body seems the least transient, the longest living component of our lives. While all else may change, our bodies will always be with us! If investment, effort and expenditure carry a risk, it may be repaid in our bodies and similarly, it will be punished through our carelessness and negligence. A great deal hangs on the body as a result and sometimes more than some bodies can bear.

Fixing intense attention on the body has its advantages. Here is a site of activity that can produce real and tangible results by watching and then measuring the results. There is no shortage of health equipment to assist in this process: blood pressure and heart monitors, plus a wealth of dietary information, to name but a few. There is no need to be a sitting target for the card that fate may deal the body, for it can become the object of desire. Doing nothing feels worse – harrowing and humiliating – than doing something, even if that proves, in the long run, not to be as effective as you wished. Yet however much care and attention are devoted to the body, when are they sufficient? The sources of the anxiety that drives us toward such concerns will not go away for they derive from something external to the relationships with our bodies – the societies in which we live. The reasons for the run to shelter will always be with us and so the demands can have an appetite that is never satisfied.

This leaves us with several possibilities. The feeling of satisfaction we may derive from the success of one or other effort at improvement, for instance, may be momentary and in no time evaporate, to be replaced by self-criticism and self-reprobation. Instead of healing the wounds left by the fickle and uncertain world 'out there', our body may well turn into one more source of insecurity and fear. Once the body is turned into a defensive stockade, all the territory surrounding it and the roads leading to it tend to become the object of intense vigilance. We must be constantly on the watch: the body is on the attack or may come under assault at any moment, even if the enemy stays as yet hidden. You need to surround the fortress with moats, turrets and drawbridges and it must fall under our gaze twenty-four hours a day. Some of the infiltrators 'settle in' and pretend to be part of the body, while in fact they are not – they remain the aliens 'inside'. For instance, fat, which we see as being 'in the body' but not 'of the body', is a good example of such a process. These crafty and deceitful traitors-in-waiting must be spied out, so that they may be 'taken out of the system' and 'removed from circulation'. There is no shortage of services offering to round up, clean, deport and squeeze it out. Never, though, are lifestyles in general the subject of reflection, debate and potential transformation, for the entire project is based on the individualization and hence internalization, of social issues. Summer camps for overweight children become the answer, not the diets, lifestyles and consumption patterns of whole groups of people.

The 'interface' between the body and the rest of the world 'out there' tends to become the most vulnerable of the frontlines we need to defend in our never-ending fight for security and safety. The border checkpoints – the orifices of the body, the passageways leading 'inside the system' – are precarious places. We should wish to watch closely what we eat, drink and breathe. Any food or air may do harm to the body or prove downright poisonous. It is not surprising, therefore, that we find a whole industry and set of marketing techniques that are part of the discourses of the body: for example, foods that are 'good' for us and others that are 'bad' for us. We should select the right kind of diet which is generous to the first and intolerant and harsh to the second, with many being on offer to fulfil these desires.

All this is easier said than done. Time and again we learn that the kinds of nourishment that were thought to be innocuous or even beneficial to the body have been found to have unpleasant side-effects, or even cause diseases. Such discoveries cannot but come as shocks since more often than not they are made after the fact, when the harm has already been done and cannot be repaired. The shocks leave lasting wounds on confidence: who knows which one of the foods now recommended by the experts will be in the future condemned as damaging? Any one of them may become so, thus no 'healthy meal' can be consumed without some degree of apprehension. No wonder that 'new and improved' diets run hard on the heels of the once favoured but now discredited ones and that allergy, anorexia and bulimia, all arising on the interface between the body and the 'world out there', have been described as disorders specific to our age. Allergy, as Jean Baudrillard observed, has wandering 'points of attachment' and is therefore difficult to pinpoint. This chimes well with the condition of diffuse and undefined anxiety which lies at the foundation of present-day concerns with the defence of the body.

If the care for the well-being of our bodies – understood as a vigilant prevention of contamination and/or degeneration – were the only motive guiding our action, then extreme reticence that borders on fasting would be a reasonable strategy to pursue. In this way we would reduce the 'border traffic' to a bare minimum by refraining from indulgence and refusing to consume those foods that are in excess of what is absolutely necessary to keep us alive. For many this is not a choice for they do not know whether they will obtain food on a daily basis. As a solution to those who enjoy such access, however, this is hardly acceptable, for it would strip the body of the major attraction it holds for its 'owner'. Quite simply, the body is a site not only of anxiety, but also of pleasure and once again, we find an industry that prompts us to seek sensation: films, soaps, glossy magazines, commercials, books and shop windows tempt us into experiences whose absence may lessen the pleasure principle. Eating and drinking are social occasions that may induce pleasurable sensations and exciting experiences. To cut down on food and drink is to reduce the number of such occasions and so the interactions that accompany them. Is it any wonder that on the list of the top twenty best-selling books you will probably find those on slimming and dieting, along with cookbooks with recipes for the most refined, exotic and sophisticated dishes?

We find a clash between two mutually contradictory motives that varies according to nations and gender, race and class. With the belief that biology is destiny for women and men tending to emphasize control and performance, for whom are these books intended and why? The body is often thought to be closer to nature than culture and whole modes of thought have unfolded that view the body as a source of mistrust. Thus, the seeking of pleasure in the body is something to be confessed by submitting ourselves to a higher authority. In the process, part of what we are is denied. These and other ways of thinking add to modes of inclusion and exclusion that surround what we may realistically hope for in our lives. The ability to enjoy food and reflect upon it, is also the capability to purchase it and be removed from the necessity of seeking food in order to survive. Similarly, surrounding ourselves with one or more of the growing armies of technicians of the body – such as personal trainers and dietary advisers – is based upon the same capabilities. For others, the 'solution' may come in a celebration of that which is commonly derided and they are determined to live with their bodies as they are and not turn them into objects of manipulation according to popular whim. A question is then raised: is all this healthy?

$$\triangledown$$

The Pursuit of Health and Fitness

If we are asked what we want to achieve when we take measures to protect our body, to train it and to exercise, we may well answer that we want to be more healthy and fit. Both aims are commendable. The problem is that they are different and sometimes at cross-purposes with each other. The idea of health, for instance, assumes that there is a *norm* that a human body should meet, with deviations being signs of imbalance, disease or danger. Norms have their top and bottom limits and so we can say that going over the upper level is, in principle, as dangerous and undesirable as falling below the lower level – for example, too high and too low blood pressure. Both call for medical intervention: for example, doctors are worried when there are too many leucocytes in the blood, but they also raise alarm when there are too few of them and so on.

We remain healthy if, and only if, we remain around a norm. The idea of health suggests the preservation of a 'constant state', with allowances for small fluctuations over time. Since we know, by and large, what the normal state is and so can measure it with some precision, we know what to strive for as an 'end state'. Taking care of our health may be quite time-consuming and aggravating and it often generates a good deal of anxiety, but at least we know how far we need to go and so there may be a happy end to our labours. Once told that we are back within an 'acceptable norm', we can be reassured that this is indeed the case by comparing the indices of our body and bodily functions with the statistics of the 'averages' for our age and sex.

The idea and practice of fitness seem to be a different story. There might be a bottom line, but the sky is the limit as far as the top line is concerned. Fitness is about transgressing norms, not adhering to them. Health is about keeping the body in a normal, functioning condition in order to work, earn a living, be mobile, engage in some kind of social life, communicate with other people and use the facilities that the society provides to serve various life tasks. However, when it comes to fitness the question may not be what the body must do, but what the body is ultimately capable of doing. The starting point is what it can do in its present state, but more can always be achieved and should in the name of fitness and so there is, or so it seems, no end in sight to the care for the fitness of our bodies.

The ideal of fitness takes the body as an *instrument* for reaching the kind of experience that makes life enjoyable, entertaining, exciting and altogether 'pleasant to live'. Fitness stands for the capacity of the body to imbibe what the world has to offer now and what it may in the future. A flabby, tame, vapid body without vigour and appetite for adventure is unlikely to stand up to such challenge. Above all, such a body would not be one that desires new experiences and this is what makes life thrilling. An old proverb suggests that it is better to travel hopefully than to arrive. We may say, therefore, that in consumer societies it is the desire that matters, not its satisfaction. Quite simply, what desire desires is yet more desire. A fit body is an adroit and versatile body, hungry for new sensations, capable of actively seeking and meeting new sensations by 'living them to the full' when they appear.

Fitness is a key ideal by which the overall quality of the body is assessed. Since the body also conveys a message, it is not enough for the body to be fit, it must be *seen* to be fit. To convince its viewers, it must be slim, trim and agile and thus possess the look of a 'sporting body' that is ready for all sorts of exercise and able to take any amount of strain that life may throw at it. Again, the suppliers of commercial goods are eager to help the body to assume such appearances and to convey the impression of fitness. So we find a wide and constantly growing choice of jogging, gym- or tracksuits and training shoes to document the body's love of exercise and its versatility. What is left to owners of the body is to find suitable shops with the right commodities and make the appropriate purchases.

Not all steps to a convincing presentation of bodily fitness are so simple and straightforward. There is a lot that the owners themselves must do: for example, weight training, jogging and playing sports are the most prominent among such tasks. Even in these cases, commercial suppliers are keen to oblige. There is a profusion of teach-yourself and do-it-yourself handbooks offering patented regimes and a huge variety of tinned, powdered or pre-cooked food made specially for the weight-lifters and fitness-watchers, to assist them in their solitary struggles. In this, as in other cases, the practice of doing things can so easily take second place to the art of shopping.

We witness here the pursuit of new sensations. The problem with all sensations, most prominently with sensual pleasures, is that they are known, so to speak, only from the 'inside'. Sensations, subjectively experienced, may not be 'visible' to others and may be difficult to describe in a manner that allows others to understand them. There are visible signs of suffering such as sad expressions on the face, tears in the eyes, sorrowful sighs or sulking silences, and happiness in smiling faces, bursts of laughter, gaiety and sudden eloquence. It is possible for us to imagine these feelings by recalling our own 'similar' experiences. Yet we cannot *feel* what others experience. Intimate friends, who wish to share all the experiences they go through separately, often ask each other, impatiently and with a whiff of despair: 'Do you *really* know what I feel?' They suspect, with good reason, that there is no way to find out whether the feelings of two different persons are 'the same' or even 'similar'.

Although we have suggested that bodily sensations are subjectively experienced and not thought to be available to others in terms of them being able to experience the same feelings, such sensations vary according to history and culture. As Rom Harré and Grant Gillett note in their study *The Discursive Mind*, historical research has shown that bodily feelings did not have much of a role in ideas of emotion among English speakers in the seventeenth century. Following those such as the Austrian-born British philosopher Ludwig Wittgenstein, who challenged the idea that there was an inner world of inaccessible experience within us all (not an 'inner life'), language becomes the means through which we express sensations and emotions. Sensations are not simply the result of bodily stimulus, but also expressions of judgements, via language, that we make about our state of being. To that extent we have to learn ways to express such emotions and an understanding of their significance is available to others through local cultural displays and expressions. Thus, even the display of emotions is a social act that varies according to the repertoire of words and actions that are available within a given culture. Given this variation, we must also be sensitive to the cultures about which we speak in understanding the idea of 'fitness'.

We have noted that the ultimate indices of fitness, unlike those of health, cannot be measured. Therefore, the potential for interpersonal comparison becomes problematic. Again, there are a number of ways in which we can seek to measure our fitness via, for example, monitoring the heart rate during strenuous exercise. The comparison, however, may come in a running race or bodybuilding competition, but there is always room for improvement. The question that then arises with fitness, in terms of its differences with health, is 'How far do we go?' Have we squeezed out of this or that experience everything that other people do and we could have done ourselves? In the pursuit of ever greater targets, these questions are bound to remain unanswered, but that does not mean we shall cease to stop looking for answers. Whether our preoccupation with the body takes the form of the care for health, or fitness training, the overall result may be similar: more anxiety rather than less, even though the prime motive to turn our attention and effort to the body was our craving for certainty and security so blatantly missing in the world 'out there'.

▽

The Body and Desire

The body is not only the site and tool of desire, but also an *object* of desire. It is our body and at the same time, what other people see of our personhood. As the French philosopher Maurice Merleau-Ponty put it: 'the body must become the thought or intention that it signifies for us. It is the body which points out, and which speaks'. The body is the site of our selves that is always on display and people tend to judge by what they can see. Even if the body is but a wrapping of what we take to be our 'inner lives', it is the attractiveness, beauty, elegance and charm of the wrapping that will entice others. How we manage our bodies is learnt while, at the same time, how others see us is also the product of common expectations. Deviations from these may cause reflection, as well as re-action in others, leaving those who are identified as being different at a disadvantage, despite the evident skills, abilities and contributions that they might otherwise make to a society. Thus, the shape of the body, the way it is dressed and made up and the way it moves, are messages to others.

Whether we find it easy or difficult to relate to other people and whether the others are willing or not to relate to us, depends on many factors – the message written by our bodies being one among many. If other people avoid us, if we are not a 'social success', if people with whom we would like to associate seem not to enjoy our company, or shun the prospect of lasting engagement, there might be something wrong with the messenger: our body. Perhaps, more to the point, there is something wrong with us as its owner, coach and guardian. Is the wrong kind of message being displayed? Or the right message, but is not salient enough or even down-right unintelligible? We may have read the clues in our social milieux incorrectly. Even ways of holding knives and forks and general bodily gestures during eating are infused with differing expectations.

We have now come full circle. We may have deployed our bodies to facilitate the vexingly confusing and insecure relations with other people, but now find that the body itself has become a source of trouble. With the body as a site of representation of ourselves, we may now have to return to the drawing board to consider another message to write, or find the way of making the present message more intelligible. It is, so we believe, the message that matters and there is nothing to stop us from writing any message we think to be right and proper. In the available repertoire there is no shortage of pre-scripted messages on offer. Indeed, our consumer-oriented society offers a multitude of 'presentation selves' to self-assemble.

The movie *Elizabeth* focused on the early years of the reign of Elizabeth I. She was perhaps the greatest monarch in English history, but found it exceedingly difficult to convince the courtiers and other high and mighty men that, as a woman, she was the proper heir to the glory of her father, Henry VIII. She sought to convince them that she had all the skills and understanding needed to rule the country with wisdom. The powerful royal ministers refused to treat her seriously for in their eyes she was just a bride-to-be, waiting for the right kind of husband who, once she married him, would be the true ruler of England. Significantly, Elizabeth dressed accordingly – the way the young women hoping to attract a 'Prince Charming' were expected to dress. During a moment in the film there comes a wondrous reincarnation. A transformed Elizabeth enters the Great Hall of the royal palace and all the courtiers and barons fall on their knees and bow. In so doing they acknowledge the monarch whose royalty they no longer doubt and whose right to rule they no longer dispute. How was this achieved?

Elizabeth changed her *appearance*. She had cut her long hair short, purchased huge jars of paint to cover her youthful face with a mask so thick that it disguised her emotions; she wore somber and sober dress and even managed to wipe the smile off her face. We, as the viewers of the movie, do not know whether Elizabeth herself had changed, but are aware that she had not changed her 'life-project': that is, a firm intention to rule England according to her own ideas and with the best of her abilities. The only thing we can be sure of is that the message sent to others by her appearance has altered. Elizabeth, it seems, sent the wrong messages and failed repeatedly, but once the right message was transmitted via her appearance, she was more successful in her quest.

We are repeatedly told such stories by all kinds of authorities. Various authorities do not necessarily see eye-to-eye when it comes to the selection of the content, but they all agree that whatever the content may be, it is the message that makes the difference between success and failure. With the body being the prime, immediately visible message, the exhibit of the self displayed for public gaze and scrutiny, it tends to be loaded with enormous responsibility for the ups and downs of social life. How aspects of our bodies are seen and endowed with particular significance effects how we see ourselves and how others see us. Our bodies, as objects of desire, are not simply tools for manipulation by some 'inner-self' of the mind, but are part of how we are constituted as selves through the reaction of others to our actions and from there, our anticipation of those responses.

In this process no aspect of the body is allowed to escape our attention and left, so to speak, to its own devices. We are responsible for every part and function of our bodies, with everything, or almost everything, having the potential to be changed for the better. This may or may not be true, particularly if we think of the ageing process, but even that is believed to be subject to change, or delay, via particular interventions. Therefore, as long as the body is a focus of constant and acute concern, its owner does not appear to be affected by the truth or untruth of that belief. What matters is that if something in our bodies, and especially in the appearance of our bodies, stops short of the ideal, the repairing of the situation seems to remain within our power to alter. In this way our bodies fluctuate between being objects of love and pride to sources of annoyance and shame. At one moment we might award our bodies for loyal service and at another, punish it for letting us down.

The Body, Sexuality and Gender

In the current climate, one aspect of our bodies that is calling for particular intense attention and care is sex. Our 'sexual assignment', like anything else concerning our bodies, is not a quality that has been determined at birth. We live in times of what Anthony Giddens termed 'plastic sex'. 'Being a male' or 'being a female' is a question of art which needs to be learned, practised and constantly perfected. Moreover, none of the two conditions is self-evident, binding us throughout our lives and neither offers a clearly defined pattern of behaviour. As far as sexual identity is concerned, the body – whatever its inherited biological traits – appears as a set of possibilities. There are options to choose from in terms of sexual identity with the possibility being open for experimentation, thereby allowing one to be taken off and replaced with something else. The original and apparent fixity for all time of 'sexual assignment' is not a verdict of fate. Our sexuality, like other aspects of our bodies, is a task that is performed. It is a complex phenomenon that includes not only sexual relations and practices, but also language, speech, dress and style. In other words, examining how sexuality is maintained and not simply given.

Sexuality is not productively seen in terms of an 'essence'. This implies a questioning of what is known as the 'essentialist' approach to sexuality. The British sociologist Jeffrey Weeks defined that in terms of seeking to explain 'the properties of a complex reality by reference to a supposed inner truth or essence'. That sexuality is not purely 'natural', but also a cultural phenomenon is not, however, a novelty of our time. Humans were always born with either male or female genital organs and male or female secondary bodily features, but at all times the culturally patterned, taught and learned habits and customs defined the meaning of being 'male' or 'female'. Nevertheless, the fact that 'maleness' and 'femininity' is human-made, non-natural and so open to change was suppressed for the most part of human history.

In this historical unfolding, culture appeared in the mask of nature and cultural inventions were seen as being on the same level with 'laws of nature'. Men were made to be men, women to be women and that was the end of the story. Nothing was left to human will and skill but to obey and live according to one's 'true' nature. After all, what nature has decided, no man (and particularly no woman) may alter! Who spoke in the name of nature was rarely contested. However, there were exceptions who are often silenced from histories. In 1694, for example, Mary Astell wrote *A Serious Proposal to the Ladies*. In this she argued that differences between the sexes were not based on unexamined ideas of 'nature', but on the power that men held over women in society.

For much of human history, hereditary distinctions in human bodies were employed as building materials to sustain and reproduce social hierarchies of power. This remains the case in terms of 'race' whenever the colour of skin is defined as a sign of superiority or inferiority and then used to explain and justify existing social inequalities. The same applies to sexual differences. Here we find biological distinctions between sexes forming the basis for gender inequality. 'Gender' is a cultural category. It entails the totality of norms to which members of the two sexual categories are obligated to conform in their performance of masculinity and femininity. Gender classifies, divides and separates via a stipulation of social activities that are considered proper or improper for each category.

It is on the basis of such a history that women may be excluded from areas of social life that are reserved for men, or that barriers are placed in the way of their participation as, for example, in politics or business. At the same time, those activities that are fundamental to society, such as reproduction, household duties and childcare, were cast aside as an exclusively feminine domain and devalued accordingly. This is not a division of labour simply given by different reproductive functions; it stands for power relations that tend to be slanted in favour of men. For instance, within organizations, as the Italian sociologist Silvia Gherardi reminded us, the position of subordination entailed by being a member of the second sex is reinforced in rituals surrounding the management of the body. This may be seen in those instances when the boss leaves the office heading for a meeting, followed by his secretary a few steps behind.

The feminist movement has challenged social inequalities based on sexual characteristics of the body. This lengthy campaign has brought its results, but legislation alone cannot achieve equality. The most it can do is to reopen for negotiation those cases previously considered 'unproblematic'. There are no sex-bound limits to which women or men must confine their life-aspirations and claims to social standing, but the question as to which of these are eventually fulfilled is often left to individual ingenuity and persistence, with the resulting effects being carried by the individuals concerned.

It is not quite clear what the effects of a shift in sexual attitudes are for the individual frame of mind and feeling. Some observers, for instance the German sexologist Volkmar Sigush, expressed concern in the following terms:

> The shadows cast by feelings of anxiety, disgust, shame, and guilt became so large and dark that many women, and consequently many men as well, saw no remaining ray of light whatsoever. Feelings of closeness, joy, tenderness, and comfort seemed doomed to suffocation in a . . . storm cloud of hate, anger, envy, bitterness, vengeance, fear, and fright.

If these circumstances predominate, then the 'fulfilment of the sexual potential of the body' becomes a more difficult task and transforms sex, and most human intercourse with it, into another source of insecurity and fear, as opposed to their potential for greater security and contentment.

Summary

As with those other topics we have considered, care of ourselves through our bodies, as well as those bodies being the objects of desire and display to others, holds out the hope for security, but is also a site of insecurity. This, in its turn, is infused with meanings that are produced within cultures that are not simply separated from biological categories, but interact and construct what we are, have been and possess the potential to become. With this comes the power to define which may be a source of comfort, but also something to resist in its invoking of norms that stifle difference. As a result, such differences are often translated as deviance, rather than being understood on their own terms and challenging for the dominant ways in which the body is considered, acted upon and deployed as a form of communication. Sexual relations then become areas of intense negotiation with results that are often unpredictable. Surrounding all of this, however, is a need for the toleration of difference.

chapter seven

TIME, SPACE AND (DIS)ORDER

'Time and space are shrinking.' This seems to be an extraordinary statement at first glance. Time and space, surely, do not shrink? From a social
point of view we think of events in terms of their occurrence within and
through time, and similarly, of being located in space. We are able to
make comparisons between ideas, attitudes and actions by charting their
historical variations within spaces that are both physical (urban and regional landscapes) and symbolic (how they are viewed and what significance is attached to relations and objects within those spaces as 'places'
of interaction). Information technologies, however, have speeded up our
communications via, for example, fax and email, while the mass media
beam themselves into all parts of the globe with effects upon how people
perceive space and place. To that extent, space and time are shrinking!
As Paul Virilio put it, the issue now is not what period in time (chrono-
logical) we find ourselves, nor in what space (geographical), but in '*what
space-time?*' This is changing at ever greater speed.

Experiencing Time and Space

Time and space seem to be independent features of the 'world out there',
but clearly they are not independent from each other in the planning, calculation and execution of our actions. We tend to measure distance by the
time needed to pass it, while our estimations of the remoteness or closeness of our destinations depends on the amount of time needed to reach
them. The result of the measurement depends, therefore, on the speed at
which we can move. That speed, in its turn, depends on the tools or vehicles of mobility to which we have routine access. If using such tools needs
to be paid for, the speed at which we move then depends on the amount of
money we can afford.

During times (not so ancient, to be sure) when human or horses' legs were the only tools of travelling, the answer you would probably get to the question 'How far it is from here to the next village?' would be 'If you start now, you would get there about midday'; or 'You won't get there before dusk, you had better stay in the inn for the night'. Later, once the 'artificial limbs' – human-made engines – had replaced human feet and horses, the answers ceased to be that straightforward. Distance then became a matter of which form of transport was used. It was not the same, and depended on whether you could afford to travel by train, coach, private car or aircraft.

The above are means of transportation that carry and shift persons and/or things from one place to another. The means of communication to which we referred in the opening paragraph, on the other hand, refer to the conveying and passing of information. We can say that for the greater part of human history there was not much to distinguish between transport and communication. Information could be carried by human carriers: for example, travellers, messengers, itinerary tradespeople and craftworkers, or those moving from one village to another in search of alms or casual work. There were a few exceptions to this general rule, such as the optical messages of the natives of the American plains or drum-telegraph in Africa. The ability to transmit information independently of human carriers, as long as it remained a rarity, gave tremendous advantage to those who had access to such means. There is a story that the pioneering use of mail-pigeons allowed Rothschild, the banker, to learn before anybody else of Napoleon's defeat at Waterloo and use that privileged information to multiply his wealth at the London Stock Exchange. Indeed, despite being illegal, the same kind of advantage still makes 'inside-trading' seductive for many who seek to advance their wealth on the stock exchanges.

For a while, the most impressive technical developments served the needs of transportation. Thus, steam, electric and internal combustion engines, rail networks, seafaring vessels and motor cars were invented. Yet alongside those inventions a new 'software' era was germinating in the discovery of things such as the telegraph and the radio. Here we find the means of transmitting pure information at long distances without a person, or any other physical body, moving from a place. In comparison, transport would be never 'instantaneous'. Except in science-fiction fantasies, it would always take time to shift humans and their belongings from one place to another and the more there was to shift and the longer the distance, the more cumbersome and costly the operation became. This is why in 'hardware' terms the place mattered and this added value to space. It was cheaper and less troublesome to be 'in place'. Owners of factories wished to produce every part of the final product under one roof and to keep all the machinery and labour necessary to produce them inside the same factory walls. This limited the need for transportation and such economies of scale reduced costs.

Around these practices forms of discipline emerged around the control of space and time. The closer the controllers were to the controlled, the more complete was their rule over everyday conduct. At the threshold of the nineteenth century, Jeremy Bentham, one of the most influential political scientists and philosophers of the time, proposed a solution to the issue of growing populations that was different from that of the economists and their concerns with poverty, food and productivity. One of his suggestions was to design a huge building in which people were under surveillance for twenty-four hours a day, but would never be quite sure whether they were being watched. The 'Panopticon' served as the ideal pattern for all modern powers from the top level to the bottom. As long as power was of the panoptical kind, the objects of constant surveillance might be obedient and refrain from insubordination, let alone acts of rebellion, because all deviation from the rule was too costly for them to be seriously considered. As a result, there was a move over the course of history, to paraphrase Michel Foucault, from the gaze of others to the interiorization of the gaze: that is, from the discipline of others to ways in which one should practise self-discipline.

The times have changed because information can now move apart from physical bodies. Given this, the speed of communications is no longer held down by the limits that are placed upon it by people and material objects. For all practical purposes, communication is now instantaneous and so distances do not matter because any corner of the globe can be reached at the same time. As far as the access and the spread of information are concerned, 'being close' and 'being remote' no longer have the importance they once commanded. Internet groups do not feel geographical distance to be an impediment to the selection of partners in a conversation. If someone happens to live in Manhattan, communicating with someone in Melbourne or Calcutta takes them no more time than doing so with someone in the Bronx.

If you were born in the 'electronic era', all this may be taken-for-granted and seem insignificant. It has become as much part of everyday life as sunrises and sunsets. You would have hardly noticed how profound has been this very recent *devaluation of space*. So stop! Let us pause for a moment and think how the human condition changes once communication takes over from transport as the prime vehicle of mobility and when the expedience and increasing urgency of information travel no longer depends on distance. What, for instance, happens to the idea of 'community'? As we have hinted at already, this is largely dependent on the idea of knowledge by acquaintance between people who are in physical proximity to each other. Community is thereby a territorial or 'local' creation because it is confined in a space that possesses boundaries drawn by the human capacity to move. The difference between the 'inside' and the 'outside' of a community is therefore one between 'the here and now' and the 'there and far away'.

The backbone of any community was the web of communication between its members in a social network informed by territory. As such, the distance at which such daily 'communicative interaction' could stretch drew the boundaries of community. Communication at a longer distance was awkward and costly and for this reason a comparatively more rare event. In this sense locality was an advantage over 'far away' with ideas being born and discussed within the locality. This situation has changed significantly. Physical closeness and frequency of communication no longer need to exist in this manner for those who are party to interactions may be mapped in terms of dots around the globe. This is not a territorial community, for these people may seldom, if ever, meet and so be unaware of each other's existence in terms of belonging to a spatially defined network of people within a common place.

A community of this type is conjured up by communicational activities and it is these that bind them together. Yet those persons are not necessarily those from whom we derive our ideas about the world. Knowledge gained by description, in contrast to acquaintance with others in situations of what Erving Goffman called 'co-presence', may not come from those who are dots on that map. After all, we read daily and weekly newspapers, from which we derive much of our knowledge. In addition, we watch television and may listen to the radio and in so doing cannot be sure where the articles have been written, or where the programmes we are watching are being broadcast from. Thanks to the electronically transmitted voices and images, it is the world which travels to us, while we remain in our place. This process of 'embedding' and 'disembedding' of knowledge means that there is no mutuality in our communication. We view people on the screen who talk to us and display themselves in front of our eyes, but they do not know 'us' among the masses of people who are their viewers.

In this way the model of the Panopticon may be reversed: the many can now watch the few. Celebrities fall into the public gaze with their importance measured by the number of books written about them, the audience ratings of their shows or films or the number of CDs they might have sold. Celebrities are not 'leaders', but are examples of success held up for public consumption. Yet in thinking about these images and their transmission and reception, while people remain in a locality the information that orients their experiences can be extraterritorial. Thus, we hear talk of information having become *global* in the sense that it has broken free from its *local* bonds. It travels freely between localities, states and continents; past boundaries are challenged and transgressed. Its speed is such that control is raised as a problem, but who can win the race when it comes to competing with electronic signals? All this has implications for the ways in which we lead our lives and the nature and distribution of power. To ignore these issues is not an option, while the questions that are raised are not easy to answer. That, however, is not a reason for inaction if we are to understand and act upon the consequences of the information age, as opposed to remaining passive through inactivity.

Risk Society

Given the issues raised by transformations in societies, Ulrich Beck proposed that we now live in a 'society of risks'. When we think of risk, we think of a danger or threat that relates to what we do or even refrain from doing. People often say 'this is a risky step to take' in order to indicate that people are exposing themselves to an undesirable state of affairs. However, in a society of risks, these issues derive not so much from what each person does in isolation, but from the very fact that because they are in isolation the actions are dispersed and uncoordinated. Given this, the outcomes and side-effects are difficult to calculate and define and so have the potential to take us by surprise. How do we cope with this state of affairs?

If we tried to prevent all undesirable consequences, we would most certainly price our actions too high and thus condemn ourselves to inactivity. At the same time risk is not the result of ignorance or a lack of skills. In fact, the opposite is the case, for risk grows out of ever greater efforts to be rational in the sense of defining and concentrating on *relevant* things that are deemed to be significant for one reason or another. As one popular saying goes: 'We will cross that bridge when we come to it.' Of course, this presupposes the existence of a bridge and has little to say about what we do when we find out it is not there!

Take the example of genetically modified (GM) food, that is, crops that are genetically modified in order that they grow more resistant to pests and diseases, or have larger yields, or a longer shelf life in the shops. Some suggest that the potential of these crops lies in the alleviation of poverty. That, however, may not be a matter of scientific advances, but to do with the relative distribution of wealth between western and majority world countries that are termed 'developing'. Others suspect that, judging by past experiences, there will be a price to pay for achieving these aims in terms of unintended consequences. They might point to the side-effects of manipulating genes in terms of the devastation of soil composition and long-term harm done to the health and life-expectations of the consumers. Therefore, the issue may be not so much one of increased production, but rather the distribution of existing resources and how crops are grown in the first place and with what effects on the environment. The debate revolves around uncertainty in terms of not knowing the price that will be paid in the future for current decisions, with views differing on the short, medium and long-term consequences of present actions.

In these situations companies with an investment in such technologies may move elsewhere, or diversify into other areas that have the potential for profit. As Barbara Adam, a sociologist of time, put it, when time becomes commodified, speed then becomes an economic value. Therefore, 'the faster goods move through the economy the better; speed increases profit and shows up positively in a country's GNP [gross national product]'. The new volatility of information also frees up movement of money with world money markets speculating (as we have noted before) on $1.5 trillion per day. These are the factors which contribute to our chances of living decent lives and our employment, education and health care opportunities, as well as the potential for clean environments.

Where gaze and proximity once mattered in the Panopticon, the technique of power now employed may be to threaten distance from those whose behaviour is to be regulated. If, for instance, a factory crew or an office staff are disaffected, unruly or demand better conditions, one would expect the outfit to be closed down, 'de-layered' or 'sold off', rather than to anticipate more surveillance and the enforcement of stricter rules. The extraterritoriality of global powers does not bind them to any particular place and they are always ready to travel away at short notice. As Richard Sennett has said of Bill Gates, the head of Microsoft, he 'seems free of obsession to hold on to things'. Nevertheless, freedom at one level does not mean freedom at another for if the 'locals' seek to follow the 'globals', they would soon find out, as Sennett warns, that the same 'traits of character begetting spontaneity become more self-destructive for those who work lower down in the flexible regime'.

Globalization is taken to be a process which no one controls. Yet this is often invoked as a reason for inaction in the face of what are seen as overwhelming and abstract forces. Government policies can and do mediate, dilute and ameliorate these effects in their resistance, or reproduce them in their passivity and indifference. Globalization affects us at an individual level in varying degrees, for we can all experience anxiety and worry when we find it difficult to understand what is going on, let alone to influence the direction in which things seem to be moving around us. An agent that has the potential to take control of its worse effects, on the other hand, is something which lies beyond the individual, group and nation-state. A willingness to act on this state of affairs requires that those who are its beneficiaries recognize they are positioned in this way only because others are excluded as a result.

There is another issue to be considered in relation to risk. We may have some idea about how to satisfy our needs, even if the means for such satisfaction is not equally distributed. However, the need to neutralize or cut down on risks is not like other needs. This is because risks are the kinds of dangers we do not see or hear coming and of which we may not be fully aware. We do not experience directly – see, hear, touch and smell – the rising carbon dioxide in the air we breathe, or the slow yet relentless warming up of the planet, or those chemical substances used to fatten up the meat we eat, but which may be undermining the capability of our immune systems to deal with bacterial infection.

Without 'experts' we may not know about these risks. These people appear on the media and interpret the world and the situations in which we find ourselves in such a way that they overcome our limited knowledge and experience. We need to trust these people to inform us about our environments, eating habits and those things we should avoid. Since there is no way we can test this advice against our own experience – at least not until it might be too late to realize our mistakes – there remains the possibility that their interpretations may be wrong. In this way, as Ulrich Beck has put it, risks may be 'interpreted away' and rendered 'non-existent' and so there will be no need for us to be spurred into action. A reaction of this type is not unusual. It may be fuelled by the belief that there is a conspiracy in which those who protect us are actually spokespersons for those who may harm us.

Hans Jonas, the German American ethical philosopher, reflected upon the consequences of technological development on a global scale. Although our actions may affect those who live in other parts of the globe, of whom we know little, our moral outlook has not kept pace with these transformations. How often is it that people speak of events as being beyond their control? This begs questions about how we may have a global ethic that also respects and recognizes the differences between people. Without this, such forces are not tamed according to our needs, but unleashed with differing consequences. This is to relieve the human race of its moral responsibility towards others. As Karl-Otto Apel, the German philosopher, expressed it, we have a responsibility for how institutions are shaped and reshaped and so for 'those institutions that facilitate the social implementation of morality'.

Even if we had a declaration of moral duties that is similar to the United Nations declaration of human rights, it would require a great change in perception to be effective. Most people do not see beyond the confines of their immediate neighbourhoods and so, understandably, tend to focus on things, events and people close to home. Vague feelings of threat can then be anchored on visible, tangible targets that are within reach. Singly or even severally, there often appears little we can do to hit distant, misty and perhaps illusive targets. Locally, people can join a patrol of concerned and active citizens who target those who are a threat to their way of life. Closed-circuit television cameras, burglar alarms, window locks and security lights can all be installed to protect local space; explanations that seek understanding of these trends beyond those confines may be ruled out as irrelevant and even irresponsible.

What will not go away are the effects of globalization. Thus, a globally induced insecurity may find its outlet in a locally produced preoccupation with safety. Perhaps we have fallen into the trap that Ulrich Beck warned against? That is, we have looked for the source of risks in the wrong place. A locally produced worry about safety exacerbates divisions that separate people – the very divisions that lead to misunderstanding and the ability to downplay the consequences of action upon others who are remote from our worlds. Those who can clearly afford to protect their properties may also be those who have something to protect that others desire, but lack the means to afford. Morally speaking, distances between people can enable them to bracket the consequences of their actions for others.

These are one set of consequences, but globalization is not only a threat, but also a great opportunity. As Karl-Otto Apel argued, we could use our reason and our will to bring into being a truly global society that seeks to be inclusive and respectful of difference and seriously attempts to eradicate war. False interpretations and allocations of blame for risks may prevent us from acting and lead to further divisions, thus worsening and not addressing the problems. This is why it is so important to 'think sociologically'. Sociology cannot correct the shortcomings of the world, but it can help us to understand them in a more complete manner and in so doing, enable us to act upon them for the purpose of human betterment. In this time of globalization we need the knowledge that sociology can provide more than ever before. After all, to understand ourselves in the present enables a hold upon current conditions and relations without which there is no hope of shaping the future.

$$\triangledown$$

Autonomy, Order and Chaos

The source of such hope may lie in the recognition of and reasons for chaos! This seems an extraordinary statement. Yet we have seen that order is enabled through boundaries and globalization itself has questioned those with differing consequences. A greater recognition of our dependence upon each other may then follow, but also an enhanced desire for separation. Which route to take (as we have suggested) depends upon a concerted effort that may start within neighbourhoods, but whose finishing point will lie way beyond them. Thus, at one level, an attempt to draw, mark and guard artificial boundaries becomes an object of ever growing concern. At another level what were once regarded as 'natural' divisions – well entrenched and resistant to change – and distances dissolve and those who were once separated now find themselves coming together in greater numbers.

We could say that the effort that goes into maintaining and defending a division grows in equal proportion to its brittleness and the extent of damage it does to the complex human reality. This situation is thought to have arisen with the type of society that established itself in the western world approximately three centuries ago and in which we still live today. Before this time – what is often referred to as 'pre-modern' – the maintenance of distinctions and divisions between categories tended to attract less attention and trigger less activity than it does today. Differences appeared self-evident and timeless because they were thought to be immune from human intervention. They were laid down by forces beyond human control; as such, a noble, for example, was a 'noble' from the moment of birth, with the same applying to peasant serfs. With very few exceptions the human condition seemed solidly built and settled in the same manner as the rest of the world. In other words, there was no distinction between nature and culture.

It was roughly towards the end of the sixteenth century that in parts of western Europe this picture of the world began to fall apart. As the number and visibility of people who did not fit neatly into any 'divine chain of being' grew, then the pace of legislative activity quickened in order to regulate areas of life that were originally left to take their natural course. Social distinctions and discriminations then became a matter of examination, design, planning and most importantly, of conscious, organized and specialized effort. Social orders emerged as human products and projects and so amenable to manipulation. Human order thereby became an object of science and technology.

We can say that order was not born in modern times, but a *concern* with order, and a fear that without intervention it would descend into chaos, certainly was apparent. Chaos in these circumstances emerges as the perceived outcome of a failure to order things. What makes it so disorderly is the observers' inability to control the flow of events, to obtain the desired response from the environment and to prevent or eliminate happenings that were not planned. Chaos, in these terms, becomes *uncertainty* and only the vigilant technicians of human affairs appear to stand between it and orderly conduct and affairs. Yet boundaries are porous and contentious. The management of order is always uncertain and incomplete. It is like erecting a building upon shifting sands. What we end up with are islands of order upon a flow of events that may achieve a temporary relative autonomy.

In saying this, we end up with a situation that we have encountered on a number of occasions. The very effort to impose order leads to an uncertainty and ambivalence that keeps the fear of chaos alive. Efforts to construe an artificial order are bound to fall short of their ideal target. They conjure up islands of relative autonomy, but at the same time can transform adjacent territories into areas of ambivalence. Questions then turn into matters of method rather than purpose: that is, how to make boundaries effective and so stop the tide of ambivalence from washing over the island of autonomy. To build order is thus to wage war against ambiguity. However, at what cost?

Lines may be drawn that physically demarcate those boundaries through which only the eligible may cross, for example passport controls between different countries. There are also more subtle examples, such as receiving an invitation that classifies you as a guest at a party. If you cannot show a passport or invitation, you may well find yourself turned away at the gate or door. Even if you get inside without such means, there is the constant fear of being spotted and asked to leave. The relative autonomy of the enclave has been compromised and corroded by your presence and this has detracted from a state of regularity and order. You then find yourself on the outside of a physical boundary, but as a means of maintaining order, this is a more straightforward matter than ensuring conformity and obedience once within its confines.

A person's character cannot be simply split into those parts that may be permitted inside and those that must remain outside (although, as the film *One Flew over the Cuckoo's Nest* demonstrated with great poignancy and Erving Goffman noted in his work on *Asylums*, total institutions may go to great lengths to ensure conformity). Total loyalty to an organization, for instance, is notoriously difficult to achieve and usually inspires the application of most ingenious and imaginative expedients. Employees of a company or an office may be prohibited from belonging to trade unions or political movements. They may be subjected to psychological tests to detect any potential resistance to the taking of orders, or they may be forbidden to discuss organizational matters with people who do not belong to the organization.

One such example is the British Official Secrets Act, which forbids particular state employees from divulging information, even if in so doing it serves the interests of those citizens whom the state is supposed to protect. Similarly, the desire for organizations to project a certain image to the public may lead to some practices within the organization that employees regard as being unethical. In the case of the British National Health Service, certain employees within hospitals adopted a practice known as 'whistle-blowing' in order to bring to public attention what they regarded as dubious practices. In order to appear to be efficient and effective in the treating and discharging of patients as an apparent measure of the organization's performance, some patients were being released back into the community without being able to recover sufficiently, only to be readmitted at a later date. The quality of individual care was then said to be undermined by a measure of the quantity of patients treated and discharged.

The desire to draw boundaries in this manner has an effect upon the dependencies and bonds between people in ways that are often unintended. What seems to be a proper, rational solution to the problem confronted from within one relatively autonomous unit, becomes a problem for another unit. As the units, contrary to their pretences, are closely interdependent, the problem-solving activity rebounds eventually on the very agency which has undertaken it in the first place. It leads to an unplanned and unpredicted shift in the overall balance of the situation that makes the continuous resolution of the original problem more costly than expected or even altogether impossible. This may be compounded by calculations of efficiency that simply examine a unit on the basis of inputs and outputs. While apparently 'rational', it has nothing to say concerning the effects of decisions of one unit upon the actions of another.

The most notorious case of such effects is the destruction of the ecological and climatic equilibrium of the planet. The natural resources of the earth are depleted in the pursuit of profit, but there is nothing inherent in such pursuit that operates as a check upon such behaviour. Large oil tankers may take short cuts in order to deliver their cargo on time, despite the risks involved, while the tankers themselves may not be designed with 'skins' in order to prevent the cargo from spilling in the event of a collision. Such design, after all, is said to be costly to a company, but at what potential cost to the environment? Industrial organizations then pollute air and water and so create many new awesome problems for those in charge of human health and urban and regional development. In their efforts to improve the organization of their own activity, companies rationalize the use of labour, by the same token declaring many of their workers redundant and adding to the problems born of chronic unemployment, such as poverty and ill-health. The mushrooming of private cars and motorways, of airports and aircraft, once expected to resolve the problem of mobility and transportation, creates traffic jams, air and noise pollution, destroys whole areas of human settlement and leads to such a centralization of cultural life and supply of services as renders many local settlements uninhabitable. In its turn, therefore, travelling becomes more necessary than ever before, while becoming more difficult and exhausting. Those things that once promised freedom, such as cars, are now contributing to a constraining of collective freedom of movement and the pollution of the atmosphere for current and future generations. Yet the solution sold to the problem is so often the building of more roads.

The roots of all this lie in the apparent relative autonomy that is promised in wrenching a part of our lives from the whole. As we all inhabit the whole, such autonomy is at best partial and at worst purely imaginary. This is achieved by being blinded to consequences or deliberately closing our eyes to the manifold and far-reaching connections between all actors and between everything each actor is doing. The number of factors which are taken into account in the planning and implementation of solutions to problems is always smaller than the sum total of factors which influence, or depend on, the situation which gave rise to the problem in the first place. We may even say that power – the capacity to design, enforce, influence and preserve order – consists precisely of the ability to disregard, neglect and push aside those factors which, if the subject of deliberation and action, would make the order impossible. To have power means, among other things, to be able to decide what is not important and what should not be a matter of concern. What rebounds upon it, however, is its inability to conjure what it has termed 'irrelevant factors' out of existence.

Matters of relevance and irrelevance are contingent: that is, there is no overwhelming reason why the line of relevance should be drawn in any particular way for it could be drawn in many ways. Given this, the decision itself is open to dispute. History is full of such examples. For instance, at the threshold of the modern era one of the most seminal power struggles developed around the passage from *patronage* to the *cash nexus*. Faced with the callous indifference of factory owners to the fate of the 'factory hands' (the name indicating that employers were interested only in the 'hands' of the workers), the critics of the nascent factory system recalled the practices of artisan workshops, or even country manors, which behaved like 'one big family' that included all people. The masters of the workshop and country squires could be ruthless, autocratic bosses and unscrupulously exploit the drudgery of their workers. At the same time the workers also expected the boss to care about their needs and, if necessary, bail them out from impending disaster.

In sharp opposition to these older habits, no such expectations were accepted as legitimate by the owners of factories. They paid their employees for the labour performed in factory hours and other aspects of their lives were their own responsibility. The critics and the people speaking for the factory workers resented such 'washing of hands'. They pointed out that the protracted, stultifying, exhausting day-to-day effort demanded by factory discipline left the workers, to paraphrase Karl Marx, 'mentally exhausted and physically debased'. Workers became commodities that were disposable because, like the other parts of the factory product, they were considered useless from the point of view of the productive plan. The critics pointed out that the relationship between the factory owners and the factory hands was not actually limited to a simple exchange of labour for wages. Why? Because labour could not be cut out and isolated from the person of the worker in the same way as a cash sum was separated from the person of the employer. 'To give away labour' means to subject the whole person, body and soul, to the task set by the employer for whom the worker becomes just the means towards the fulfilment of their ends. In this way, despite protestations to the contrary, workers were being asked to give in exchange for wages the whole of their character and freedom.

The power of the factory owners over the workers was thereby given in this asymmetry of power. It was for this reason that Karl Marx remarked that at least in conditions of slavery in contrast to capitalism, the owners had some interest in the well-being of their slaves. What was substituted for this relationship was an abstract form of exchange in which employers had no interest in the physical and mental well-being of the workers. The employers defined the meaning of employment and reserved the right to decide what was and what was not a matter for their concern – a right they denied to their employees. By the same token, the workers' fight for better labour conditions and more say in the running of the productive process then had to turn into a struggle against the employer's right to define the limits and the contents of the workplace order.

The conflict between workers and factory owners about the definition of the boundaries of the factory system is just one example of the kind of contention that all definitions of order must necessarily trigger off. Since any definition is contingent and in the last account rests solely on someone's power to enforce it, then it remains, in principle, open to challenge. Indeed, it tends to be contested by those who fall victim to its damaging effects. Such debates can then enter the public arena as calls for action to ameliorate the effects of such boundaries. A classic example is that of the British welfare state. Born but a short time ago in history, in the late 1940s, its purpose was to provide a safety net against the vagaries and fluctuations of a system that was uninterested in the well-being of those who promoted its cause. As one of its key founders, William Beveridge, expressed it: 'If full employment is not won and kept, no liberties are secure, for to many they will not seem worth while'. For some, it seems, these debates are no longer relevant. For others, those who forget the lessons of history are bound to repeat its mistakes in their denials of its contemporary relevance.

Nowadays we hear, time and again, heated debates about who should pay for, say, polluting the supplies of fresh water, disposing of toxic waste, or the damage caused to the landscape by new open-cast mines or motorways. Someone's waste may well become an important element of someone else's life condition. The objects of dispute look different depending on the vantage point from which they are contemplated and their meanings derive from the place they occupy in those partial orders. Buffeted by what are often contradictory pressures, they can assume a shape that no one has planned in advance and no one finds acceptable. Affected by many partial orders, no one seems to assume responsibility for their existence and consequences.

In modern times the problem has tended to become ever more acute as the power of technological instruments of human action has grown and with it the consequences of their application. As each island of order gets more streamlined, rationalized, better supervised and more effective in its performance, the multitude of perfected partial orders can result in overall chaos. Distant outcomes of planned, purposeful, rationally designed and tightly monitored actions may hit back as unpredictable, uncontrollable catastrophes. Think of the prospect of the greenhouse effect. This is the unanticipated product of numerous efforts to harness ever more energy in the name of increasing efficiency and production. Each effort, in isolation, may be hailed as a breakthrough and a technological advancement, justified according to short-term goals. Similarly, discharges of toxic substances into the atmosphere or rivers may be justified as rare events in otherwise safety-conscious processes that are hailed as beneficial to the public good. Each of these may be indicative of an earnest search for the best, most 'rational' solution to a specific task faced by this or that relatively autonomous organization. Each newly engineered virus or bacteria has a clearly defined purpose and a concrete useful job to perform. Until, that is, it is found to have undesirable side-effects as a result of its application.

Much of the argument around such consequences falls into the domain of 'ownership'. While private enterprise is thought to be able to produce outcomes that are generally beneficial – judging, that is, by how few seem to challenge this assumption – such motivations may find themselves questioned by democratically elected governments. One such area is the mapping of human genes and their potential for manipulation. Large pharmaceutical companies claim that they are ultimately acting with the public good in mind, but who owns the patent to human genes? Are they something that can be 'owned' in the sense that they are commodities to be bought and sold on the market place and manipulated according to the capability to pay? This is being challenged in a struggle that has fundamental consequences for us all.

At the same time, the results of such work may be aimed at what are seen as desirable, immediate targets, for example, vulnerability to a specific disease. Yet changes in the situation 'in focus' cannot but affect those things that are left 'out of focus'. Artificial fertilizers used to enhance agricultural crops illustrate the issue very vividly. Nitrates fed into the soil may achieve their declared effect because they multiply the crops. Rainfall, however, washes away a good portion of the fertilizers into the underground supplies of water, thereby creating a new and no less sinister problem that requires rendering the water supply suitable for consumption. Sooner or later it will be discovered that the new processes have polluting effects of their own: for example, they are lush feeding grounds for toxic algae.

In these ways the struggle against chaos continues. There is no doubt that, given a willingness to think and act differently, there are ways to reduce future risks. Nevertheless, chaos that waits to be contained and conquered in the future will be a product of particular, order-constructing human activity. Problem-solving activity can lead to the creation of new problems and thus inspire the search for new solutions. All too often this has taken the form of appointing a team charged with the task of finding the shortest, cheapest and 'most reasonable' way of disposing of the current problem. The more uncomfortable and more searching questions and solutions are left out of this process, the shorter, cheaper and seemingly more rational – at least according to the logic of short-termism and particular ideas of cost – will be the recommendations provided.

$$\bigtriangledown$$

Summary

We have suggested that struggles to replace chaos with order through making the parts of our worlds rule-abiding, predictable and controllable are bound to remain inconclusive. This results as the struggle for order is itself the most important obstacle to its own success because the disorderly phenomena arise precisely from narrowly focused, targeted, task-oriented, single-problem-solving actions. Each new attempt to make a part of the human world, or a specific area of human activity, orderly creates new problems as it seeks to remove the old ones. Each attempt gives rise to new types of ambivalence and so renders further attempts necessary with what may be similar results.

In this way the search for artificial orders appears as the cause of its deepest, most worrying ailments. Splitting the unmanageable totality of the human condition into a multitude of small, immediate tasks, which because they are small and confined in time can be fully scanned, monitored and managed, has rendered human action more efficient than ever before. The more precise, limited and clearly defined is the task at hand, the better it may be performed. Indeed, this way of doing things is strikingly superior to any that has existed before – as long as it is measured in terms of value for money and expressed in terms of particular definitions of costs and benefits. This is precisely what is meant by what people often refer to as rational. It is an instrumental reason that measures the actual results against the intended end in terms of particular inputs and outputs.

These calculations appear oblivious, in their exercise of rationality, to those costs that scream out for attention. Those that are borne by actors who are not party to its conception and those results that are not monitored in order to prove its efficiency, bear these costs, along with the environment as a whole. If, on the other hand, a more inclusive measure of losses and gains were taken into account, the superiority of the modern way of doing things would look less certain. It might well transpire that the ultimate outcome of the multitude of partial and separate rational actions is more, not less, irrationality. This is an irksome yet inescapable tension in the search for order, as it is with the struggle against ambivalence that has marked so much of human history in the modern era.

The problem–solution connection is a feature of the human condition. What must be asked, from the sociological vantage point, is to whom is this a problem? Why is it a problem for them and what are the consequences of this problematization and its corresponding solutions? We are all trained to think of our lives as a collection of tasks to be performed and problems to be solved. We are used to thinking that once a problem has been spotted, the task is to define it in a manner that can render it the subject of immediate intervention according to certain criteria. We assume that once this has been done, doing away with the irritating problem is just a matter of finding the right resources and applying oneself diligently to the task. If nothing happens and the problem does not go away, we blame ourselves for ignorance, neglect, laziness or ineptitude, while if our low spirits continue, we explain it either by our own lack of resolve in fighting the blues, or by wrongly defining their cause – the 'problem' to be handled. No amount of disappointment and frustration, however, is likely to undermine the belief that each situation, whatever its complexity, may be disassembled into a finite set of problems and that any of those problems can be effectively dealt with via an application of the proper knowledge, skill and effort. In brief, the business of life may be split up into single problems, for each of which there is a solution given the proper application of method which so easily subsumes more general questions of purpose.

There is no doubt that modern times have given rise to spectacular achievements. Denying those is not the issue. The issue is that we are now facing not only the benefits, but also the costs of technological progress. These are not restricted to small enclaves of order, as they affect our entire futures. What is now required is some understanding of the weaknesses, as well as strengths, of the ways in which we view each other, our ways of thinking and acting and the environments that we all inhabit. In this process of rethinking, established ways of viewing the world may find themselves questioned by new sets of circumstances that call for new ways of thinking. To some this may be a threat and to others an opportunity for indulgence. Yet there is an urgency given by those conditions and this requires a willingness to change: no more, of course, than humankind has changed so many times before in the course of its history.

chapter eight

DRAWING BOUNDARIES: CULTURE, NATURE, STATE AND TERRITORY

At the end of chapter 7 we explicitly opened up an issue that has been implicit throughout the book. This may be expressed in the following terms: the way in which we think about and examine a problem will itself give rise to what are seen as appropriate solutions. From this viewpoint, thinking differently is not an indulgent activity. On the contrary, it is often the first step towards the construction of more practical and long-lasting solutions to the issues we face in contemporary times.

Nature and Culture

Consider the issues we raised in chapter 7 concerning a 'modern' way of thinking about the differences between nature and culture. This new image set nature and society sharply apart. One can say that nature and society were 'discovered' simultaneously. What was in fact discovered was neither nature nor society, but the *distinction* between them and especially the distinction between the practices that each one enabled or gave rise to. As human conditions appeared more and more to be products of the legislation, management and intervention in general, 'nature' assumed the role of a huge depository for everything which human powers could not yet or had no ambition to mould; everything, that is, which was seen as being ruled by its own logic and left by humans to its own devices.

Changes in social thought also occurred at this time. Philosophers began to talk about 'laws of nature' by analogy with the laws promulgated by kings or parliaments, but also to distinguish them from the latter. 'Natural laws' were like the laws of the kings and thus obligatory, but unlike the royal decrees they had no conceivable human author. Their force was therefore 'superhuman', whether they had been established by God's will and inscrutable purpose or were causally determined, with an unassailable necessity, directly by the way cosmic matters were arranged. These distinctions (as we have suggested earlier) also gave rise to a manner of social boundary formation: for example, the assumption that men were 'rational' and so able to transcend the demands of nature, while women were 'emotional' and subject to nature's impulsive forces. Similarly, there were developed countries that exhibited certain principles that distinguished them from those other countries that were 'uncivilized' in their outlook.

These changes gave rise to transformations in both our ways of seeing and doing. Consider, for example, the distinctions we employ between what is thought to be within 'human power' to alter according to our desires, ideals and aims. These are informed by the question of whether there is a standard, a norm, to which that 'something' should submit. In other words, there are things that may be changed by human intervention and fashioned according to particular expectations. These are to be treated differently from other things, which stay beyond human power. The first we call *culture* and the second, *nature*. Thus, when we think of something as being a matter of culture, rather than nature, we are implying that the thing in question is manipulable and further, that there is a desirable, 'proper' end-state for such manipulation.

Culture concerns making things different from what they are and otherwise would be and about keeping them in this made-up, artificial shape. Culture is about introducing and keeping an order and fighting everything that departs from it as indicative of a descent into chaos. Culture is about supplanting or supplementing the 'order of nature' (that is, the state of things as they are without human interference) with an artificial, designed one. Culture not only promotes, but also evaluates and orders. Thus, the 'solution' sold to many businesses in the name of productivity is an introduction of the 'correct' culture into an organization that, in turn, permeates throughout the organization enabling each person to evaluate themselves according to their abilities to live up to its expectations. In the process that which does not accord with the ideals that inform these transformations, or even questions them, is regarded as 'disorderly' impediments to the pursuits of such ends as 'quality', 'efficiency' and 'effectiveness'.

Where exactly the dividing line between nature and culture falls depends, of course, on what skills, knowledge and resources are available and on whether there is an ambition to deploy them for previously untried purposes. On the whole, the development of science and technology widens the scope of possible manipulation and thus extends the realm of culture. To return to one of our original examples, the know-how and the practice of genetic engineering, together with the chemical industry and members of the medical profession, may well transfer the standards that inform what it is to be a 'normal' human being. Taking this one step further, if genetic control is applied to the regulation of height, it will be the parents who will decide how tall their offspring will be, or a law passed and enforced by the state authority that will decide the normal and thus acceptable height of the citizens. In this way culture may appear to the individual in much the same way as the laws of nature: it is a fate against which one cannot rebel, or against which rebellion is, ultimately, a futile gesture.

Let us take a close look at the 'human-made elements' in our own lives. They may well enter into the space we occupy in two ways. First, they regulate and so render orderly the context in which our individual life-processes are conducted. The second may shape the motives and purposes of our life-process itself. One enables us to rationalize our actions by rendering some more sensible and reasonable in comparison to other forms of conduct. The other orients us in terms of being able to select particular motives and purposes from what are innumerable, general others that may even lie beyond our imagination. These are not distinct from other environments that we come across, for each of our actions has effects upon other environments that we inhabit and interact with in our everyday lives. Thus, to take one example of modern technology, the introduction of mobile phones is said to afford their owners improved communication, but in some contexts have been regarded as antisocial and even damaging in their use.

We may distinguish the order that is enabled by cultural intervention from randomness or chaos by observing that in an orderly situation not everything may happen. Out of a virtually infinite set of conceivable events, only a finite number may take place. Different events thus carry different degrees of probability, leaving a criterion of success for the establishment of order being the transformation of what was once improbable into the necessary or inevitable. In this sense, to design an order means to manipulate the probability of events. Preferences and priorities according to particular values that stand behind and are eventually incorporated into all artificial orders inform this process. Once this order has become well entrenched, solid and secure, this truth may be forgotten by perceiving the order as the only one imaginable.

As human beings, we all have a vested interest in creating and maintaining an orderly environment. This is because of the fact that most of our behaviour is learned and this learning accumulates over time thanks to memory passed on through such means as narratives and documentary records. These accumulated knowledges and skills remain beneficial as long as the context in which they were formed remains unchanged. It is thanks to the constancy of the world around us that the actions that were successful before are likely to remain so if repeated today and tomorrow. Just imagine what havoc would occur if, for instance, the meaning of the colours of traffic lights were changed without warning. In a randomly mutable world, memory and learning would turn from a blessing into a curse. In this context, to learn through past experience would be truly suicidal.

The order of the world around us has its counterpart in the orderliness of our own behaviour. On the whole, we choose different lanes for walking and driving. We do not behave at a party in the same fashion as we do at a college seminar or business meeting. We conduct ourselves differently at our parental home during the holidays and at a formal visit among people whom we do not know. We use a different tone of voice and different words, depending on whether we are addressing our boss or chatting to our friends. There are words we say on one occasion but avoid on another. There are things we do in public, but also 'private' activities which we do only when we are sure that we are not being watched. The remarkable thing is that while choosing a conduct 'proper' for the occasion, we find ourselves in the company of others behaving exactly like us. As such, departures from what are apparently rules are infrequent and this provides for a degree of *predictability* in the conduct of ourselves, others and the institutions with which we deal and that run our lives.

Culture, as the labour that makes up artificial order, requires distinctions: that is, setting things and people apart through acts of segregation and discrimination. In a desert, untouched by human activity and indifferent to human purpose, there are neither signposts nor fences making one stretch of land different from another. In other words, it is formless. In an environment subjected to the work of culture, on the other hand, a uniform, flat surface is divided into areas which draw some people but repel others, or into strips fit only for vehicles and those that are suitable solely for walkers. The world thus acquires a *structure* that orients activities. People are divided into superiors and inferiors, agents of authority and lay persons, and those who speak and those who listen and are expected to take notice of what is said. Similarly, time occurs in a uniform flow via a division into designated activities, for example, breakfast-time, coffee break, lunchtime, afternoon tea and dinner. Spatially there is demarcation according to the 'physical' composition and place of particular gatherings – being in a seminar, a conference, a beer festival, a dinner party or a business meeting.

These distinctions are drawn on two planes. The first is the 'shape of the world' in which the action takes place and the second is the action itself. Parts of the world are made different from each other, as well as different in themselves, depending on the periods distinguished in the flow of time (the same building may be a school in the morning and a badminton court in the evening). The actions within them are equally differentiated. Conduct at the table differs sharply depending on what has been put on the table, in what circumstances and who is sitting around it. Even table manners differ according to the formality and informality of the meal, as well as the class location of the participants as both Erving Goffman and Pierre Bourdieu, among others, have reminded us as a result of their sociological studies. Let us note, however, that the setting apart of the two planes is a product of abstraction. After all, they are not really independent from each other for there would be no formal dinner without the diners behaving in a formal manner.

We can express these acts of coordination in another way by observing that both the culturally organized social world and the behaviour of culturally trained individuals are structured in terms of being 'articulated', with the help of oppositions, into separate social contexts. In turn, these contexts call for distinctive manifestations of conduct and separate patterns of behaviour that are deemed suitable for each occasion. In addition, these two articulations 'correspond' to each other or, to employ a more technical term, they are isomorphic. The device that secures the 'overlap' between structures of social reality and of culturally regulated behaviour, is the cultural *code*. As you have probably guessed by now, the code is first and foremost a system of oppositions. Indeed, what is opposed in this system are *signs* – visible, audible, tactile, olfactory objects or events like lights of different colours, elements of dress, inscriptions, oral statements, tones of voice, gestures, facial expressions, scents and so on. These link actors' behaviour and the social figuration sustained by this behaviour. The signs, as it were, point in two directions at the same time: towards the intentions of the actors and towards the given segment of social reality in which they act. Neither of the two is just a reflection of the other, or is primary or secondary. Both, permit us to repeat, exist only together, grounded in the same facility of the cultural code.

Think, for instance, of a 'no entry' notice fixed to an office door. Such a notice appears, as a rule, on one side of the door only and the door on which it appears is usually unlocked (were the door impossible to open, there would hardly be a need for the notice). The notice is not, therefore, giving information on the 'objective state' of the door itself. It is, rather, an instruction, meant to create and sustain a situation which otherwise would not occur. What the words 'no entry' do, in fact, is to distinguish between the two sides of the door, between the two kinds of people who approach the door from the opposite sides and the two kinds of conduct in which those people are expected or permitted to engage. The space behind the marked side of the door is barred to those who approach it from the side of the notice, but for the people on the other side, on the contrary, no such restriction has been imposed. The sign stands precisely for this distinction. Its achievement is to make discrimination in an otherwise uniform space among equally uniform people.

From the above we can say that to know the code is to *understand* the meaning of signs and this, in turn, means knowing how to go on in a situation in which they appear, as well as how to use them to make such a situation appear. To understand is to be able to act effectively and thereby sustain coordination between the structures of the situation and our own actions. It is often said that to understand a sign is to grasp its meaning. However, this does not mean that a thought is then invoked as a mental image within our own mind. A thought, manifested perhaps in terms of a sort of 'reading aloud' of the sign in our head, may indeed accompany the sight or the sound of the sign, but to grasp meaning means no more and no less than to know how to go on. What follows is that the meaning of a sign resides, so to speak, in the difference its presence or absence makes. To put this in another way, the meaning of a sign resides in its relation to other signs. Some, such as Jacques Derrida, take this one step further and argue that because meanings derive only from the relation between signs, they can never be fixed. We are left with an inability to decide based upon the idea of *différance*. In this way fixed meanings always allude us over time because of the necessity for continual clarification and definition.

In practice, one sign does not usually carry enough information to make a relation fix sufficiently to enable action. One sign may be read incorrectly and if such an erroneous reading does happen, there will be nothing to correct the mistake. For instance, the sight of a military uniform tells us in unambiguous terms that the person in front of us is a member of the armed forces. For most civilians, this information would be quite sufficient to 'structure' the encounter. Nevertheless, for members of the armed forces, with their complex hierarchy of power and division of duties, the information conveyed by the uniform might not be enough and so other rank-showing signs are 'piled up' on the primary and general sign (the uniform) to provide further information. In certain instances such are the surplus of signs that they add little to the information already conveyed. Certain marketing tactics, for example, in their search for distinction between one product and another, merely replicate the information already conveyed by other signs.

In these cases we may refer to the *redundancy* of signs. Here we find an insurance against mistakes through the elimination of potential ambivalence through misreading. Were it not for redundancy, the accidental distortion or overlooking of just one sign could prompt the wrong kind of behaviour. We could even suggest that the more important are the oppositions between signs for the maintenance and furtherance of the established order, the more redundancy we can expect. At one level this reduces the problems associated with mistaken readings and so seeks to reduce *mis*understanding via a surplus of signs. Yet, at the same time, this surplus can heighten ambiguity and render alternative meanings more likely. Thus, while pursuing the effectiveness of communications to coordinate activities, to push this venture too far can risk introducing ambiguity and hence, distorted communications.

Let us repeat: it is the *opposition* between signs which is meaningful, not a single sign taken apart. This implies that the meanings to be 'read out' and understood reside in the system of signs – in the cultural code as a whole, in the distinctions it makes, not in the assumed special link between the sign and its referent. As noted in relation to the arguments of Derrida, among others, the signs are *arbitrary*. This quality of arbitrariness sets the culturally produced signs (the whole human-made system of signification) apart from anything one can find in nature. Therefore, the cultural code is truly unprecedented.

In terms of the way in which we gain knowledge of natural phenomena, we often refer to 'signs' through which nature 'informs' us of itself and which have to be read in order to extract the information they contain. Thus, we look at the drops of water flowing down the window pane and say, 'it's raining'. Or we observe a wet pavement and we conclude that it must have been raining and so on. What is characteristic about signs like these is that unlike the cultural signs we discussed before, they are all *determined*: that is, they are effects of their respective causes. Rain sends drops of water down the window pane and leaves the roads wet; illness changes the temperature of the body and makes the head feel hot, leading us to conclude that someone has a fever. Once we know of such causal connections, we can reconstruct the 'invisible' cause from the observed effects. To avoid confusion, it would perhaps be better to speak of *indices*, rather than signs, when referring to causally determined clues in our reasoning.

We have suggested that the natural causes noted in our above example place limitations on the interpretations that can then be made of the phenomenon in question. Two qualifying points need to be made here. First, social studies of the practice of science have suggested that much of what appears as the unproblematic interpretation of so-called natural events is, in fact, socially produced. Work conducted in scientific laboratories, for example, is a social activity in which social meanings play a large and important role, while much inference in the physical sciences concerns unobserved phenomena. In this latter instance there is not a placing of limitations, through observation, on possible interpretations. Second, while noting the arbitrary character of cultural signs, this does not suggest they are not real in their effects: that is, they place constraints upon our behaviour and the possibilities with which we are all faced in social life. To this extent they both enable and constrain our activities and the manner of their effects can vary according to the context and the power we may possess to alter their effects. Being defined as 'poor', for example, refers not simply to an arbitrary cultural category, but to the capability that people have, materially speaking, of being able to have sufficient money to meet their everyday needs according to the basic standards of the society in which they find themselves.

The observation that cultural signs are arbitrary is thus not equal to complete freedom of choice. The most free are signs that perform none but their cultural discriminatory function and serve no other need but that of human communication. These are, first and foremost, the signs of *language*. Language is a sign-system specialized in the function of communication. In language (and in language only), therefore, the arbitrariness of signs has no constraints. Those vocal sounds that humans are capable of producing can be modulated in an infinite number of utterly arbitrary ways, provided there is enough of them to produce the required oppositions. The same opposition, in various languages, may be construed with the help of pairs such as boy and girl, hot and cold, large and small and so on. Language and power, as Michel Foucault, Pierre Bourdieu and critical linguists have all pointed out, also go together in such a way as to limit what may be spoken.

Sign systems can be closely related to other human needs and thus be tied down by other functions. Dress, for instance, is fraught with arbitrary signs, yet it also offers shelter from the vagaries of an inclement climate, protects the body heat, offers an additional protection to vulnerable parts of the skin and upholds what may be binding standards of decency. Similarly, however rich and precise are the signifying distinctions impressed upon various kind of food and meals, there are limits to the material in which cultural discriminations may be expressed, as not every stuff can be made edible given the peculiarities of the human digestive system. Besides, tea or dinner, formal or informal, must, apart from signifying the specific nature of the occasion, provide nourishing substances; it is, after all, also a food intake. While the capacity for human speech is utilized solely for communicative purposes, other media of communication share their *semiotic* (meaning carrying and transferring) function with servicing other needs. Their code is carved, as it were, on the surface of other, not primarily communicative, functions.

As we have continually noted, those things that provide for the possibility for action are also those that may serve to constrain our potential as they set limits on possibilities. To this extent, culture is most effective when it is disguised as nature. What is artificial appears to be rooted in the very 'nature of things' and so becomes something that no human decision or action may possibly change. Sharply distinct practices of the placement and treatment of men and women, inscribed from an early age, become truly well established and secure once it is accepted as beyond question that the relation between sexes is somehow predetermined.

Culturally produced, social differences between men and women appear as natural as the biological differences between the male and female sexual organs and procreative functions.

Such processes occur as long as the arbitrary character of the norms that culture propagates are not exposed. Culture looks and acts like nature as long as no alternative conventions are seen and known. Yet virtually every one of us knows that there are many different ways of life. We look around us at people who dress, talk and behave differently from ourselves. We know that there are *cultures* rather than one single culture. Thus, culture is unable to hold the same firm grip on human conduct as if it were a universal condition free from alternative orders. In the process we may come across periods and times of doubt that require explanations and justifications for an existing state of affairs. These questions may be met through an open and inquiring culture, but equally may prompt an even more forceful imposition of what is assumed to be the natural order of things.

State, Nations and Nationalism

During a process of questioning and the pursuit of justifications, uncertainty can occur. This is seldom a pleasant condition and so attempts to escape from it are not uncommon. The pressure to conform to the norms promoted by cultural training may therefore be accompanied by efforts to discredit and denigrate the norms of other cultures. A 'naturalness' is propagated aided by the rhetoric of 'purity' and 'contamination' at one end of the spectrum and a right to live a culture, separately from others, at the other end. Even if other ways of life are acknowledged as viable cultures in their own right, they may be portrayed as bizarre and vaguely threatening. They may be acceptable for those who demand less of their people, but are not sufficient for those persons of distinction. What we witness here are varying degrees of *xenophobia* (dread of the alien) or *heterophobia* (dread of the different) as methods for defending an order against ambivalence.

With the distinctions between 'us' and 'them', 'here' and 'there', 'inside' and 'outside', 'native' and 'foreign', we often see the drawing of a territory over which there is a claim for undivided rule and an intention to guard against all competition in the name of an established and unproblematic culture. Cultural tolerance is often exercised at a distance. When that is threatened a rhetoric of invasion and purity is often thinly disguised by another that proclaims the right of all people to live their life as they wish – as long as it is in their 'own country'.

This sort of activity has been referred to as a process of cultural *hegemony*. What is indicated by this term is a subtle but effective process aimed at securing a monopoly of the norms and values upon which particular orders are erected. Hence, culture can become a proselytizing activity that aims at conversion by inducing its objects to abandon their old habits and beliefs and embrace others instead or, alternatively, by castigating other cultures based upon the assumed superiority of its own. On the other hand, in those situations where cultural designs coexist without clear demarcation lines separating their fields of influence, we find conditions of 'cultural pluralism'. In these situations, mutual tolerance, exemplified in a recognition of the other side's worthiness and validity, is an attitude that is necessary for constructive and peaceful coexistence.

Citizenship and the State

These kinds of issues are linked to matters of identity that, in turn, relate to citizenship. Citizenship may be something to which a person is entitled by virtue of their place of birth. In addition, it may be conferred upon someone as a result of an application to a country, or by virtue of a past association and service to a country that is rewarded accordingly. In other instances, people may be refugees from persecution and so apply for political asylum and residence. In considering such issues, culture, nation and beliefs concerning nationalism will inform the status conferred upon the person and the granting or refusal of their application. If granted, what may then occur is a link between personal identity and belonging in terms of being part of a nation.

Consider all the forms that we are routinely asked to complete when making particular applications. They ask many details about us and may often include a question about nationality. To this question a person may answer 'American', 'British', 'German', 'Italian', 'French', 'Portuguese' and so on. However, if answering British, the person may also answer 'English' (or 'Welsh', or 'Scottish', or 'Jewish', or 'Greek'). As it happens, both answers are proper responses to the question of nationality, but refer to different things. When answering 'British' they are indicating that they are a 'British subject', that is, a citizen of the *state* called Great Britain or the United Kingdom. When answering 'English' they are reporting the fact that they belong to the English *nation*. A question about nationality makes both answers possible and acceptable and demonstrates how the two memberships are not clearly distinguished from each other and thus may become confused. Yet while state and nation may overlap, they are quite different things and a person's membership of each involves them in very different kinds of relationships.

We may first observe that there is no state without a specific territory held together by a centre of power. Every resident of the area over which the authority of the state extends belongs to the state. Belonging in this case has first of all a legal meaning. 'Authority of the state' means the ability to declare and enforce, the 'law of the land'. These are the rules that must be observed by all subjects of this authority (unless the state itself exempts them from such an obedience), including those persons who may not be its citizens but fall within its territory by virtue of their physical presence. If the laws are not observed, the culprits are liable to be punished. They will be forced to obey, whether they like it or not. To paraphrase Max Weber, the state has a monopoly over the legitimate means of violence. Therefore, the state claims the sole right to apply coercive force (to use weapons in defence of the law, to deprive the law-breaker of freedom through imprisonment and ultimately to kill if the prospect of reform is nil, or if the breach of the law was so grave that the form of punishment is death). In these instances when people are executed by the order of the state, the killing is regarded as legitimate punishment and not murder. Clearly, however, that interpretation is open to considerable debate. The other side of the state monopoly of physical coercion is that any use of force which has not been authorized by the state, or committed by anyone other than its authorized agents, is condemned as an act of violence. Note, of course, that none of this is to suggest that those acting on behalf of the state may not engage in illegitimate acts of violence and terror.

The laws announced and guarded by the state determine the duties and the rights of the state subjects. One of the most important of these duties is the payment of taxes – giving away a part of our income to the state, which takes it over and puts it to various uses. The rights, on the other hand, may be *personal*. Here we might include the protection of our own body and possessions, unless ruled otherwise by the decision of authorized state organs, as well as the right to profess our own opinions and beliefs. They may also be *political* in terms of influencing the composition and the policy of state organs: for example, by taking part in the election of the body of representatives who then become rulers or administrators of the state institutions. They may also include, as the sociologist T. H. Marshall argued, *social* rights. These refer to those rights that are guaranteed by the state in terms of a basic livelihood and essential needs such as cannot be attained by the efforts of given individuals.

We should note at this point that social rights may challenge property rights in that they are associated with, to employ the British philosopher Isaiah Berlin's famous distinction between two concepts of liberty, both 'positive and negative liberty'. 'Negative liberty' denotes a freedom from interference based upon ownership of property. This is argued to grant a person entitlement to their land and possessions and a minimal state involvement in the means through which they dispose of their wealth. 'Positive liberty', on the other hand, is about providing people with certain entitlements regardless of such ownership which may, of course, simply be an accident of birth. Charitable giving may be associated with the former whereby those with wealth choose to give a small proportion of their income to worthy causes. However, for the recipients, this comes in the form of a 'gift', rather than an 'entitlement' as a result of their citizenship. Such issues inform the campaigning slogans that often surround the erosion or claim to rights: for example, 'rights not charity' and 'education is a right, not a privilege'.

It is a combination of rights and duties that makes the individual a subject of the state. The first thing we know about being state subjects is that however much we might dislike it, we have to pay income tax, local tax or value added tax. Yet we can also complain to the authorities and seek their assistance if our bodies are assaulted or possessions stolen. We can also, depending on the country in which we live, expect to have access to primary and secondary education regardless of the ability to pay, as well as a health service (the British National Health Service, for example, is an extraordinary institution that was set up precisely in order that all people could have access to health care and thus seek to ensure a more healthy population for general economic and social well-being).

What we see in the above is the potential for people to feel simultaneously protected and oppressed. We enjoy the relative peacefulness of life which we know we owe to the awesome force always waiting somewhere in the wings to be deployed against the breakers of peace. During the Cold War this balance was determined in our nuclear age by a process that came to be known as MAD (mutually assured destruction). As the state is the only power permitted to set apart the permissible from the impermissible and as law enforcement by the state organs is the only method of keeping this distinction permanent and secure, we believe that if the state withdrew its punishing fist, universal violence and disorder would rule instead. We believe that we owe our security and peace of mind to the power of the state and that there would be no security or peace of mind without it. On many occasions, however, we resent the obtrusive interference of the state into our private lives. If the *protective* care of the state enables us to do things – to plan our actions in the belief that the plans may be executed without obstacle – the *oppressive* function of the state feels more like disablement. Our experience of the state is, therefore, inherently ambiguous: we may like and need it and dislike and resent it at the same time.

How these two feelings are balanced depends upon our circumstances. If we are well off and money is not a problem, we might relish the prospect of securing for ourselves a better health service than that offered to the average person. Therefore, in the British context, we might resent the fact that the state taxes us and runs the National Health Service. If our income, on the other hand, is too modest to buy exclusive health services, we might welcome the state as a device that protects us in times of ill-health. That noted, we may fail to see how, in general, the tax and benefit systems associated with the nation-state, affect life-chances in different ways. Our focus is upon ourselves and how we are affected by our circumstances. Of course, this is perfectly understandable. However, how would a person be able to afford private health care in the British context if it were not for the National Health Service training doctors and nurses and so providing the skills and knowledge that the private sector requires? Similarly, how would the economy be able to perform effectively if it were not for the state education sector furnishing the job market with skilled and knowledgeable individuals?

We can see from this discussion that, depending on their situation, some people may experience an increase in freedom as a result of state actions thus widening their choice, while others may consider such action as constraining and so narrowing their range of choice. However, on the whole, everybody would prefer as much enabling as possible and as little oppression as is truly necessary. What is perceived as enabling and what as oppressive will differ, but the urge to control, or at least to influence the composition of the mixture, does not. The greater the part of our lives that depends on state activities, the more widespread and intense is likely to be this urge.

To be a citizen means, in addition to being a subject as the bearer of rights and duties as the state has defined them, having a say in determining the state policy that informs those rights and duties. In other words, citizenship now refers to a capability to influence the activity of the state and thus to participate in the definition and management of 'law and order'. To exercise such influence in practice, the citizens must enjoy a degree of autonomy regarding the state regulation. There must, in other words, be limits to the capability of the state to interfere with a subject's actions. Here, once again, we confront the tensions between the enabling and oppressive aspects of state activity. For instance, citizens' rights cannot be exercised fully if the activities of the state are surrounded by secrecy and if the 'ordinary people' have no insight into the intentions and the doings of their rulers. A government that confuses its aims with those of the state, in terms of the rights of its citizens, can undermine those rights by denying them access to the facts which allow them to evaluate the real consequences of the state's action.

For these and other reasons, the relations between the state and its subjects are often strained, as the subjects find themselves obliged to struggle to become citizens or to protect their status when it is threatened by the growing ambitions of the state. The main obstacles they encounter in this struggle are those related to the tutelage complex and therapeutic attitudes of the state, respectively. The first refers to a tendency to treat subjects as if they were unable to determine what is good for them and act in a manner that serves their best interests. The second refers to the inclination of state authorities to treat subjects in the same manner that doctors treat their patients. In this way they become individuals who are burdened with problems that they cannot resolve on their own. What is then assumed to be required is expert guidance, along with surveillance to resolve problems that, as it were, reside 'inside' the patient. The treatment is then instruction and supervision in order that they work on their bodies in accordance with the doctor's orders.

Here we can see a tendency, from the state's point of view, to see subjects as objects of regulation. The subjects' conduct may then be regarded as being in constant need of proscription and prescription. If the conduct is not what it should be, then there is something wrong with the subject themselves, as opposed to the context in which they find themselves. This tendency to individualize social problems takes place against a background of asymmetrical relations. Even if patients are allowed to choose their doctors, once the doctor has been chosen, the patient is expected to listen and to obey. The doctor expects discipline, not discussion. The state then justifies its own call for the uncontested implementation of its instructions by allusion to what is in the best interests of the citizen. This is what may be termed the exercise of *pastoral power* in order to protect the individual against their own inclinations.

In this process there may be justifications invoked concerning the need to withhold information for the good of the citizen. This practice of secrecy surrounds the detailed information that the state gathers, stores and processes. Much of this, of course, is information designed to assist in policy formulation and implementation. Yet, at the same time, data about the state's own actions may be classified as 'official secrets', whose betrayal is prosecuted. As most subjects of the state are denied access to this type of information, those few who are so permitted gain a distinct advantage over the rest. State freedom to collect information, coupled with the practice of secrecy, can further deepen the asymmetry of the mutual relations.

Given this potential, citizenship carries a tendency to resist the commanding position aspired to by the state. These efforts may be manifest in two related, but different directions. The first is *regionalism* in which state power may be seen as an adversary of local autonomy. The specificity of local interests and issues become singled out as sufficient reasons for aspirations to the self-management of local affairs. Accompanying this is a demand for representative local institutions that will stand closer to the people in the area and be more sensitive and responsive to their regional concerns. The second manifestation is *de-territorialization*. Here we find the territorial basis of state power being open to challenge. Other traits are then promoted as being of more significance than mere place of residence. For instance, ethnicity, religion and language may be singled out as attributes that possess a heavier bearing on the totality of human life. The right to autonomy, to separate management, is then demanded against the pressure for uniformity from the unitary territorial power.

As a result of these propensities and even under the best of circumstances, there remains a residue of tension and distrust between the state and its subjects. The state therefore needs to secure its *legitimacy* by convincing the subjects that there are valid reasons why they should obey the commands of the state. Legitimation is meant to secure the subjects' trust in that whatever comes from state authorities deserves to be obeyed, along with the conviction that it also must be obeyed. To this extent legitimation aims at developing an unconditional allegiance to the state in which security is apparent in belonging to a 'homeland' in which the individual citizen can benefit from its wealth and might. With this may come *patriotism* as a guide to actions seen in terms of a love of the homeland and a general will to keep it strong and happy. A combination of consensus and discipline are thought to make all citizens better off and concerted actions, rather than rifts, are held to be beneficial to all citizens.

If patriotic obedience is demanded in the name of reason, one may well be tempted to subject the argument to a test of reason on the basis that all calculation invites a counter-calculation. One may count the costs of obedience to an unpopular policy against the gains that an active resistance may bring. One may then find out, or convince oneself, that resistance is less costly and damaging than obedience. Civil disobedience cannot be simply written off as the distorted aspirations of those who are misled, for it takes place in those spaces created by efforts to legitimize state activities. As this process is hardly ever conclusive and without end, these kinds of actions can act as a barometer for the extent to which policies become too oppressive. This is an insight which Emile Durkheim was particularly concerned to emphasize when writing about such matters as the state, crime and deviance. Indeed, Durkheim's lasting legacy was to argue that society is an active moralizing force and this, of course, may be undermined or promoted by state activities and policies, as well as economic interests.

Nations and Nationalism

An unconditional loyalty to a nation, in contrast to the above, is free from the inner contradictions which burden discipline towards the state. *Nationalism* does not need to appeal to reason or calculation. While it may appeal to gains that can be afforded by obedience, it is normally characterized by obedience as a value in its own right. Membership of a nation is understood as a fate more powerful than any individual and as such, is not a quality that cannot be put on or taken off at will. Nationalism implies that it is the nation which gives individual members their identity. Unlike the state, the nation is not an association entered into in order to promote common interests. On the contrary, it is the unity of the nation, its common fate, that precedes all consideration of interests and, further, gives the interests their meaning.

Depending upon its composition and the situation it confronts, a national state can exploit the potential of nationalism instead of trying to legitimize itself by reference to the calculation of benefits. The national state demands obedience on the grounds that it speaks in the name of the nation. In this form discipline towards the state is a value which does not serve any objective other than the pursual of its own purpose. In this situation, to disobey the state becomes something far worse than a breach of the law. It becomes an act of betrayal of the national cause – a heinous, immoral act which strips the culprits of dignity and casts them outside the bounds of the human community. It is perhaps for the reasons of legitimation and more generally, of securing the unity of conduct, that there is a sort of mutual attraction between the state and the nation. The state tends to enlist the authority of the nation to strengthen its own demand for discipline, while nations tend to constitute themselves into states to harness the enforcing potential of the state to the support of their claim to loyalty. That noted, not all states are national and not all nations have states of their own.

What is a nation? This is a notoriously difficult question, with no single answer being likely to satisfy everybody. The nation is not a 'reality' in the same way in which the state may be defined. The state is 'real' in the sense of having clearly drawn boundaries, both on the map and on the land. The boundaries are on the whole guarded by force, so that random passing from one state to another, entering and leaving the state, encounters very real, tangible resistance which makes the state itself feel real via its bounded practices. Inside the boundaries of the state, a set of laws is binding which, again, is real in the sense that disregarding its presence, behaving as if it did not exist, may 'bruise' and 'hurt' the culprit in much the same way as disregarding any other material object might.

The same cannot be said about the nation. A nation is an 'imagined community' because it exists as an entity in so far as its members mentally and emotionally 'identify themselves' with a collective body. True, nations usually occupy a continuous territory which, as they may credibly claim, may lend them a particular character. Seldom, however, does this provide the territory with a uniformity that is comparable with that imposed by the unity of the state-sponsored 'law of the land'. Hardly ever can nations boast a monopoly of residence on any territory. Within virtually any territory there are people living side-by-side who define themselves as belonging to different nations and whose loyalty is thus claimed by different nationalisms. In many territories no nation can really claim a majority, much less a position sufficiently dominant to define the 'national character' of the land.

It is also true that nations are usually distinguished and united by a common language. Yet what is deemed a common and distinct language is to a large extent a matter of a nationalist (and often contested) decision. Regional dialects may be so idiosyncratic in their vocabulary, syntax and idioms as to be almost mutually incomprehensible and yet their identities are denied or actively suppressed for fear of disrupting national unity. On the other hand, even comparatively minor local differences may well be played up, their distinctiveness exaggerated, so that a dialect may be elevated to the rank of a separate language and of a distinctive feature of a separate nation (the differences between, say, the Norwegian and Swedish, Dutch and Flemish, Ukrainian and Russian languages are, arguably, not much more conspicuous than the differences between many 'internal' dialects which are represented – if acknowledged – as varieties of the same national language). Besides, groups of people may admit to sharing the same language and still consider themselves separate nations (think of the English-speaking Welsh or Scots people, the sharing of English by many nations of the former Commonwealth and the sharing of German by the Austrians and Swiss).

There is a further reason why territory and language are insufficient as defining factors that make up the 'reality' of the nation. Quite simply, one can move in and out of them. In principle, a person can declare a change of national allegiance. People move homes and acquire residence among a nation to which they do not belong and may then learn the language of another nation. If the territory of residence (remember, this is not a territory with guarded borders) and participation in a linguistic community (remember, one is not obliged to use a national language by the fact that no other languages are admitted by power-holders) were the only constituting features of the nation, the nation would be too 'porous' and 'underdefined' to claim the absolute, unconditional and exclusive allegiance that all nationalisms demand.

This latter demand is at its most persuasive if the nation is conceived of as a fate, rather than a choice. It is then assumed to be so firmly established in the past that no human intervention can change it. As it is deemed to lie beyond what may be viewed as the arbitrary character of culture, nationalisms aim to achieve this belief with the *myth of origin* serving as the most potent instrument towards this end. This myth suggests that even if it were once a cultural creation, in the course of history the nation has become a truly 'natural' phenomenon and so is something beyond human control. The present members of the nation – so the myth says – are tied together by a common past from which they cannot escape. The national spirit is then regarded as a shared and exclusive property that not only unites people, but also sets them apart from all other nations and all individuals who may aspire to enter their community. As Craig Calhoun, the American sociologist and historian, put it, the idea of nation then becomes established 'both as a category of similar individuals and as a sort of "supra-individual" '.

The myth of the origin, or the claim to 'naturalness' of a nation and the ascribed and inherited nature of national membership cannot but embroil nationalism in a contradiction. On the one hand, it is held that the nation is a verdict of history and a reality that is objective and solid as any natural phenomenon. On the other hand, it is precarious because its unity and coherence is constantly under threat by virtue of the existence of other nations whose members may become part of its ranks. The nation may then respond by defending its existence against the encroachments of the 'other' and thus cannot survive without constant vigilance and effort. Therefore, nationalisms normally demand power – the right to use coercion – in order to secure the preservation and continuity of the nation. State power is then mobilized and (as we have seen) this means monopoly over the instruments of coercion; only the state power is capable of enforcing uniform rules of conduct and promulgating laws to which its citizens must submit. So, much as the state needs nationalism for its legitimation, nationalism needs the state for its effectiveness. The national state is the product of this mutual attraction.

When the state has been identified with the nation – as the organ of self-government of the nation – the prospect of nationalist success increases considerably. Nationalism no longer has to rely solely on the persuasiveness of its arguments as state power means the chance of enforcing the sole use of the national language in public offices, courts and representative bodies. Public resources become mobilized in order to boost the competitive chances of the preferred national culture in general and national literature and arts in particular. It also means, above all, control over education which is made simultaneously free and obligatory, so that no one is excluded and no one is allowed to escape its influence. Universal education permits all inhabitants of the state territory to be trained in the values of the nation that dominates the state. With varying degrees of success, there is the seeking to accomplish in practice what has been claimed in theory, namely the 'naturalness' of nationality.

The combined effect of education, of ubiquitous though diffuse cultural pressure and of the state-enforced rules of conduct, is the attachment to the way of life associated with the 'national membership'. This spiritual bond may find itself manifest in a conscious and explicit *ethnocentrism*. The characteristics of this attitude are the conviction that our own nation, and everything which relates to it, is right, morally praiseworthy and beautiful. In terms of being constituted through contrast, this is also exemplified in the belief that it is vastly superior to anything that may be offered as an alternative and further, that what is good for our own nation should be given precedence over the interests of anybody and anything else.

Ethnocentrism may not be overtly preached, but it remains pervasive for those who have been brought up in a specific, culturally shaped environment and who tend to feel at home and secure in it. By default, therefore, it may be perpetuated; conditions that deviate from the familiar devalue the acquired skills and may cause feelings of unease, vague resentment and even an overt hostility that is focused upon the 'aliens' who are assumed to be responsible for the confusion. It is then 'their ways' that require changing. Here we can see how nationalism inspires a tendency towards cultural crusades via efforts to change the alien ways, to convert them, to force them to submit to the cultural authority of the dominant nation.

The overall purpose of the cultural crusade is one of *assimilation*. The term itself originally came from biology in order to denote how, in order to feed itself, a living organism assimilates elements of the environment and so transforms 'foreign' substances into its own body. In so doing it makes them 'similar' to itself and so what used to be different becomes similar. To be sure, all nationalism is always about assimilation, as the nation which the nationalism declares as having a 'natural unity' has first to be created by rallying an often indifferent and diversified population around the myth and symbols of national distinctiveness. Assimilatory efforts are at their most conspicuous and fully expose their inner contradictions when a triumphant nationalism, which has achieved state domination over a certain territory, meets among the residents some 'foreign' groups: that is, those who either declare their distinct national identity, or are treated as distinct and nationally alien by the population that has already gone through the process of cultural unification. In such cases assimilation can be presented as a proselytizing mission in much the same way as the heathen must be converted to a 'true' religion.

Paradoxically, efforts at conversion can be half-hearted. After all, too much success can bear the mark of the inner contradiction always present in the nationalist vision. On the one hand, nationalism claims the superiority of its own nation, of its national culture and character. Therefore, the attractiveness of such a superior nation to the surrounding peoples is something to be expected and in the case of a national state, it also mobilizes the popular support for state authority and undermines all other sources of authority resistant to the state-promoted uniformity. On the other hand, the influx of foreign elements into the nation, particularly when made easy by the 'open arms', hospitable attitude of the host nation, casts doubt on the 'naturalness' of national membership and thus saps the very foundation of national unity. People are seen to change places at will: 'them' can turn into 'us' under our very eyes. It looks, therefore, as if nationality were simply a matter of a choice which could, in principle, be different from what it was and even revoked. Efforts at assimilation that are effective thereby bring into relief the precarious, voluntary character of the nation and national membership – a state of affairs that nationalism seeks to disguise.

As a set of practices, assimilation breeds resentment against the very people the cultural crusade aimed to attract and convert. In the process they are constructed as a threat to order and security for, by their existence, they challenge that which is believed to be outside human power and control. An allegedly natural boundary is exposed not only as artificial but, worse still, passable. Acts of assimilation are, therefore, never complete for in the eyes of those who seek their transformation, assimilated persons will appear as potential turncoats. After all, they may pretend to be what they are not. Despite its aims, the success of assimilation gives credence to the idea that boundaries are permanent and that 'true assimilation' is not, in fact, possible.

Recognition and respect for difference do not then become an option for those with nationalist tendencies who, when faced with an absence of success, may retreat to a tougher, less vulnerable and racist line of defence. Unlike the nation, *race* is perceived overtly and unambiguously as a thing of nature and so provides for distinctions that are neither human-made nor subject to change by human efforts. Often race is given a purely biological meaning in, for example, the idea that individual character, ability and inclination are closely related to observable, extrinsic characteristics that are genetically determined. In all cases, however, its concept refers to those qualities that are seen to be hereditary and so when confronted with race, education must surrender. What nature has decided, no human instruction may change. Unlike the nation, race cannot be assimilated and so among those who seek to maintain or construct boundaries upon such a basis the language of 'purity' and 'pollution' is apparent. To stave off such a morbid event, alien races must be segregated, isolated and, best of all, removed to a safe distance to make mixing impossible and thus protect one's own race from the effects of 'others'.

Although assimilation and racism seem to be radically opposed, they stem from the same source: that is, boundary-building tendencies inherent in nationalist preoccupations. Each one emphasizes one of the poles of the inner contradiction. Depending on circumstances, one or the other side can be deployed as tactics in the pursuit of nationalist objectives. Yet both are always potentially present in any nationalist campaign and so rather than excluding, they may mutually boost and reinforce each other. Here also we find the strength of nationalism being derived from the connecting role it plays in the promotion and perpetuation of the social order as defined by the authority of the state. Nationalism 'sequestrates' the diffuse heterophobia – the resentment of the different that we discussed earlier – and mobilizes this sentiment in the service of loyalty and support for the state and discipline towards state authority.

Utilizing the above means, nationalism makes the state authority more effective. At the same time it deploys the resource of state power in shaping the social reality in such a way that new supplies of heterophobia, and hence new mobilizing opportunities, may be generated. Given that the state guards its monopoly of coercion it prohibits, as a rule, all private settling of accounts, such as ethnic and racial violence. In most cases, it would also disallow and even punish private initiative in petty discrimination. Like all the rest of its resources, it would deploy nationalism as a vehicle of the one and only social order that is sustains and enforces, while simultaneously persecuting its diffuse, spontaneous and thus potentially disorderly manifestations. The mobilizing potential of nationalism may then be harnessed to the appropriate state policy. Examples of such activity include inexpensive yet prestigious military, economic or sporting victories, as well as restrictive immigration laws, enforced repatriation and other measures ostensibly reflecting, while certainly reinforcing, the popular heterophobia.

Summary

We have discussed various forms of boundaries, how they are constructed, with what effects and mobilizing what resources. In each case they have tangible effects on how we view the social and natural worlds. The activity of cultural building is one aimed not only at achieving a unity among a population, but also at control of environments. These, however, have a way of reminding us of their force via floods, earthquakes, volcanic eruptions and famines. Yet cultures inform not only actions, but also reactions. Given our relationship to the planet we inhabit and its finite resources, just what is an appropriate and sustainable way of living together?

In examining these kinds of questions we find extraordinary variations in national uses of energy, as well as having access to things that many cannot take for granted, such as clean drinking water. These raise questions about the effects of cultures upon environments and the distribution of resources between nations. Issues such as these refer to the need to recognize different cultures *and* the distribution of resources between them. It is no surprise, therefore, that how much we have to change is a hotly disputed matter as it threatens those countries who have enjoyed a relationship to the environment that is not sustainable.

When it comes to nations, the state and nation historically merged in large parts of the world. In this way the states have been using national sentiments to reinforce their hold over society and strengthen the order they promote. Each was self-congratulatory regarding the order it had created by alluding to a unity that was allegedly natural. Enforcement, therefore, was not required in such situations. Let us note, however, the fact that the merger of state and nation did occur historically is not proof of its inevitability. Ethnic loyalty and an attachment to particular languages and customs are not reducible to the political function to which they have been put by their alliance with state power. The marriage between state and nation is not in any way preordained – it is one of convenience. As a result, its fragility can be manifested in both covert and overt acts of violence with what are disastrous consequences. However, as this relationship has changed in the past, so it may in the future and the judgement as to the beneficial and detrimental effects of any new configurations will be made in times to come.

chapter nine

THE BUSINESS IN EVERYDAY LIFE: CONSUMPTION, TECHNOLOGY AND LIFESTYLES

Each of us exhibits, in the daily routines of our lives, extraordinary abilities and different characteristics. We eat, drink, communicate, move through time and space utilizing our bodies in various ways, experience times of happiness and sadness, stress and relaxation, engage in working activities that utilize various skills and finally, rest and sleep. In the process of which, we engage with our environments and deploy the resources to which we have access in our actions.

As sociologists of everyday life have demonstrated, our abilities to get on with our tasks and interact with one another requires a tacit knowledge without which the fabric of social life would not be possible. We take these things for granted except, however, when they go wrong. At these times there are moments of reflection that may lead us to consider, or question, the conditions, hopes, fears, aspirations and desires that inform our lives. These acts of questioning may be temporary, only to take us back into the routines that are part of our lives, or have more profound effects and lead us to alter the trajectories of our life-courses. Whatever may be the result, when reflecting upon our actions, we often regard ourselves as being self-determined: that is, autonomous beings who have both the ability and capability of acting according to the ends we seek. Yet this presumes it is we who manipulate our environments. However, what if our environments manipulate us, or we are the product of the interaction between ourselves, others and the environments we inhabit?

▽

Technology, Expertise and Skills

These are fundamentally important questions, for they are about the ways in which we organize our lives and what we may realistically hope for not only for ourselves, but also for others. Take, for example, the numerous technologies that surround those persons living in countries where they are now taken for granted. Do we utilize and manipulate those technologies to our advantage, or do they have the effect of making us increasingly reliant upon them so diminishing our independence? After all, in their design, purchase and maintenance they make us totally reliant upon shops, electricity plants and companies who distribute the electricity for profit and on the experts and designers who built them. Computers are purchased, but are immediately rendered obsolete as the speed of processors and the capacity for memory increases by the month. Can people live with these changes? Indeed, can they afford to live without them?

Thinking in these terms, we can see how our dependence on technologies may have grown over time. They inevitably go wrong and when they do, we are often greeted with salespersons saying new models are now on the market, while parts are no longer available to repair 'outdated' items. It is not unusual to be told that it is cheaper to buy a new item than to get the old one repaired. Yet what idea of cost is being invoked here? Cost to the environment in terms of raw materials and the disposal of what then becomes 'rubbish' are not factors in these calculations. Thus, we are locked into a cycle of purchasing goods if we regard them as essential to our lifestyles. However, is this really a choice designed to enhance our freedom that occurs independently of the seduction of consumerism and the enormous industry that has grown up around the marketing of goods and services? There are even studies being conducted on the relationship between background music played in supermarkets and patterns of consumer purchasing. Nothing, in the desire to influence consumers, is now left to chance.

With each technological purchase, new skills are required and these may enhance our general abilities. Nevertheless, just how many functions does a mobile phone require? Is it necessary that games may be played on them? Similarly, with computer software coming on to the market, there is a need to update our equipment. However, is the learning how to interact with new technologies a means to an end, or an end in itself? For instance, both of us write on computers, but have different systems and have had to respond to different demands. Zygmunt has an older machine that was designed for word-processing and he does not wish to alter his system. Why? Because that would require learning new software programs and his concern is to produce more writings on various topics, which would detract from that overarching purpose. Tim, on the other hand, has recently moved jobs and the institutional requirements, as well as the expectations placed upon him in his new position, require that he learn new ways of interacting with technology. Therefore, while he is also committed to the same ends, the context in which they both work and their interactions with new technologies are very different. Neither of us would be prepared to say that these conditions are simply the result of free choice, nor are our interactions with new technologies simply one-way. Our actions are, in other words, modified and constrained in different ways by our relations with technologies and the situations in which we find ourselves working.

With each change we have had to acquire new skills but how they impact upon our lives depends upon the social conditions in which we find ourselves. At the same time, we still have to take on board that with each step we come to 'need' more complex technologies that make more demands upon our skills. Because we have other reasons for using these technologies aside from understanding their inner workings, we know less about their mode of operation and so are less able to fix them if they go wrong. As a result, our dependency upon others grows as more sophisticated tools are required for their repair and maintenance. Yet we also have to acquire ways of interacting with these technologies and so they render our old skills outdated, making us more dependent on the need to change in order to keep apace with developments. These skills, focused on new tools, chase away our 'old' abilities. As such, our skills become absorbed into the tools of new technologies and it is questionable whether this leads to a growth in our autonomy, or an increase in our dependence.

A growth in expertise now appears to fill the gap between expectation and actuality in the service of the promises that come with the information age. Everyday skills that were once assumed to be fairly widespread, or at least within grasp, given time, are now subjected to careful scientific study. Tasks are split into elementary parts and each one examined in detail and represented as a problem with its own intrinsic requirements. To every problem, there is now a solution given time, effective design and experimentation through comparison. New products are the culmination of the effort of specialists who participate in the production of the ultimate goods. Cars, for example, are now replete with various gadgets designed to maximize the comfort of the driver and passengers, but are also marketed as a means of projecting and enhancing a particular lifestyle.

However, when it comes to car maintenance, an increase in computer-controlled engine management leads to a need for more complicated diagnostic equipment – to say nothing of the increasing expense of repairs. Mechanics, who once performed diagnostic work and made repairs accordingly, can then find themselves replaced by 'fitters' who change entire components because their repair is not possible given their complicated functioning and/or the fact that they are 'sealed units'.

Lives have transformed like this in advanced industrial societies in so many spheres of everyday activities: for example, sweeping the floor, mowing the lawn, cutting the hedge, cooking a meal or even washing the dishes. In all these functions expertise, locked in technological implements and gadgets, took over, polished and sharpened the skills once in everyone's possession. We now need that expertise and that technology to achieve the task at hand. We also need new skills to replace the old, obsolete and forgotten ones: this time we need the skills of finding and operating the right technological instruments. Nevertheless, not all the technology that is now deployed simply replaced tasks that were previously accomplished in different ways. There are things, quite central to many people's lives, which we would never do without the technology that makes them possible. Think of radios, music towers and TV sets. Their introduction opened new possibilities which did not previously exist. As spending our evenings watching sitcoms or drama serials was not a feasible idea, there was no need for it, but now people may feel deprived if the TV set goes wrong. A *need* has now developed where previously it did not exist. In such cases technology seems to have created its own need. These technological objects did not replace older ways of doing things, for they have induced people to do things they did not before.

Expertise and technology do not necessarily appear as a response to our needs. It is often the case that those who offer us their expertise and products must first go to great lengths to persuade us that we actually have a need for the goods they sell. However, even in cases where new products are addressed to well-established needs they could continue to be satisfied were we not tempted by the allurements of a new gadget. Thus, new technologies are not simply a response to a need: in no way has its appearance been determined by popular demand. It is rather the demand that has been determined by the availability of new technology. Whether the need did or did not exist before, the demand for new products comes after their introduction. In this way the presumption that demand creates supply is reversed by the suppliers actively creating demand via their marketing strategies.

Consumption and Advertising

So what causes ever new, deeper, more focused, more specialized expertise and ever more sophisticated technological equipment to appear? The probable answer is that the development of expertise and technology is a self-propelling, self-reinforcing process which does not need any extra causes. Given a team of experts supplied with research facilities and equipment, we can be pretty sure that they will come up with new products and propositions, guided simply by the logic of activity in an organization. This logic is characterized by a need to excel, to prove our superiority over competitors, or just the all-too-human interest and excitement in the performance of our work. Products may become scientifically or technologically feasible before their uses have been ascertained: we have this technology, how can we use it? Further, since we have it, it would be unforgivable not to use it.

Solutions are then held to come before problems and so seek the problems they might be able to solve. To put it in a different way: an aspect of life is frequently not perceived as a problem, as something that cries for a solution, until expert advice or technological objects appear claiming to be the solution. The project of persuading the prospective users that the object in question has use value is then mobilized. Such users must be convinced of this or they will not part with their money. 'Interest free' purchasing terms, glossy advertising targeted at particular groups, allusions to lifestyle 'choices', tactics to distinguish the product from others, plus 'free' goods with purchases made by a certain date, are just some of the tactics of persuasion that are mobilized in this process.

We become, via these kinds of methods, consumers of expertise. This may be in the form of verbal instruction or locked inside the technological implement we purchase and then use. Even the experts succumb to this when venturing outside the narrow fields of their own specialism, with much of the expertise entering our lives without being invited, or seeking our permission. Think, for instance, of the increasingly sophisticated technology that is deployed for the purposes of routine surveillance. At one level this is justified according to the greater freedom of movement that is afforded by their presence. Yet that may also mean the power to exclude certain persons who are considered 'undesirable' and restrictions over freedom of movement. In extreme cases, therefore, they may even make us helpless victims of someone else's arbitrary decisions. Nevertheless, much of the technology that is used in everyday life is meant to enhance, not limit our range of choices. It is sold to us on the basis of providing more freedom by exercising more control over our lives. By and large, we welcome new technological offers as liberating or making life richer and allowing us to do old things faster and with less fatigue. They even enable people to do things they never did, or could not achieve, before their invention.

We need to be persuaded of this potential. So many experts, armed with numerous tactics and enormous sums of money, are routinely deployed in order to convey the belief that we can trust what we hear and see. After all, what other ways do we have of knowing? In the gap between new products and their potential to create and satisfy needs, marketing steps in to induce a process in which needs melt into desires which, if not met, will lead potential consumers to be unfulfilled in their aspirations. We may not even know what need the latest product on offer is meant to satisfy. Take, for example, the idea of something being a threat, but whose existence is beyond our senses to comprehend. Washing ourselves with 'ordinary' soap may not remove the 'deep dirt' which can apparently be remedied by using special washing lotions. What about those invisible bacteria that accumulate on our teeth which ordinary brushing cannot remove and so require a special liquid with which to gargle every day? Perhaps we also did not know that our camera is absurdly primitive and unable to respond to the 'normal' demands which we place on it and so often leads to disappointment when we see the results. In this case we need a new fully automatic one that will enable us to become better photographers and enjoy better photographs that capture important and memorable moments.

Once told all those things, perhaps we might wish to obtain the products in order to satisfy our needs, and once those are identified, to fail to act seems wrong. When opportunities are presented, doing nothing will be evidence of our negligence and will somehow detract from our self-esteem and the respect we might command from others. These objects become indicative of what we are and offer something in terms of what we might become. Think of this relationship in terms of a scale. At one end we may view objects as things to be utilized in the service of our ends. In the middle of the scale this relationship is modified as we interact with objects such that they co-construct our identities and our skills and characteristics are modified as a result. At the other end of the scale, things are very different. This position was expressed by Marshall McLuhan, a leading analyst and commentator on the growth of electronic media and communications, when he observed that we cannot escape the embrace of new technology unless we escape from society itself and so 'By consistently embracing all these technologies, we inevitably relate ourselves to them as servomechanisms'.

In most cases to obtain something means to purchase it. Those wonderful, skilful and powerful things tend to come as commodities in that they are marketed, sold and paid for with money. Someone wants to sell them to us in order to make a profit. To achieve this, they first have to convince us that parting with our money is worth our while. This requires that the commodity has the *use value* that justifies its *exchange value*. Use value relates to the utility that a commodity has in relation to satisfying a human need, while exchange value refers to its ability to be exchanged for other goods or services. People who want to sell their products must therefore seek a distinction for their commodities by making the old products seem out of date, obsolete and inferior. Now, as we have indicated, a desire for the product must be created whereby any sacrifice that is incurred in its purchase is sidelined in favour of the wish to possess the commodity.

Advertising is central to this process and must aim to achieve two effects. First, our own understanding of our needs and the skills that satisfy them should be rendered at least questionable and, at most, inadequate. As a result we feel we are not good judges of what we truly need and what we should do to address the problem. Second, that there exists solutions that are dependable methods for addressing our ignorance or poor judgement. In these two aims we see the fine line that exist between the dissemination of information and the numerous techniques of persuasion that are routinely employed to target particular groups of consumers. In commercials, for example, those who seek to achieve their tasks employing 'old-fashioned' methods may be the subject of ridicule or, alternatively, the product on offer is sold as a means of realizing their dreams.

These forms of advertising often employ a trustworthy authority who testifies to the reliability of the product on offer. Such an authority may be embodied in a number of ways: for example, the dispassionate scientist who makes a judgement on the quality of a product apparently free from the influence of the fee they are paid for such a purpose; a dependable expert in car technology who was once a racing driver; testimony from an avuncular, well-wishing character who speaks about the wonders that some banking or insurance package offers the normal 'person in the street'; the trust in a product that comes from the endorsement of a caring and experienced mother; the use of an acknowledged, seasoned expert in the kind of job the product is meant to serve; a famous person that the viewer knows is also known to millions of other people and finally, in the striving for distinction in order to capture attention, the juxtaposition of unlikely pairs such as a bishop or nun driving a fast car in order to show that the product can unleash a part of people that was hitherto repressed. These are just some of the myriad of ways in which advertisers, as technicians of persuasion, seek to seduce audiences into the need for their products and an enormous amount of time and money is devoted to this effort.

Advertising copy and commercials are meant to encourage us and prompt us to buy a specific product. Between them, however, they promote our interest in commodities and the marketplaces (department stores, shopping malls) where the commodities may be found, as well as the desire to possess them. A single commercial message would hardly have an effect on our conduct if general interest were not already well entrenched and shopping turned into a daily fact of life. In other words, the 'persuading efforts' of advertising agencies appeal to what is assumed to be an already established consumer attitude and, in so doing, reinforce it.

To endorse such an attitude means seeing everyday life as a series of problems which can be specified and clearly defined in advance and thus singled out and acted upon. Nothing, in other words, is beyond control and even when such a situation might arise, there are ways of ameliorating or even rectifying its effects. This induces a sense of responsibility in that dealing with actual or potential problems is one's duty which ought not to be neglected without incurring guilt or shame. For every problem, therefore, there is a solution that is prepared for the needs of the individual consumer who needs only to go shopping and exchange money for goods and services. If they cannot afford it now, they can always pay later through various schemes that can be tailored to their income. Aside from gaining the power to possess them once found, the main focus is upon translating the task of learning the art of living as the effort to acquire the skill of finding such objects and recipes. Links are established in such an attitude between identity, shopping skills and purchasing power. Through advertising, a mother's identity may therefore become bound up with the ability to locate the best washing powder and the best washing machine to satisfy the needs of her family from which she derives her pleasure, as well as the capability to afford them in order to meet such needs. Other needs and forms of recognition are bracketed in the process of persuading consumers of the connections between identity, need, product, fulfilment and satisfaction through purchase.

The consumer attitude concerns the apparently inextricable relationship between life and the marketplace. It orients every desire and each effort in the search for a tool or an expertise one can buy. The problem of control over the wider setting of life – something which most of us will never achieve – is subsumed into a multitude of small purchasing acts that are, in principle, within the reach of the majority of consumers. In this way, issues that are not assumed to be *public* in that they are shared and *social*, are *privatized* and *individualized*. Thus, it becomes each person's duty to improve themselves and their lives, to overcome their shortcomings, *as if* all had equal access to the means for this purpose and our relations with others and the environments which we inhabit were not of fundamental significance in this process. Thus the unbearable din of heavy traffic is translated into the urge to install double-glazing and polluted urban air is dealt with by the purchase of eye drops and facemasks. The oppressed conditions of an overworked wife and mother is ameliorated by packets of painkillers and/or prescribed anti-depressants, while the dilapidation of public transport is responded to by purchasing a car and thereby adding to noise, pollution, congestion and stress. However, these situations can always be responded to via references to the 'freedom to choose' that underpins the sovereignty of the consumer.

Lifestyles, Products and the Market

Our lives are thus forged into individual affairs and to call attention to extra-individual factors is believed to deny responsibility for the situations in which we find ourselves. The activity of being a consumer makes us into an individual, yet almost always what we create and produce takes place in the company of others. Reproduction is the most important thing that occurs in a society because without this, there would be no future generations and the economy would perish. Yet what recognition is afforded by the economy to motherhood and parenthood in general? This is translated into a consumer attitude whereby responsible parenting is the purchase of the latest baby products. It seems in the end that the message is that we are made up of the things we buy and own. Tell us what you buy, why you buy it and in what shops you make your purchase and we can tell who you are, or wish to become. Just as dealing with our problems is increasingly privatized, so too is the shaping of our personal identities. Our self-assertion, self-esteem and the task of forging ourselves into concrete persons are ours alone. We stand as testimonies to our intentions, diligence and persistence and are accountable for whatever is the product of our actions.

We are ably assisted in this task for there are plenty of models from which we can choose and many more that will arrive tomorrow. They come complete with all that is required to assemble them: they are genuine DIY 'identikits'. Even when the technicians of persuasion, via carefully crafted advertising, offer us single, specific products ostensibly addressed to a single, specific need, they are on the whole shown against a clearly portrayed background of the lifestyle to which they 'naturally' belong. Just compare the dress, language, pastimes and even physical shapes of the people in adverts that are meant to encourage us to drink a given brand of beer with the equivalent features of those in commercials selling an exquisite brand of perfume, luxury car, or even cat and dog food. What is being sold is not simply the value of a product, but its symbolic significance as a building block within a particular lifestyle.

The models fluctuate according to *fashion*. Any sense of complacency is the enemy of production and consumption and to keep its wheels moving forward requires that the consumer attitude is relentless in its desires. Were we to keep products as long as they served their ostensible uses, market activity would soon grind to a halt. The phenomenon of fashion prevents this from happening. Things are discarded and replaced not because they have lost their usefulness, but because they went out of fashion. Products then become easily recognizable, from their looks, as goods chosen and obtained by consumers whose tastes are clearly outdated and so their presence casts doubt on the status of their owners as respectable and responsible consumers. To retain this status, one must keep up with the changing offers of the market and to obtain them means to reconfirm a social capacity – only, that is, until many other consumers do the same. At that point the fashionable items that originally bestowed a distinction become 'common' or 'vulgar' and are ready to go out of fashion, only to be eagerly replaced by something else.

Models also vary in the degree of popularity that they enjoy in particular social circles and the amount of respect that they are likely to bestow upon their owners. They possess, therefore, differential rates of attraction according to the social position in which consumers finds themselves. By selecting a given model, purchasing all its necessary accoutrements and diligently practising it, we portray an image as being a member of a group that approves of such a model and adopts it as its trademark; it becomes a visible sign of belonging. To render oneself a visible member of a group is to wear and own the right signs: the appropriate dress, the correct CDs and watching and discussing the recognized TV programmes and films. Bedroom walls become embellished with the group-specific adornments and evenings are spent at specific places and exhibit particular patterns of behaviour and conversation.

The 'tribes' we join in search of our identities are totally unlike those that explorers are said to have discovered in 'distant lands'. What makes the tribes we join by purchasing their symbols superficially similar to these is that both set themselves apart from other groups and seek to underline their separate identity and avoid confusion; both cede their own identity to their members – define them by proxy. Nevertheless, here the similarity ends and a decisive difference begins, for these consumer-oriented *neo-tribes* have no councils of elders or boards or admission committees to decide who has the right to be in and who ought to be kept out. They employ no gatekeepers and no border guards. They have no institution of authority – no Supreme Court which may pronounce on the correctness of members' behaviour. In short, the form of control is dissimilar and they do not undertake to monitor degrees of conformity at a collective level. Thus, it seems that one can wander freely from one neo-tribe to another by changing one's dress, refurbishing one's flat and spending one's free time at different places.

These differences appear as a result of what is only a casual glance. After all, if neo-tribes do not guard entry in a formal manner, there is something else which does – *the market*. Neo-tribes are, in essence, lifestyles and these relate to styles of consumption. Access to consumption leads through the market and to acts of purchasing commodities. There are few things one can consume without first buying them and these products are often deployed as the building blocks of recognizable lifestyles. If some of them do contribute to a specific lifestyle, they may be looked down on, deprived of glamour and prestige, disdained, considered unattractive and even degrading. Indeed, wearing the wrong type of training shoe has been linked to bullying in school playgrounds. What, therefore, of those who lack the means to exercise the choices that are apparently open to all? They cannot afford to be choosy and their acts of consumption are thereby limited. The silence surrounding those who find themselves in conditions of poverty in a consumer-oriented society becomes deafening.

The apparent availability of a wide and growing range of neo-tribes, each sporting a different lifestyle, has a powerful yet ambiguous effect on our lives. On the one hand, we experience it as the dismantling of all limitations to our freedom. We are apparently free to move from one personal quality to another, choose what we want to be and what we want to make of ourselves. No force seems to hold us back and no dream seems to be improper in that it is at odds with either our existing or potential social position. This feels like liberation from constraint: an exhilarating experience in which everything, in principle, is within our reach and no condition is final and irrevocable. Nevertheless, each new point of arrival, no matter how lasting or temporary, appears as a result of the way in which we have exercised our freedom in the past. Thus, it is us and us alone who can be blamed for where we stand, or praised depending on the degrees of satisfaction that are derived from recognition from others mediated via the objects we possess.

We are all 'self-made persons' and if not, have the potential to become those to whom we should aspire to be. Repeatedly we find ourselves reminded that there is no justification for cutting our ambitions short and that the only constraints we face are those that reside within us as individuals – in *isolation* from one another. We thus face challenges in which the only impediment to achievement is a matter of individual attitude. Every lifestyle is a challenge. If we find it attractive, if it is more vaunted than ours is, proclaimed more enjoyable or respectable than our own, we can feel *deprived*. We feel seduced by it, drawn to it, prompted to do our best in order to become part of it. Our current lifestyle begins to lose its allurement and no longer brings us the satisfaction it once provided.

As the wheels of production and consumption are lubricated by the frenetic activity that guards against the dangers of complacency, there is no apparent halt to efforts directed at finding suitable lifestyles. At what point can we say 'We have arrived, achieved all we wanted and so can now relax and take it easy'? Just when this may be possible, a new attraction will appear on the horizon and celebration feels like an indulgence that derives from an unjustified contentment. The result of this freedom to choose in pursuit of the unattainable appears to be condemned to remain forever in a state of deprivation. The sheer availability of ever-new temptations and their apparent accessibility detract from any achievement.

When the sky is the limit, no earthly destination seems pleasant enough to satisfy us. Publicly flaunted lifestyles not only are numerous and varied, but also are represented as differing in value and so in the distinctions that they bestow on their practitioners. When we settle for less than the best in the pursuit of cultivating our selves, we may then believe that our not very prestigious social standing is a natural effect of a half-hearted self-cultivating diligence.

The story does not end at potential accessibility, but at the temptations that derive from visibility. What makes other lifestyles so temptingly close and within reach is that they are not practised in secrecy. On the contrary, they appear so seductively open and inviting because neo-tribes do not live within fortresses guarded by impregnable walls and so they may be reached and entered. That said, despite appearances to the contrary, entry is not free for the gatekeepers are invisible. What are referred to as part of everyday parlance as 'market forces' do not wear uniforms and they deny all responsibility for the final success or failure of the escapade. The effects of global market forces, for instance, not only are a description for a state of affairs, but also may be appealed to as having consequences for which no one has responsibility, or to which a response is demanded that necessitates transformations in attitude and organization. In contrast, state regulation of needs and their satisfaction, which cannot but stay visible, are more vulnerable to public protest and an easier target for collective efforts aimed at reform.

Of course, exceptions occur as is evident from protests in different countries against the effects of globalization. In the absence of effective collective resistance, however, the hapless walker must believe that it was their own fault, pure and simple, for their inability to achieve their desires. The stakes are high for the individual and so for the society of which they are a part, for they risk losing faith in themselves, in the strength of their character, intelligence, talents, motivation and stamina. Internalization of blame is manifest in self-questioning and if they can afford the cost and/or have access to such a service, they might seek the services of an expert to repair their faulty personality. What might result from this process?

Suspicions are likely to be confirmed during the consultations. After all, the identification of any cause beyond that which an individual can act upon may be considered an indulgence for it is not within the power of the individual to alter. An inner flaw, something hidden in the broken selves of the defeated that prevented them from availing themselves of the opportunities which were undoubtedly there all along, will be revealed. Anger born of frustration is not likely to spill over and be directed at the outside world. The invisible gatekeepers barring the intended way will remain invisible and more secure than ever. By default, the dream-states that they so alluringly paint will not be discredited as a result. The unsuccessful are thus also denied the tempting consolation of decrying in retrospect the value of the lifestyles they sought to adopt in vain. It has been noted that the failure to reach the goals that are advertised as superior and richly satisfying results in feelings of resentment that are aimed not simply against the goals themselves, spread to those people who boast of having attained them, or stand as symbols of their achievement. However, that too can be constructed as the response of an individual who, when abstracted from the social conditions of which they are a part, is held fully responsible for their actions. Any striving for understanding in these terms is then taken to be an excuse for their behaviour, as opposed to a constructive attempt to find more longer-term solutions to such problems.

Even the most elaborate lifestyles must be represented as universally available if they are to be successfully marketed. It is their alleged accessibility that is the necessary condition of their seductiveness. They inspire the shopping motivation and interest of the consumers because the prospective buyers believe that the models they seek are attainable. In addition they must be admired in order that the models are legitimate objects of practical action and not merely of respectful contemplation. These forms of presentation, which the market can ill afford to abandon in its claims, imply an *equality* of consumers in terms of their capacity freely to determine their social standing. In the light of such assumed equality, the failure to obtain goods that others enjoy is bound to create feelings of frustration and resentment.

This failure seems unavoidable. The genuine accessibility of the alternative lifestyles is determined by the prospective practitioners' ability to pay. Quite simply, some people have more money than others and thus more practical freedom of choice. In particular, those with the largest amount of money, who possess the true passports to the wonders of the market, can afford the most lauded, coveted and hence most prestigious and admired styles. Yet this is a tautology, that is, a statement which defines the things it speaks about while pretending to explain them. This occurs because the styles which can be obtained by relatively few people with particularly large stocks of wealth are by the same token seen as the most distinguished and worthy of marvel. It is their rarity that is admired and practical inaccessibility that makes them wonderful. Therefore, once acquired they are worn with pride, as distinctive marks of exclusive, exceptional social position. They are the signs of the 'best people' as occupants of the 'best lifestyles'. Both the commodities and the people who use them – display being one of the main uses – derive the high esteem they enjoy precisely from this 'marriage' to each other.

All commodities have a price tag. These tags select the pool of potential customers. They draw boundaries between the realistic, unrealistic and feasible which a given consumer cannot overstep. Behind the osten-

sible equality of chances the market promotes and advertises lies the practical *inequality* of consumers in terms of sharply differentiated degrees of
practical freedom of choice. This inequality is felt as oppression and a
stimulus at the same time. It generates the painful experience of deprivation, with all the morbid consequences for self-esteem which we have
surveyed before. It also triggers off zealous efforts to enhance one's consumer capacity – efforts that secure an unabating demand for what the
market offers.

Its championship of equality notwithstanding, the market thereby produces and reinstates inequality in a society made of consumers. The typically market-induced or market-serviced kind of inequality is kept alive
and perpetually reproduced through the price mechanism. The marketed
lifestyles bestow the sought-after distinction because their price tags put
them out of reach of the less well-off consumers. In turn, this distinction-
bestowing function adds to their attraction and supports the high price
attached to them. At the end of the day, it transpires that with all the
alleged freedom of consumer choice, the marketed lifestyles are not distributed evenly or randomly; they tend to concentrate in a particular part
of society and acquire the role of a sign of social standing. Therefore,
lifestyles tend to become class-specific. The fact that they are assembled
from items that are all available in shops does not make them vehicles of
equality. This, however, makes them less bearable, more difficult to endure for the relatively poor and deprived, than it was when possessions
were overtly ascribed to the already occupied, often inherited and immutable, social ranks. Beneath the claim that suggests achievement is within
the reach of all lies the reality of ascription that is set according to an
unequal distribution of the ability to pay. The struggle for recognition, in
this sense, may arrive only with redistribution.

The market thrives on the inequality of income and wealth, but it does
not appear to recognize ranks. All vehicles of inequality are denied but
those of the price tag. Goods must be accessible to everybody who can
afford to pay their price. A purchasing ability is the only entitlement that
the market can recognize. It is for this reason that in a market-dominated
consumer society the resistance to all other, ascribed inequality grows to
unprecedented proportion. Exclusive clubs that do not accept members
from certain ethnic groups and/or women, restaurants or hotels that bar
access to customers because they have the 'wrong colour of skin', estate
developers who will not sell property for a similar reason, all find themselves under attack. The overwhelming power of market-supported criteria of social differentiation seemingly invalidates all its competitors. Quite
simply, there should be no goods that money cannot buy and the market
is not assumed to be the embodiment of particular values and prejudices,
but a universal and value-free force that all reasonable people ought to
accept.

Despite claims to the contrary, market-oriented and ethnicity-grounded deprivations overlap. The groups that are held in an inferior position by 'ascriptive' restrictions are usually also employed in poorly paid jobs, so that they cannot afford the lifestyles destined for those who benefit from their labours. In this case, the ascriptive character of the deprivation remains hidden. Visible inequalities are explained away as the results of the lesser talents, industry or acumen of the members of the deprived group; were it not for their innate faults, they would succeed like everyone else. To become like those who they should envy and wish to imitate would be within their reach if they acted on their wishes. The inequality upon which the market relies is thereby enabled by the barriers to entry that such groups routinely encounter, thus giving further rise to explanations that are targeted not at the conditions in which such groups find themselves and the prejudices they encounter, but at the characteristics assumed to be peculiar to 'their' group.

Even those members of the otherwise depressed category who succeed in market terms still find the gates to certain styles of life firmly shut. They have the financial power to afford the high fees of the club or hotel, but are barred entry. The ascriptive character of their deprivation is thereby exposed and they learn that, contrary to promise, money cannot buy everything and so there is more to human placement in society, to their well-being and dignity, than diligently earning money and spending it. As far as we know, people may differ in their abilities to buy tickets, but should anyone be refused a ticket if they can afford one?

Given the claim in a market society that goods and services are open to those who can afford them, ascriptive differentiation of opportunities is unjustifiable. This is why a rebellion against discrimination on any but 'purchasing ability' grounds tends to be led by the better-off, more successful members of the discriminated groups. The era of 'self-made persons', of the proliferation of lifestyle 'tribes', of differentiation through styles of consumption is also an era of resistance to racial, ethnic, religious and gender discrimination. Here we find struggles for *human rights* expressed in terms of the removal of any restrictions except those which may be overcome by the effort of any human being as an individual.

Summary

Our identities are being transformed in various ways not only through the introduction of new technologies, but also through the increasing role that markets play in our everyday lives. For those who can afford and have access to them, new technologies require a constant updating of skills. Nevertheless, there is a question over whether we use such means towards our ends, or the means becomes an end in itself. As we orient ourselves towards the future, some science-fiction writings seem to become more pertinent as strict demarcations between humans and machines increasingly blur. The implantation of mechanical valves and the fitting of artificial limbs to the human body may be more than just the recovery of 'natural' functioning, but have the potential to serve as enhancements to human-mechanical capabilities. Technological innovations may permit greater control, but with what consequences and for whom? These matters require an understanding that is derived from outside of a process that recognizes nothing other than its own rationalizations.

Important ethical issues are raised by such questions. Yet in societies driven by the logic of consumerism, where do the resources lie from which to draw for this purpose? Apparently, the only thing that is recognized here is the ability to pay, but we have seen that this is a supposed equality that is met by the prejudices that exist within a society. Equality of opportunity and outcome are differentially distributed, so not only do people bring different capacities to choose to the marketplace, but also it rewards them according to their acceptability within the order of things. Thus even the possession of money may not be sufficient to benefit from such arrangements and protests against such inequity are hardly universal, but far from unusual. In the mean time, we are continually encouraged to consume in the pursuit of the unattainable – the perfect lifestyle in which contentment reigns supreme.

part three

LOOKING BACK AND LOOKING FORWARD

chapter ten

THINKING SOCIOLOGICALLY

Chapter by chapter, we have travelled together through a world of daily experience in terms of the changing issues that both surround and inform our lives. With sociology as our guide in this journey, it was offered the task of commenting on what we see and do. As on any guided tour, we hoped that our guide would not miss anything of importance and would bring to our attention those things which, if left to ourselves, we might pass by unnoticed. We might also expect our guide to explain things that we knew only superficially and even provide a perspective that, hitherto, we had not considered. At the end of our tour we might realistically hope that we would know more and will have improved our understanding as a result.

The Sociological Eye

Understanding is at the core of social life. Following the philosopher Charles Taylor, we may speak of understanding in two senses. First, there is an understanding of things in terms of their place in a meaningful order. What may at first seem puzzling and even threatening may then be understood in terms of its relations with those aspects of our lives that are more familiar to us. As we have also seen in our journey, there are events and practices that are often taken to be alien and threatening. For this reason, to seek to explain those may well prove challenging to existing ways of seeing. These ways of seeing relate to a second sense of understanding that informs our knowledge of an environment that enables us to get on and practise within it. This is the tacit knowledge that we routinely draw upon in our actions without which we could not accomplish and orientate our lives.

Between these two senses of understanding there is a tension. Both display a complexity that is indicative of the richness of the human condition. The former, however, can appear as a critique of the latter through its potential to question that which is taken-for-granted in our everyday lives. It is a form of understanding via a *relationism* that situates people in terms of how their lives are bound up with others. In the process it shows not only how our lives are achievements, but also how they relate to events and processes that are not normally part of our everyday understandings.

Our focus in this book has been informed by both of these dimensions of understanding. After all, how we get on with others and how that relates to us as persons, as well as the role that social conditions and relations in general play in our lives, better enables us to cope with the issues we face in everyday life. We are not suggesting that our attempts to solve them will automatically be more successful as a result, but we may then know how to frame problems in ways that can provide more long-lasting solutions. Thinking sociologically, therefore, is central to that task, but its success is dependent upon factors that lie outside the influence of any discipline. Framing problems that require action and finding appropriate solutions is an ongoing task and this requires a willingness to listen and act, as well as the capability to bring about change. The role of sociology as a disciplined way of thinking is to inform this process. To this extent, it offers something that is fundamental to social life in general: that is, an interpretation of experiences through the processes of understanding and explanation. For this task, it has acquitted itself very well.

Let us characterize sociology as a commentary on social life. While providing a series of explanatory footnotes to our experiences, it also raises implications for how we conduct our lives. In this way it acts as a means for refining the knowledge we possess and employ in our daily life by bringing into focus not only our achievements, but also the constraints and possibilities we face by connecting our actions to the positions and conditions in which we find ourselves. Sociology is a disciplined eye that both examines 'how' we get on in our daily lives, and locates those details onto a 'map' that extends beyond those immediate experiences. We can then see how the territories we inhabit fit into and relate to a world that we may have no opportunity to explore ourselves but which, nevertheless, may inform and structure our lives.

The differences we might experience before and after reading sociological studies are not simply the same as those between error and truth. While sociology may correct our impressions and challenge our opinions, our actions can be described and explained at different planes of experience. This, after all, is exactly what happens in social life when we find ourselves in different contexts: for example, when working, being at home, shopping or with friends at a party. To say, therefore, that there is one explanation that will suffice for all times and places is not only inaccurate, but also forecloses differences within the present and possibilities for the future. People do act contrary to expectations and that is part of what it is to exercise freedom. Sociology can explain the reasons for this, but because of its modes of study it is an inducement to go on searching in the quest for understanding. There is no end to this as there is no final resting-place where the *absolute* truth resides. Instead our knowledge as in all spheres of scientific endeavour, improves in terms of its adequacy to explain those things that were previously undiscovered or little understood.

Going back to our two senses of understanding, sociology not only illuminates the means through which we conduct our lives, but also has the effect of questioning such adequacy through the production of studies and works that prod and challenge the imagination. This may be a demanding process in that it views what are familiar things from unexpected and unexplored angles. Feelings of confusion can then arise because of the beliefs that we carry about forms of knowledge and what we can expect of them. We often expect them to justify our existing ideas, or provide new knowledge which does not disturb our understandings, but adds to them in significant ways. Of course, sociological knowledge may fulfil both of these expectations. Yet (as we have said) it may also question these by its refusal to close down that which is open or ambivalent in our lives. Because of this it raises possibilities for thinking differently by including those aspects of our lives that are normally bracketed from consideration. For us, this makes it a very practical discipline, but perhaps not in the ways that this term is often invoked by those who seek to make their visions of society into comfortable realities that, as we have seen, include by virtue of being exclusive.

▽

Social Expectations and Sociological Thought

The tensions between the above forms of understanding and the expectations that are often made of scientific knowledge are manifest in what is expected of sociological thinking. First, that it is a 'science'. Although it has been shown that the actual practice of science does not live up to these criteria, this frequently takes the following form: science is a collection of practices that claims, or ought to claim, a clear and so unproblematic superiority over forms of knowledge and can therefore produce reliable and valid information in the name of *the* truth. Using this as a basis for judgement, sociologists can then be placed alongside other experts who can tell us what our problems are and what we must do about them.

This expectation is born of a belief in 'scientism' which, as Jürgen

Habermas put it, is 'the conviction that we can no longer understand science as one form of possible knowledge, but rather must identify knowledge with science'. Sociology is then viewed as a form of DIY briefing, with its textbooks containing foolproof information about how to succeed in life, where success is measured in terms of how to get what we want and how to jump over or bypass anything that may stand in our way. This is informed by the belief that freedom derives from the ability to control a situation and thereby subordinate it to our purposes. The promise of knowledge is then taken to be its ability to tell us, beyond any doubt, what will happen and that this, in turn, will enable one to act freely and rationally in the pursuit of particular ends. Armed with this knowledge, the only moves that will be made are those guaranteed to bring about the desired results.

For a person to be in control must mean, in one way or another, luring, forcing or otherwise causing other people, who are always part of the social conditions, to behave in a way that helps them obtain what they want. As a rule, control over a situation cannot but mean control over other people. Such expectations translate into the belief that the art of life involves how we can both win friends and control people. Despite these aims being in clear tension, sociology can then find its services being enlisted in the efforts to create order and evict chaos from social situations. As we have noted in previous chapters, this is a distinctive mark of modern times. By exploring the hopes, wishes, desires and motivations that inform human action, sociologists may be expected to provide information about the way things need to be arranged in order to elicit the kind of behaviour that people ought to exhibit. This entails the elimination of any conduct that the designed model of order would render unsuitable. For instance, the managers of call centres and factories may enlist the help of sociologists in order to extract more productivity from their employees; army commanders may ask them to conduct surveys and observation studies that enable greater discipline within the ranks or reveal information concerning enemy targets; police forces may commission proposals on how to disperse crowds and deploy methods of surveillance effectively; supermarkets may send their security officers on courses designed to detect and reduce shoplifting; companies may seek expertise in order to seduce prospective customers into buying their products and public relations officers may want to know the best methods for rendering politicians more popular and electable by appearing to be 'in touch' with the people.

All these demands amount to the same thing: sociologists should offer advice on how to combat those things that are already defined as problems by particular groups in ways that ignore, or find 'irrelevant', alternative explanations and solutions. One outcome may be to reduce the freedom of some people so that their choices are confined and their conduct controlled according to the desires of those who commission the studies. Knowledge is required on how to transform the people in question from *subjects* of their own action into *objects* of intervention or manipulation. Understanding in terms of the relations that exist between a person and their environment is then subordinated to the wishes and images of those who seek control in the first place. Any subsequent deviations from those expectations are likely to demand ever greater forms of control, rather than a questioning of the whole enterprise itself. Indeed, the latter may be considered an indulgent attitude that is deemed a luxury in the face of situated 'necessities'.

These expectations amount to the demand that sociological thinking should produce recipes for the control of human interaction. What we see here is the desire to possess control over the objects of study. This, as we saw in relation to the interactions between culture and nature, has a long history whereby the latter was to become an object of intervention so that it could be subordinated to the will and purpose of those who sought to utilize resources for the better satisfaction of their own needs. A language, purified of intent and embroiled in technicalities that appeared to be distanced from emotion, then emerged in which the objects of intervention received, but did not generate or question, actions. They were devoid of being related in an overall balance and so having been compartmentalized were amenable to manipulation in order to fulfil particular ends. So described, the natural world was conceived as a 'free for all': a virgin territory waiting to be tilled and transformed into a purposefully designed plot better suited to human habitation. At no time were questions of balance raised until, that is, they were recognized to be near to exhaustion and the results of such intervention led to the extinction of whole species and vital habitats. In the mean time, a whole history about the alternative sources of energy and practices that were available, but remained subordinated to the pursuit of particular ends, awaited its emergence.

The social world can be explored with this purpose in mind. It may be studied so that *some* human beings may give it the shape they desire and a knowledge can emerge that not only explains, but also justifies this process. In the process reality can be seen as something that is resistant to purposeful activity. More knowledge may then be deployed and nurtured in order to find out how the resistance can be broken. In the mean time, raising any doubts about such a process can be turned into the questioning of a conquest that means the emancipation of humanity from constraints and the apparent enhancement, so to speak, of collective freedom. Of course, this may be the result in some areas of activity, but the assumed neutrality of this model of knowledge production is devoid of the very issues that render human life purposeful and meaningful: that is, the ethical and moral dimensions to our existence.

Sociology: Three Strategies in Emergence from the Shadows

Any discipline that seeks legitimacy in such a context must seek to anticipate this model of knowledge production. Any kind of knowledge that aspires to obtain public recognition through a place in the academic world and a share in public resources needs to prove that it can deliver a similarly useful model. Thus we find that even if the role of architects or builders of the social order did not cross the minds of the early sociologists (for some it did) and even if the only thing they wanted was to comprehend the human condition more fully, when they sought to construct the discipline of sociology they could hardly avoid the dominant conceptions of what was held to be 'good knowledge'. Therefore, at some point a construction and demonstration were needed that human life and activity could be studied under the same conditions. Not surprisingly, therefore, they felt it incumbent upon them to prove that sociology could elevate itself to a status whereby it would be recognized as a legitimate activity in the terms expressed earlier.

Within the institutions where the struggle for disciplinary recognition took place, we find sociological discourse taking a particular shape, with the effort to make sociology accord to the discourse of scientism becoming a task that took pride of place among the concerns of the participants. Among these we can discern strategies that were an interpretation and subsequent response to these new demands. We are not suggesting that these are exhaustive of the diversity of sociological perspectives that are currently on offer. We are, however, saying that elements of all three have converged to inform and shape the dynamics of sociology as it is currently constituted and the expectations that people have of its knowledge.

Our first strategy is concerned with a *replication* of the scientific enterprise as laid down by these dominant expectations. Our leading thinker here is one whose intellectual legacy is still being considered, given not only the breadth and depth of his interests, but the relation between his writings and the social context in which he found himself. Emile Durkheim sought nothing less than a basis for sociology within a united set of social disciplines aimed at providing a rational, systematic and empirical basis for society's civil religion. In the process he pursued a model of science which was characterized first and foremost by its ability to treat the object of study as strictly separate from the studying subject. The subject thus gazes upon an object 'out there' that can be observed and described in a neutral and detached language. From this point of view scientific disciplines do not differ in method, but in their attention to distinct areas of reality. The world is thereby partitioned into plots with each being researched by a scientific discipline that draws boundaries around its object of curiosity. Researchers employ the same kind of tools and command the same kind of technical skills when engaged in an activity that is subject to the same methodological rules and codes of behaviour. A scientific gaze is then cast upon those things that are separate from their activities and simply await observation, description and explanation. What demarcates scientific disciplines is solely the division of the territory of investigation, with each taking care of its own 'collection of things'.

Sociology, according to this model, is like a seafaring explorer, seeking to discover a terrain over which no one has claimed sovereignty. Durkheim found this in *social facts*. These are collective phenomena that are irreducible to any one individual. As shared beliefs and patterns of behaviour, they can be treated as things to be studied in an objective, detached fashion. These things appear to individuals as a reality that is tough, stubborn and independent of their will. They cannot necessarily be recognized, nor wished away. To that extent, they replicate the characteristics of the physical world in much the same way as a table or chair might occupy a room. To ignore them is akin to assuming that one can ignore gravity. In this sense, to transgress a social norm can result in punitive sanctions as a reminder not to transgress that which no person may alter.

We can say, therefore, that social phenomena, though obviously not existing without human beings, do not reside *inside* human beings as individuals, but *outside* them. Together with nature and its inviolable laws, they constitute a vital part of the objective environment of every human being. There would be no point in learning about those social phenomena by simply asking those people who are subjected to their force. The information would be hazy, partial and misleading. They might, instead, be asked about their reactions to the environment in order to see how changes in those situations might improve behaviour, or be indicative of those forces that reside within the environment itself.

In one important respect, as Durkheim agreed, social facts differ from the facts of nature. The connection between violating a law of nature and the damage that follows it is automatic: it has not been introduced by human design (or, for that matter, by anyone's design). The connection between violating the norm of society and the sufferings of norm-breakers is, on the contrary, 'human-made'. Certain conduct is punished because society condemns it and not because the conduct itself causes harm to its perpetrator (thus, stealing does no harm to the thief and may even be beneficial to them; if the thief suffers as a consequence of their actions, it is only because social sentiments militate against thieving). This difference, however, does not detract from the 'thing-like' character of social norms or from the feasibility of their objective study. Such thing-like social facts and not the states of mind or emotions of individuals (such as are avidly studied by psychologists) offer a genuine explanation of human conduct. Wishing to describe correctly and to explain human behaviour, the sociologist is thus entitled (and exhorted) to bypass the individual psyche, intentions and private meanings that only the individuals themselves can tell us about and concentrate instead on studying phenomena which can be observed from outside and would, in all probability, look the same to any observer watching them.

A very different strategy is to pursue a scientific status, but without replicating existing practices. We may term this one *reflection* and *modification*. Mainly associated with the work of Max Weber, the idea that sociology should selflessly imitate the practices of the physical sciences is rejected. Instead, it is proposed that sociological practice, without losing the precision expected from scientific knowledge, should be as different from that of the natural sciences as the human reality investigated by sociology is from the world studied by the sciences of nature. It is this reality that should drive sociology which, as a discipline, should be sensitive to the changes that take place within societies as a whole.

Human reality is different from the natural world because human actions are meaningful. People possess motives and act in order to reach the ends they set for themselves and these ends explain their actions. For this reason, human actions, unlike the spatial movements of physical bodies, need to be understood rather than explained. More precisely, to explain human actions means to understand them in the sense of grasping the meanings invested in them by actors. That human actions are meaningful is the foundation of *hermeneutics*. This refers to the theory and practice of a 'recovery of meaning' that is embedded in literary texts, paintings or any other product of a human creative spirit. In order to understand its meaning, the interpreters of the text must put themselves in the author's 'place': that is, to see the text through the author's eyes and think the author's thoughts. They should then link the author's actions to the historical situation in which they find themselves.

The hermeneutic circle – from the particularity of the author's experiences and their writings to the general historical context in which they wrote – does not depend on a uniform method that any person can apply with equal success, but on the talents of a single interpreter. If interpreters come forward with sharply different interpretations, one may choose one of the competing proposals because it is richer, more perceptive, profound, aesthetically pleasing or otherwise more satisfying than the rest. Clearly, this knowledge does not afford a sense of certainty that comes with the desire to mould order in the name of a power that demands unambiguous prescriptions. Despite these differences, however, Weber still argued that sociology can achieve a basis that is 'scientific'.

Not all human actions may be interpreted in this manner. As we have seen, much of our activity is either traditional or affective in the sense it is guided by habits or emotions. In both cases action is *unreflective*. When, for example, we act out of anger or follow a routine, we do not calculate our actions, nor pursue particular ends. Traditional and affective actions are determined by factors outside of our direct control and may be best comprehended when their cause is pointed out. What requires an understanding of meaning rather than a causal explanation are *rational* actions because they are calculated, controlled and oriented towards consciously considered ends (the 'in order to' actions). Thus, while traditions are manifold and emotions are thoroughly personal and idiosyncratic, the reasons we deploy to measure our ends against the means we select in order to achieve them, is common to all human beings. We can then wrest meaning out of observed action not by guessing what has been going on in the actors' heads, but by matching to the action a motive that makes sense and thus renders the action intelligible.

In this manner Weber argued that one rational mind may recognize itself in another rational mind. Further, that as long as the studied actions are rational, in the sense of being calculated and oriented towards a purpose, they can be rationally understood by postulating a meaning, not a cause. Therefore, sociological knowledge has a clear advantage over science in that it can not only describe, but also understand its objects. However thoroughly explored the world described by science, it remains meaningless, but sociology in the process of its discoveries recovers the meaning of reality.

There is also a third strategy that is not replication, nor reflection and modification, but what may be characterized as *demonstration by effect*. The aim here is to show that sociology had direct and effective practical applications. It was the pioneers of sociology in the USA that tended to pursue this end. Why? Because the USA is a country prominent for its pragmatic frame of mind and for viewing practical success as the supreme criterion of value and in the end, also of truth. As the pragmatist philosopher William James put it, 'It is quite evident that our obligation to acknowledge truth, so far from being unconditional, is tremendously conditioned'. With such arguments in mind, sociological research can provide knowledge whose results can be judged by those in pursuit of particular ends. In this way it can be employed to 'manipulate' reality and to change it in a way that agrees with needs and intentions whatever they may be and however they have been defined and selected.

From the start we see this strategy giving sociology a practical edge in its mission of social diagnosis. Its insights were sharpened in the study of recognized social problems like rising criminality, juvenile delinquency and gang behaviour, alcoholism, prostitution, the weakening of family ties and so on. Sociology thereby grounded its bid for social recognition in a promise to assist the administration of social processes. Sociology then places itself at the service of the construction and maintenance of social order and is seen to share the concerns of social administrators whose task it was to manage human conduct. The services of sociologists may then be deployed to defuse antagonism and prevent conflicts in factories and mines; to facilitate the adaptation of young soldiers in warweary army units; to promote new commercial products; to rehabilitate former criminals and to increase the effectiveness of social welfare provisions.

This strategy comes closest to the philosopher Francis Bacon's formula 'to subdue nature by submission'. Here we see a blend of truth with usefulness, information with control and knowledge with power. We also witness the judgement of sociological knowledge according to the practical benefits that it may bring to the management of social order. So we find ourselves, once again, confronting the idea that sociology provides solutions to the problems that are seen and articulated by the technicians of order. Society can then be viewed from the top, as an object of manipulation that throws up resistant material whose inner qualities must be known better in order to be made more pliable and receptive to the final shape that is desired.

Tensions within these expectations of sociological knowledge always return in a form that seeks to question its status. This is not surprising for the merger of sociological and managerial interests remains core to those who conceive of human relations in an instrumental form. The justification of knowledge is then seen to lie in terms of its application according to narrowly defined interests. Yet, as with the criticisms that have been made of the early pioneers of US sociology, for a discipline to define its success in terms of servicing the requirements of the powerful is, by default, to ignore alternative values, as well as to set the limits of its investigations within narrowly confined boundaries. What is then foreclosed is an understanding of potential alternative visions of social relations, as well as the possibilities for change that are pregnant within all contemporary arrangements.

Critics of this third strategy have pointed out that its pursuit amounts to taking sides and an active support for the extant asymmetry of social power. After all, not everyone can use knowledge construed from the managerial perspective as its application demands resources that only the managers command and may deploy. Sociology thus enhances the control of those who are already in control and further shifts the stakes in favour of those who already enjoy a better hand. The causes of inequality, misunderstanding and social injustice are thereby served.

Because of the above reasons, sociology attracts controversy. It becomes a target for ambivalence within society and its work becomes subjected to pressures that are not within its power to reconcile. What one side may ask sociology to achieve, the other side may view as an abomination and is determined to resist. Therefore, conflicting expectations are bound to inform its practice, whatever may be the evident rigours of its methodology, methods and the refinement of its theoretical insights. It can then fall victim to real social conflicts that are part of the tensions, ambivalence and contradictions within society at large. Sociology, in its raising of social issues through systematic investigation, may find itself used as a convenient target that displaces the need for serious debate and action. However, let us now turn our gaze outwards towards society itself to seek an understanding for this state of affairs.

Social Tensions, Forms of Life and Sociological Targets

We can see this resulting from the project of *rationalization* that is inherent in modern society, with rationality presenting itself as a two-edged sword. On the one hand, it clearly assists in the process of obtaining more control over actions. Rational calculation (as we have seen) informs actions in a manner that is better suited to selected ends and thus increases its effectiveness according to selected criteria. On the whole, it seems that rational individuals are more likely to achieve their ends in comparison to those who do not plan, calculate and monitor their actions. Placed in the service of the individual, rationality may increase the scope of individual freedom. There is also another side to rationality. Once applied to the environment of individual action – to the organization of the society at large – rational analysis can serve to limit choices or diminish the range of means from which individuals may draw in order to pursue their ends. Therefore, it may constrain individual freedom. Sociology reflects this tension, while also providing the means through which to understand its effects better and so more effectively address the issues and problems it raises in modern society. As Marshall McLuhan wrote in relation to new technologies, if we understand the ways in which they are transforming our lives, 'we can anticipate and control them; but if we continue in our self-induced subliminal trance, we will be their slaves'.

Given these pressures and despite the evident methodological rigours of Weber and Durkheim, they both exhibited a concern with freedom. Durkheim was critical of a utilitarianism informed by calculations aimed at maximizing the ends of individual actors. How, he asked, could this provide a societal basis for happiness and contentment within the individual? Weber was also concerned for those values that were core to the human condition, but found themselves increasingly subjected to the calculation of instrumental rationality. Similarly, Robert Park, one of the early pioneers of sociology in the USA, wrote about how new forms of communication created associations that not only intensified competition between people, but also brought with them the potential to increase understanding.

In our present times these same concerns are being voiced. Thus we hear of how trust is fundamental to human relations, but often finds itself undermined by the calculations of global businesses who command power and wealth that is equivalent to some nations, yet they remain democratically unaccountable. For them, any resistance to encroachments on ways of life may be nothing more than manifestations of local impediments to the realization of their global goals. We also hear about community values and their importance for social solidarity. Yet, as we have seen in our journey, this often translates into a defensive attitude towards the 'other'. As Richard Sennett notes, the most important aspects of community architecture then become 'the walls against a hostile economic order'. As a result, to paraphrase Paul Virilio, politics becomes linked with a freedom from fear, while social security becomes associated with the right to consume.

What we see here are the deployment of resources according to the realization of particular goals and boundary-making activities as responses to social conditions. These, in turn, are informed by knowledges that are visions containing interpretations of the world. Knowledge, in this sense, does not, as is often believed, simply reflect things as they are by themselves. Instead, it sifts, orders and compartmentalizes into containers in the form of categories, classes and types. The more knowledge we have, the more things we see and the greater number of different things we discern in the world. To study the art of painting, for example, leads us not to see 'red' in a picture, but different forms of red such as Adrianople red, flame red, hellebore red, Indian red, Japanese red, carmine, crimson, ruby, scarlet, cardinal red, sanguine, vermilion, damask, Naples red, Pompeian red, Persian red and so on. The difference between the trained and untrained eye becomes manifest in the power to discern and explore in a methodical manner.

In all areas, acquisition of knowledge consists of learning how to make new discriminations. In the process the uniform is rendered discrete, distinctions made more specific and large classes are split into smaller ones, so that the interpretation of experience gets richer and more detailed. We often hear of how educated people can be measured by the richness of the vocabulary they deploy in their discriminations and descriptions. Things may be described as 'nice', but then elaborated upon in terms of being enjoyable, savoury, kind, suitable and tasteful or 'doing the right thing'. Yet language does not come into life from 'outside' to report experiences and events that have already occurred. Language is in and reflective of life, from the start. As Pierre Bourdieu put it, 'social uses of language owe their specifically social value to the fact that they tend to be organized in systems of differences' and these, in turn, reproduce 'the system of social differences'.

From this we may say that language is a *form of life* and every language – English, Chinese, Portuguese, working-class and middle-class language, 'posh' language, the argot of the underworld, the jargon of adolescent gangs, the language of art critics, of sailors, of nuclear physicists, of surgeons or miners – is a form of life. Each brings together its map of the world and a code of behaviour. Inside each form of life, the map and the code intertwine. We can think of them separately, but in practice we cannot pull them apart. Distinctions made between the names of things reflect our perception of the difference in their qualities. At the same time our recognition of the difference in quality reflects the discrimination we make in our actions towards them and the expectations from which our actions follow. Let us recall an earlier observation: to understand is to know how to go on and if we know how to go on, we have understood. It is precisely this overlapping, this harmony between the two – the way we act and the way we see the world – that makes us suppose that the differences are in the things themselves.

There is an ease and certitude that accompany the discriminations that are routinely employed in the service of everyday understanding. As we have noted, there is a richness in this form of understanding and sociologists have explored this with extraordinary insight. In the process, they render manifest what is latent. Practice itself must, to some degree, be indifferent to the conditions of its possibility in the normal course of events. Without this in place, how could we act if we spent all of our time thinking about our actions and their relation with the conditions of which we are a part? To do this would be a recipe for inaction and uncertainty. Nevertheless, the forms of life that allow for this are not simply removed from one another. Sociological understanding is not simply about how we get on in life, but how our lives are bound up with others even if, in the normal course of events, this does not appear to be the case. Actions may be based on local information, but they have the potential to be transported and represented in ways that cross boundaries.

This is exactly what the armies of those who market goods and services do in the name of consumption. Boundaries between forms of life then find themselves subject to images and possibilities that come from different media and, as we have seen during our guided tour, have different effects. The resultant form of understanding cannot be interpreted as simply coming from 'within' in the sense of adding to the local pool of knowledge in terms of knowing how to get on in a form of life. These are not simply confirming instances of new knowledge that can be unproblematically incorporated into our lives, but represent interpretations that can make demands upon us to accord them recognition in a way that, by default, we recognize as our own. Understanding in this form is knowing that our distinctions are not the *only* ones that exist. As such, we are not separated from each other by impermeable walls in which we can unproblematically take inventories of the contents and their owners.

One reaction to this state of affairs (as we have seen) is to resort to boundary enforcement with ever greater means being employed to ensure the walls are impervious to outside influences. Nevertheless, while forms of life may be orderly and share patterns of action, they are often superimposed on each other, overlap and vie for selected areas of the total life experience. They are, so to speak, different selections and alternative arrangements of the same portions of the total world and the same items drawn from the shared pool. In the course of one day we move through many forms of life, yet wherever we go we carry a piece of other forms of life with us. In every form of life through which we pass during our lives we share knowledge and behavioural codes with a different set of people and each of those possess a combination of the forms of life of which she or he partakes.

For these reasons no form of life is 'pure' and as history has demonstrated on so many occasions, attempts at purification lead to catastrophic results. Our entry into forms of life is, however, not a passive process in the sense of twisting and moulding our identities and skills so that they conform to sets of rigid rules. We are both co-authors and actors in social life and so as we enter forms of life, we both utilize and change them by bringing with us other forms of life. These, in turn, orient our actions and inform our judgements and decisions, but may not be suited to these new settings. Each act of entry is thus creative *and* transformational. The sociological eye then turns to such questions as at what levels, to what extent, for what reasons and utilizing what resources and with what consequences?

This is why issues of understanding constantly arise, along with feelings of confusion, threat and possible breakdowns in communication, because they are part of the human condition. To ignore this in the name of closing down social orders is to ignore a central aspect of the process of understanding in which meanings undergo a subtle, yet steady and unavoidable transformation. We can say that the process of communication – that action aimed at achieving joint understanding – prevents any form of life from being static. Just think of whirls in a stream. Each one looks as if it possesses a steady shape and so remains the same over a protracted period of time. Yet (as we know) it cannot retain a single molecule of water for more than a few seconds and so its substance remains in a permanent state of flux. Just in case it is tempting to think that this is a weakness of the whirl and it would be better for its 'survival' if the flow of water in the river were stopped, remember that this would mean the 'death' of the whirl. It cannot keep its shape or its form as a separate and persistent identity without a constant influx and outflow of ever new quantities of water. Remember, too, that the water itself bears different ingredients!

Forms of life, like whirls, stay alive precisely because they are flexible, permanently in flux and able to absorb new material and discard that which is no longer thought to be useful. This means, however, that forms of life would die were they ever to become closed, static and repellent to change. They would not survive final codification and that precision which prompts the attempts at codification. To put it differently, languages and knowledge in general need ambivalence to remain alive, to retain cohesion, to be of use. Despite this, however, the powers concerned with ordering reality cannot but view the same ambivalence as an obstacle to their aims. They tend to seek to freeze the whirl, to bar all unwelcome input into the knowledge they control and attempt to seal the 'form of life' over which they wish to secure a monopoly.

Concerns for order underpinned by limited views of social life lead to searches for unambiguous knowledge. The expectation is that this knowledge should be exhaustive and final and also serve as a justification for subsequent actions. Allusions to its neutrality can then alleviate those who apply it of the burden of judgement, but it cannot live up to such ideals for the effects will be there for all to see. To want full control over a situation is to strive for a clear-cut map in which meaning is cleansed via the purification of ambiguity and all links are binding upon all those who constitute the form of life. Over a given terrain different strategies will emerge according to the investment that people have in the order of things. On the one hand, we may find acceptance by virtue of practices remaining unquestioned. This enables (as we have suggested) a disposition that informs actions in everyday life. On the other hand, those unaccustomed to the accepted ways of thinking who then enter these relations carrying other forms of life may find, by default, that they question and so disrupt the accepted ways. They may question themselves in the process, but their actions may also have a transformative effect on the form of life itself.

Resulting efforts to preserve orthodoxy, and to prevent or eliminate heresy, have control over interpretation as their objective. The power in question aims at gaining an exclusive right to decide which of the possible interpretations ought to be chosen and made binding as the true one. The quest for a monopoly of power expresses itself in casting the proponents of alternatives in the role of dissidents and is accompanied by an intolerance that may be exemplified in persecution. Any discipline, from this point of view, that seeks something other than the production of knowledge for the purposes of control, will find itself a target of attack from those who have an investment in the given order of things.

Sociology and Freedom

Sociology produces a sense of understanding that we may call the interpretive-relational. It is not content to see things in isolation, because that is not how social life exists. Because of this, it is ill suited to the demands of 'closing down' that which is not, nor could be, hermetically sealed from outside influences. Sociology is an extended commentary on the experiences that arise in social relations and is an interpretation of those experiences in relation to others and the social conditions in which people find themselves. This is not to suggest that it possesses a monopoly of wisdom in respect to those experiences – even though it undoubtedly enriches them through helping us to understand ourselves better through and with others. If anything, thinking sociologically broadens our horizons of understanding because it is not content with the exclusivity and completeness that comes with any one interpretation. It also highlights the cost of attempts to bring about such a situation in the first place.

This is a long way from suggesting that sociology is not 'practical'. By enlarging the scope of our understanding it is capable of bringing into focus those things that might otherwise go unnoticed in the normal course of events. These include a plurality of experiences and forms of life and how each exhibits and deploys its forms of understanding, while also demonstrating how each cannot be a self-contained and self-sufficient unit. Quite simply, we are all bound up with one another, albeit in different ways. This is the challenge to thinking sociologically because it does not stem, but facilitates the flow and exchange of experiences.

For some this means that sociology can add to ambivalence because it will not join those who seek to 'freeze the flux' in pursuit of limited ends. Approached in this way, it can be viewed as part of the problem, not the solution. However, if a society is serious about its wish to learn, it will give licence to a form of understanding that better equips us to face the future. The great service that sociology is well prepared to render to human life and human cohabitation is the promotion of mutual understanding and tolerance as a paramount condition of shared freedom. Because of the form of understanding that it deploys, sociological thinking cannot but promote the understanding that breeds tolerance and the tolerance that makes understanding possible. As we have suggested throughout this book, how we view problems will influence what are seen as appropriate solutions. Between our expectations for the future and experiences obtained from the past and present, lies a space that thinking sociologically illuminates and from which we can learn more about ourselves, others and the relations between our aspirations, actions and the social conditions that we create and inhabit. Sociology is therefore central to the endeavour of coming to understand ourselves in better ways.

questions for reflection and further reading

Our intention in this section is to provide a structure for seminar discussions, reading groups, or those individuals who have read the book and wish to explore further the issues we have raised in the book. For this purpose we have provided a series of questions for each chapter, along with suggestions for further reading. These are bound to be selective when it comes to areas of interest that have often generated a considerable amount of writings. After all, sociology is a growing and dynamic discipline that is producing new studies all the time. This is not surprising given our lives are changing in different ways and at different times. We have selected these books in terms of the topics they cover and the issues we have examined in the individual chapters. As a result, they are not always the easiest books, but we hope they prove to be of sufficient interest to prompt further thought on core social issues.

When you consider these texts and read them, do not feel depressed or surrender to the temptation to quit. Sociological knowledge may seem overwhelming, but you will find the effort richly rewarding and certainly not beyond your power. Besides, there are sociological publications that are specifically produced to help you and others move into the main body of sociological knowledge. Note that reading can be a passive exercise in which the reader acts as a recipient of the text and does not engage with it in criticizing, analysing, cross-referencing and bringing prior learning and experiences to the text. It is for these reasons that you should read using an 'interrogative style' where you 'engage' with the text and constantly ask questions, bearing in mind the aims of your reading. We have produced the questions to assist in this process, but your interrogative abilities will clearly develop as you accumulate an ever-widening depth and breadth of knowledge. It only remains for us to say that we hope you enjoy the continuing sociological journey.

Introduction

Questions for Reflection

1 Do you think there can be a science of common sense and/or a common-sense view of science?
2 If you were asked to define the discipline of sociology in no more than two sentences, what would you say and why?
3 What are the benefits and pitfalls associated with the process of 'defamiliarization'?
4 Is sense 'common'?

Suggested Further Reading

Berger, P.L. and Kellner, H. (1982) *Sociology Reinterpreted: An Essay on Method and Vocation* (Harmondsworth: Penguin). This book, following on from the earlier *Invitation to Sociology*, examines topics such as freedom and the 'scientization' of social life.
Giddens, A. (2001) *Sociology*, fourth edn (Cambridge: Polity). A comprehensive and general overview of sociology.
May, T. (2001) *Social Research: Issues, Methods and Process*, third edn (Buckingham: Open University Press). While we have not examined research methods, this book provides a tour of methods and perspectives employed in social research for those interested in these areas of activity.
Mills, C.W. (1970) *The Sociological Imagination* (Harmondsworth: Penguin; originally published in 1959). Although this seems dated, it is still a sociological classic and the last chapter anticipates the theme of 'ambivalence'.

Chapter 1

Questions for Reflection

1 What goals do you have in your life and what means might you have access to in order to attain them?
2 Who are the reference groups in your life and what is the relationship between your actions and their expectations?
3 How do you understand the relationship between freedom and dependence?
4 What would you consider to be the relations that exist between families, communities and organizations and how do these affect the goals we set for ourselves and whether they are attainable or not? Consider this in relation to the 'criteria of relevance'.

Suggested Further Reading

Bauman, Z. (1988) *Freedom* (Milton Keynes: Open University Press). This study considers the issues we have addressed in this chapter.

Griffiths, M. (1995) *Feminisms and the Self: The Web of Identity* (London: Routledge). Ideas on the self are considered in relation to belonging, authenticity, politics and autobiography.

Mead, G.H. (1964) *Selected Writings: George Herbert Mead*, edited by A.J. Reck, (Chicago: University of Chicago Press). An edited collection of Mead's original writings that are worth reading in themselves, rather than via secondary sources.

Skeggs, B. (1997) *Formations of Class and Gender: Becoming Respectable* (London: Sage). A sociological study tracing the lives of women and how they struggle to make their social identities.

Chapter 2

Questions for Reflection

1   The boundaries between 'us' and 'them' provide for the maintenance, via distinction, of identity. How does this occur and with what consequences for how we see others and ourselves?

2   Is there a 'togetherness' or 'common bond' that humanity, as a whole, shares?

3   What practices of segregation and entitlement do you see within the City? Would you regard yourself as the beneficiary or victim of these and why?

4   What did Erving Goffman mean by 'civil inattention' and how is it manifested?

Suggested Further Reading

Bourdieu, P. et al. (1999) *The Weight of the World: Social Suffering in Contemporary Society*, translated by P. P. Ferguson, et al. (Cambridge: Polity). A study based on detailed empirical investigations, conducted over several years, into the issues that people face in their everyday lives.

Frisby, D. and Featherstone, M. (eds) (1997) *Simmel on Culture: Selected Writings* (Thousand Oaks, Calif.: Sage). Simmel was a great sociologist and this edited collection of his works enables the reader to gain an insight into the range and depth of his interests.

Goffman, E. (1984) *The Presentation of Self in Everyday Life* (Harmondsworth: Penguin; originally published in 1959). This book has sold a great many copies, probably because of the insights that its author brought to our interactions.

Miller, T. and McHoul, A. (1998) *Popular Culture and Everyday Life* (London: Sage). Interesting insights into everyday practices.

Chapter 3

Questions for Reflection

1 In what ways are communities and social identities linked?
2 What do you think Raymond Williams meant by 'the remarkable thing about community is that it always has been'?
3 Do sects and organizations differ? If so, in what ways?
4 Would you consider exposing those practices in organizations that you consider unethical? If so, when, why and under what type of circumstances?

Suggested Further Reading

du Gay, P. (2000) *In Praise of Bureaucracy: Weber – Organization – Ethics* (London: Sage). The author argues that bureaucracy can have an important role to play in a society that seeks responsible government.
Gerth, H. and Mills, C.W. (eds) (1970) *From Max Weber: Essays in Sociology* (London: Routledge and Kegan Paul). As with our suggestions on Simmel and Mead, it is often worth returning to original materials to gain the best insights into the ideas of leading sociologists.
Jenkins, R. (1996) *Social Identity* (London: Routledge). A very useful overview of both sociological and anthropological views on identity, mixed with the author's own analysis and interpretations.
Lyon, D. (2001) *Surveillance Society: Monitoring Everyday Life* (Buckingham: Open University Press). Increasing areas of our lives are subject to routine surveillance and this study illuminates how this takes place and discusses its implications.

Chapter 4

Questions for Reflection

1 What are the differences between coercion and choice?
2 What does it mean to say that people are ends in themselves, rather than means towards the ends of another?
3 Traditionalist legitimations play an important role in our lives. Can you think of some examples and how they relate to your actions?
4 Are there such things as 'universes of obligation'?

Suggested Further Reading

Bauman, Z. (1989) *Modernity and the Holocaust* (Cambridge, Mass.: Polity). An in-depth examination of some of the themes we have raised in this chapter.
de Beauvoir, S. (1994) *The Ethics of Ambiguity* (New York: Citadel; originally

published in 1948). A highly insightful essay by a leading figure from the French existentialist movement which examines the choices we face in situations of ambiguity.

Bellah, R.N., Madsen, R., Sullivan, W.M., Swidler, A. and Tipton, S.M. (1996) *Habits of the Heart: Individualism and Commitment in American Life* (updated edition; Berkeley, Calif.: University of California Press). A study that sparked a wide-ranging debate about contemporary values and ways of life.

Sennett, R. (1998) *The Corrosion of Character: The Personal Consequences of Work in the New Capitalism* (London: W.W. Norton). This book looks at political and economic changes in terms of their affects in relation to trust, integrity and belonging.

Chapter 5

Questions for Reflection

1 Does the idea of a 'pure' gift in a social relationship make sense to you?
2 Jürgen Habermas wrote about the 'colonization' of the lifeworld by money, power and bureaucracy. Do you think this is an increasing trend in contemporary society? If so, what effects does it have on everyday life?
3 Is there identity outside of commodification?
4 Is the impersonality of exchange underpinned by social relationships such as emotional attachment and trust? If so, in what ways and what does this mean for the idea of 'exchange'.

Suggested Further Reading

Beck, U. (1992) *Risk Society: Towards a New Modernity* (Thousand Oaks, Calif.: Sage). Ulrich Beck characterizes contemporary society in terms of its propensity to produce risks that have effects upon the conduct of our lives.

Hochschild, A.E. (1983) *The Managed Heart: Commercialization of Human Feeling* (Berkeley, Calif.: University of California Press). The title speaks enough of the content and is written in an engaging style.

Jamieson, L. (1998) *Intimacy: Personal Relationships in Modern Societies* (Cambridge: Polity). Is the desire for intimacy a basic human need? To what extent is it shaped by social and economic conditions? These are some of the main questions addressed in this book.

Luhmann, N. (1998) *Love As Passion: The Codification of Intimacy* (Stanford, Calif.: Stanford University Press). An insightful examination of love, emotion and attachment in terms of its evolution over the course of history.

Chapter 6

Questions for Reflection

1   In seeking security are we in search of the unattainable?
2   How are habits and bodily postures and mannerisms related? How do they manifest themselves in everyday life?
3   In what ways are bodies represented in the popular media and for what reasons and utilizing what means?
4   Are the ideas of health and fitness different because of the existence and absence of a 'norm' against which they can be measured?

Suggested Further Reading

Burkitt, I. (1999) *Bodies of Thought: Embodiment, Identity and Modernity* (Thousand Oaks, Calif.: Sage). This book engages with arguments around the mind-body issue and concludes that having a body, acting and thinking of ourselves as persons are inseparable.

Delphy, C. and Leonard, D. (1992) *Familiar Exploitation: A New Analysis of Marriage in Contemporary Western Society* (Cambridge, Mass.: Polity). A comparative analysis of how the organization of the family is related to labour, production and consumption.

Foucault, M. (1979) *The History of Sexuality, Volume 1: An Introduction*, translated by R. Hurley, (Harmondsworth: Penguin). The first of Michel Foucault's studies on sexuality not only is accessible, but also requires the reader to examine what may be habitually held beliefs from a very different perspective.

Nettleton, S. (1995) *The Sociology of Health and Illness* (Cambridge, Mass.: Polity). A comprehensive overview of perspectives on medical sociology.

Chapter 7

Questions for Reflection

1   We spoke of 'hardware' and 'software' times. What did we mean by this and what consequences does it have for the ways in which we lead our lives?
2   Are communications freed from the limits placed upon them by 'people and material objects'?
3   Is 'threat' targeted at that which lies within a neighbourhood, but whose actual source is more distant?
4   What are the relations between problem-solving activities and boundaries?

Suggested Further Reading

Adam, B. (1995) *Timewatch: The Social Analysis of Time* (Cambridge: Polity). One of the foremost social theorists of time, Barbara Adam examines the ways in which time informs our lives in a number of areas, for example, health and work.

Bauman, Z. (2000) *Liquid Modernity* (Cambridge, Mass.: Polity). An examination of the fluidity of life, which we have discussed here, in relation to such topics as work, time and space, community, emancipation and individuality.

Waters, M. (1995) *Globalization* (London and New York: Routledge). A good overview of this concept and its implications for our lives.

Williams, R. (1989) *Culture* (London: Fontana). Raymond Williams devotes his attention to the idea of culture and why it has become so important to an understanding of social relations, as well as how this relates to his own 'cultural materialist' position.

Chapter 8

Questions for Reflection

1   Is nature anything more than the material upon which culture fashions itself?
2   Is the genetic control of crops a step forward in the process of controlling nature for human purposes?
3   What do the terms 'xenophobia' and 'heterophobia' refer to? Give two examples of each in everyday life.
4   What are the differences between citizenship, state, nation and nationalism and how do they relate to each other?

Suggested Further Reading

Calhoun, C. (1997) *Nationalism* (Buckingham and Minneapolis, Minn.: Open University Press and Minnesota Press). The importance of national boundaries, states, identities and nationalism is evident in contemporary times. This book examines these issues and how they interact and are used in different ways.

Delanty, G. (2000) *Citizenship in a Global Age* (Buckingham: Open University Press). Defining the term 'citizenship', the author examines the implications of de-territorialization and argues for a 'cosmopolitan' form of citizenship.

Gilroy, P. (2000) *Between Camps: Nations, Cultures and the Allure of Race* (London: Allen Lane, The Penguin Press). An examination of identity, ethnicity and race in modern times and the issues they present for living our lives with others in improved ways.

Segal, L. (1999) *Why Feminism? Gender, Psychology, Politics* (Cambridge: Polity). Lynne Segal's writings resonate with contemporary issues and this collection of essays is no exception.

Chapter 9

Questions for Reflection

1 In what ways are new technologies informing and shaping your life?
2 Is advertising simply a means of conveying information, or does it determine what we buy?
3 Are public problems becoming private ills?
4 Is there more to life than shopping?

Suggested Further Reading

Featherstone, M. (1991) *Consumer Culture and Postmodernism* (London: Sage). A review of the idea that we can characterize modern societies in terms of consumption, while also being the author's own evaluation of a global order and its implications for cultural practices.

Klein, N. (2000) *No Logo* (London: Flamingo). A revealing set of insights into the power that large corporations have over everyday lives.

MacKenzie, D. and Wajcman, J. (eds) (1999) *The Social Shaping of Technology*, second edn (Buckingham: Open University Press). An edited collection of original articles by thinkers reflecting upon the interactions between technology and human relations.

Slevin, J. (2000) *The Internet and Society* (Cambridge, Mass.: Polity). A detailed study on the rise of the internet and its implications for identity and the organization of social relations.

Chapter 10

Questions for Reflection

1 What do you hope for in studying sociology?
2 What are the issues that have informed the development and practice of sociology as a discipline?
3 In what ways can thinking sociologically assist us in improving our understanding of ourselves, others and the social conditions that we inhabit?
4 Is no 'form of life' pure?

Suggested Further Reading

Fraser, N. (1997) *Justice Interruptus: Critical Reflections on the 'Postsocialist' Condition* (London: Routledge). Nancy Fraser has the ability to reach to the core of arguments and set out the ways in which we might constructively find solutions to the problems they raise. This set of essays is no exception and in here she makes the point, apparently so often forgotten, that recognition walks hand in hand with redistribution.

May, T. (1996) *Situating Social Theory* (Buckingham: Open University Press). Utilizing a basis in the history of social theory and traditions of social thought, this book situates contemporary schools of thought and discusses their strengths and weaknesses.

Williams, M. (2000) *Science and Social Science: An Introduction* (London and New York: Routledge). A guide to the debates on science and how these relate to the practice of the social sciences. The author also considers the important issue of values and scientific practices.

Young, J. (1999) *The Exclusive Society: Social Exclusion, Crime and Difference in Late Modernity* (Thousand Oaks, Calif.: Sage). This book examines the transition from stability to change and division. Noting that 'there is no going back', the author considers the possibilities for the future and in so doing, utilizes the sociological gaze in a manner that is not dissimilar to the one we have suggested in this final chapter.

index